THE PROCEEDINGS OF THE 16th INTERNATIONAL HUMANITIES CONFERENCE

ALL & EVERYTHING 2011

John Amaral
Seymour Ginsburg
Dimitri Peretzi
Michael Readshaw
Arkady Rovner
Paul Taylor

Published by All & Everything Conferences
2011

First Edition Published 2011
Published by All & Everything Conferences (on behalf of the Planning Committee)
© Copyright 2011 by Seymour B. Ginsburg and Ian C. MacFarlane

The contents of this publication may not be reproduced or copied in whole or part in any book, magazine, periodical, pamphlet, circular, information storage or data retrieval system, or in any other form without the written permission of the Planning Committee.

Any profit from the sale of these Proceedings will be devoted to the funds for the organization of future Conferences of a similar nature.

Published by All & Everything Conferences

Website: www.aandeconference.org
Email: info@aandeconference.org

First Edition Print

ISBN-10: 1-905578-30-X
ISBN-13: 978-1-905578-30-6

Also Published as
First Edition eBook

ISBN-10: 1-905578-31-8
ISBN-13: 978-1-905578-31-3

Cover Photo © Copyright 2011 by Bonnie Phillips

Table of Contents

Foreword 4
Conference Program 5
Planning Committee 13
Speakers 14
Why is that Transformation, which Gurdjieff so wished for us with all his Being, and to achieve which he wrote Beelzebub's Tales to His Grandson, necessary, and how is it achieved? 16
    Why is that Transformation…? - Questions & Answers 26
Some Explorations of I Am, I Wish, I Can 29
    Some Explorations of I Am, I Wish, I Can - Questions & Answers 39
Seminar 1: Chapter 32 - Beelzebub's Tales 45
Conscience and Consciousness in the Tales 62
    Conscience and Consciousness in the Tales - Questions & Answers 73
Gurdjieff's Beelzebub's Tales - A Landmark in the Spiritual History of Humanity 77
    Gurdjieff's Beelzebub's Tales - A Landmark in the Spiritual History of Humanity - Questions & Answers 93
Seminar 2: Chapter 7 - Meetings with Remarkable Men 97
The Ray of Creation Revisited 113
    The Ray of Creation Revisited - Questions & Answers 118
Beelzebub Alien 127
    Beelzebub Alien - Questions & Answers 138
Seminar 3: Chapter 33 - Beelzebub's Tales 140
Seminar 4: Where Do We Go From Here? 151
Appendix 1: List of Attendees 155
Index 156

Foreword

The Planning Committee would like to take this opportunity of thanking all the Presenters for their help in producing these Proceedings. We have all done our best to produce a permanent record of what some of us believe to have been the sixteenth important and definite Conference under the title of All and Everything 2011.

It is hoped that this will lead to further creative interaction of those in the Work in the near future.

The 16th International Humanities Conference - All & Everything 2011 convened on April 6, 2011 in Prague, Czech Republic. The conference was attended by thirty three delegates travelling from Greece, Russia, Norway, Germany, Czech Republic, Canada, the Netherlands, the United Kingdom and the United States.

From the Conference's inception, it's members have worked toward making this "gathering of the Companions of the Book" to become more and more just that - a gathering of people from all over the world who come together for the purpose of "fathoming the gist" of Gurdjieff's writings, of sharing our insights and experiences, our questions, and our efforts to understand and grow into becoming remarkable men and women.

Six papers were presented. Abstracts of the papers are located on the Abstracts 2011 page. Three Seminars were also conducted in which were discussed various issues and questions relating to the books and ideas of Gurdjieff. Seminars included: Chapter 32 ("Hypnotism") and 33 ("Beelzebub as a Professional Hypnotist") of Beelzebub's Tales and chapter 7 of Meetings with Remarkable Men – Prince Yuri Lubovedsky.

An excellent performance of Gurdjieff/deHartmann music by Tao McQuade followed the end of the formal proceedings on Friday.

The final session of the conference on Sunday morning, traditionally entitled "Where Do We Go From Here," provided an opportunity to discuss the achievements of the conference and the challenges facing its future editions.

The availability of the Proceedings of All & Everything 2010 was announced. New and past editions of the Proceedings are available from Amazon.com.

Conference Program

all & everything

the 16th international humanities conference 2011

Wednesday, April 6 through Sunday, April 10

Hotel Extol Inn, Prague, Czech Republic

Conference Program

"And so even during the last century, it occasionally happened there that such a one from among your favorites who had already reached responsible age completely formed and prepared in the said manner for external perceptions, constating by chance a certain law-conformable particularity among the cosmic results around him, began to study it in detail and from every aspect and having ultimately attained, after long persevering labors, to some objective truth or other, initiated other beings around him and similar to him, into this truth."

All and Everything, "An Objectively Impartial Criticism of the Life of Man" or Beelzebub's Tales to His Grandson, page 818

Visit the All and Everything Conference website at: www.aandeconference.org

All & Everything Conference 2011

Conference Program

8:00 AM - Each morning an unguided sitting / meditation / morning preparation room will be available for all to use.

Wednesday
   8:30 PM - Informal Session: Getting to Know You - facilitator Nick Bryce

Thursday
   9:15 - Opening Remarks – Nick Bryce
   9:30 - Paper: Michael Readshaw – What is that transformation?
   10:45 - Coffee Break
   11:15 - Paper: John Amaral - Some Explorations of I Am, I Wish, I Can
   12:30 - Lunch
   2:30 - Seminar 1: Ch. 32 of *Beelzebub's Tales* – "Hypnotism" facilitated by Steve Aronson
   3:45 - Coffee Break
   4:15 - Seminar 1: continued
   Thursday Evening 7 PM – Deciphering de Hartmann's Message
     A Concert by Elan Sicroff – NÁRODNÍ MUZEUM

Friday
   9:30 - Paper: Dimitri Peretzi – Conscience and Consciousness in *The Tales*
   10:45 - Coffee Break
   11:15 - Paper: Arkady Rovner - Gurdjieff's *Beelzebub's Tales*: A Landmark of the Spiritual History of Humanity
   12:30 - Lunch
   2:30 - Seminar 2: Ch. 7 of *Meetings with Remarkable Men* – Prince Yuri Lubovedsky – facilitated by Dimitri Peretzi
   3:45 - Coffee Break
   4:15 - Seminar 2: Continued
   8:30 - Musical performance by Tao McQuade or an informal Talk on the relationship between ancient Chinese philosophy and *Beelzebub's Tales*

Saturday
   9:30 - Paper: Sy Ginsburg - The Ray of Creation Revisited (via Skype)
   10:45 - Coffee Break
   11:15 - Paper: Paul Beekman Taylor – Beelzebub Alien
   12:30 - Lunch
   2:30 - Seminar 3: Chapter 33 *Beelzebub's Tales* – Beelzebub as a Professional Hypnotist – facilitated by Terje Tonne
   3:45 - Coffee Break
   4:15 - Seminar 3: Continued
   7:30 - Conference Banquet

Sunday
   9:30 - Seminar 4: Where Do We Go From Here? - facilitated by Bonnie Phillips

Conference Programme

Michael Readshaw
Transformation and How It Is Achieved

Why is that transformation, which Gurdjieff so wished for us with all his Being, and to achieve which he wrote Beelzebub's Tales to His Grandson, necessary, and how is it achieved?

As soon as he can, in *Beelzebub's Tales to his Grandson*, Gurdjieff makes the following claim:

> "Concerning all this it must be said that neither the organ Kundabuffer which their ancestors had is to blame, nor its consequences which, owing to a mistake on the part of certain Sacred Individuals, were crystallised in their ancestors and later began to pass by heredity from generation to generation.
>
> "But they themselves were personally to blame for it, and just on account of the abnormal conditions of external ordinary being-existence which they themselves have gradually established...
> (chapter 13, "Why in Man's Reason Fantasy may be perceived as Reality," pp 104-05)

And then this:

> "You yourself will very well understand that although the fundamental causes of the whole chaos that now reigns on that ill-fated planet Earth were certain 'unforseeingnesses,' coming from Above on the part of various Sacred Individuals, yet nevertheless the chief causes for the developing of further ills are only those abnormal conditions of ordinary being-existence which they themselves gradually established and which they continue to establish down to the present time.'
> (chapter 16, "The Relative Understanding of Time," pp132-33)

In this talk, Mike analyses the expression ' the abnormal external conditions of ordinary being-existence established by them themselves,' – a phrase which Gurdjieff uses 153 times, in one form or another, in *The Tales*, to completely define the causes of our present sorry state – word for word, in order to find out what are these conditions, that is, what is wrong with us, how and why we establish these conditions ourselves, and hence he establishes why Gurdjieff wrote *Beelzebub's Tales* in order to transform us, and how that transformation is achieved.

~ Mike Readshaw first read *Beelzebub's Tales* at University, where he obtained a degree in Mathematics, specializing in Mathematical Logic. A meeting with Rina Hands indirectly led to him producing a number of audio talks, the first of which, "Reading Gurdjieff," exposed the difference between Gurdjieff's own writings and the established Gurdjieff canon of thought. This was much praised by Mrs. Annie Staveley, but after a serious climbing accident in the Alps, Mike was distracted and had to re-learn to walk, married, and trained as a teacher. He lived in France for a number of years before family circumstances forced him back to England. Mike is a widower, with five children in his care, and teaches Mathematics in the north of England. Knowing that personality has ideas whilst essence has insights, his most recent work consists of devising 365 completely original sayings with the intention of raising the overall level of awareness of those in contact with him, based upon the principle that: A good saying stops all thought so that understanding can fill that vacuum.

John Amaral
Some Explorations of I Am, I Wish, I Can

In the daily self-re-membering exercise "I am, I wish, I can," specific expressions are evoked. What are the meanings of these expressions? For example, if "I am" is an expression evocative of potential "Will-Being," what does this mean for me in the exercise, and what do the other expressions in the exercise mean to me? In this paper, I intend to give a sense of possibilities in the exercise, some of which may have been ordinarily missed.

~ John Amaral was born in Long Beach, California, raised by Catholic nuns, and trained in Electrical Engineering and Music. He has studied Gurdjieff with students of Mr. Nyland, Mrs. Staveley and Mrs. Popoff, and began to attend the A&E Conferences in 2003. "Perhaps the most useful aspect of the Conference for me has been that it has helped me to develop a more inclusive perspective about ways of Working. It has also opened for me new vistas of interesting inspiring contacts."

Dimitri Peretzi
Conscience and Consciousness in *The Tales*

The talk traces the way the author applies these two terms, "Conscience" and "Consciousness", in the text of *Beelzebub's Tales to his Grandson* and compares the connotations of their use with the meaning given to them by contemporary Science and Philosophy of Mind. The importance of the philosophical study of Consciousness, over the last two decades, has rendered the concept a key for the formation of any theory about the Mind and the operation of the brain. The way the two terms are used in *The Tales* gives clues about the way Gurdjieff views the Mind and point toward a coherent and quite advanced theory proposed for its structure.

~ Mr. Peretzi is the president of the Gurdjieff Foundation of Greece. With reference to his personal contacts with eminent students of Gurdjieff, Lord Pentland, Madame de Salzmann, Dr. Welch and others, he has authored a number of books and articles that study the problem of consciousness, relating views from the esoteric traditions to those of the contemporary philosophy of mind. Mr. Peretzi did graduate work in Philosophy, at Yale, where he received his Master of Architecture. Having settled since 1974, he established his own Construction and Prefabrication Company.

Arkady Rovner
Gurdjieff's *Beelzebub's Tales* – A Landmark of the Spiritual History of Humanity

One of the most important books written in the last century, "*Beelzebub's Tales*" is, according to its genre an epic poem – comparable with the number of works pertaining to the same genre, such as: the Hebrew Bible, the New Testament, the Koran, the Upanishads, the Mahayana Sutras, the Ramayana, the Mahabharata, Homer's Iliad and Odyssey, Dante's Divine Comedy, François Rabelais' Gargantua and Pantagruel, Nietzsche's Also Sprach Zarathustra, Helen Blavatsky's The Secret Doctrine and some others. Most of these works are considered to be landmarks of the spiritual history of humanity, albeit in different degrees.

These works often carry in themselves new metaphysical principles, new cosmological and historical concepts, new codes of behavior and ideals of human existence, predictions and prophecies said to be obtained through spiritual revelation. The authorship of or inspiration for many of these works has been ascribed to Almighty God or to the Spirits closest to Him, as well as to Archangels, Angels, prophets or legendary beings.

A special kind of sacredness has been attributed to these works, and they have been made objects of exclusive reverence and worship as well as of systematic study and commentary, the latter sometimes leading to creation of special kinds of disciplines, e.g. Christian theology, midrashim, kalam, etc. Special rituals for handling these books and special manners of recitation have been created and particular schedules and orders of their private and communal recitation have been established. Many of these works have been considered to contain special and secret content, a "bone" or "a dog" buried in them which the devoted reader is supposed to dig out. Some of these works have been engaged in the process of enculturation, i.e. incorporation of their content and style into the various layers of existing culture. As a result of constant recitations, quoting and references, some of these poems acquire the character of a warrant of objective Truth, as they have solidified in an inert culture and their ideas have ceased to develop and grow, thus becoming an infallible dogmas.

The aim of this presentation is to pose and to make attempt of answering the following question: How could we avoid the danger of pitfalls contained in the uncritical attitude towards Gurdjieff's main work?

~ Arkady Rovner was born in 1940 in Odessa, USSR and spent his youth in Tbilisi, Georgia. He studied at Moscow State University and Columbia University, New York. He taught numerous courses on world religions and contemporary mysticism at the New York University, the State University of New York, the New School for Social Research and the Moscow State Humanitarian University.

He was introduced to Gurdjieff's ideas and practices in Moscow, Russia in 1965 and has been an adherent of the Gurdjieff Work ever since then. During the years 1975-1984 he was in constant communication with Lord Pentland, the head of the

American branch of Gurdjieff Foundation. In the summer of 1980, with a letter of reference from Lord Pentland, he travelled to London and Paris where he met and interviewed a number of Ouspensky's and Gurdjieff's former disciples, including Mr. Tilley and P. L. Travers, as well as Michael de Salzmann.

Sy Ginsburg
The Ray of Creation Revisited

The purpose of this suggested revision to the presentation of the Ray of Creation is two-fold:

1. To accommodate the idea that the descending Ray of Creation in the materialization descends in the first instance into multiple universes. Recent theories in astrophysics suggest that there are multiple universes just as there are multiple galaxies within our universe. William James in 1895, coined with word "multiverse" to describe multiple simultaneous universes.

2. To eliminate the idea that the planets taken as a whole represent a greater level of freedom from the operation of the Sacred Triamazikamno (law of 3 forces) than does Earth taken as a single planet. All our planets revolve around the Sun. Therefore, all of them are subject to the same level of limitation of freedom. The group is no more free than is an individual planet.

Like most students of Gurdjieff's teaching, I was introduced to the concept of the Ray of Creation through the book In Search of the Miraculous, by P.D. Ouspensky, who recorded it as part of the oral teaching given him by Gurdjieff in 1915 and which is recounted in this book. I was at once excited and dismayed by this presentation of the Ray of Creation. (See Figure 1.)

I was excited because of the idea of scale and relativity that was presented. The Ray shows that at each level higher, there is a marked increase in the relativity of freedom, or operation under a significantly reduced number of orders of laws which restrict that freedom. While the Ray is presented astronomically in terms of the relativity of freedom of cosmic entities, of even more importance for us, is the idea that the Ray can be seen as presenting relative degrees of freedom in our inner world, the world of the psyche. The Gurdjieffian idea is that in our state of "ordinary consciousness" in which we identify with everything, we are under 48 orders of laws, equivalent to the number of laws under which is also the Earth. In the state that Gurdjieff calls "self-consciousness" or "self-remembering" we are under only 24 orders of laws, equivalent to the number of laws under which are the planets of the Sun when taken as a whole. In the state that Gurdjieff calls "objective-consciousness" we are under only 12 orders of laws, equivalent to the number of laws under which is our Sun as it relates to greater and lesser cosmic bodies. Our Milky Way Galaxy, for example, is said to be under only 6 orders of laws. The Sun is a captive of the Milky Way and is therefore less free than is the Milky Way Galaxy, just as our Earth is a captive of the Sun and is therefore less free than is the Sun.

But as valuable as is the insight into scale and relativity of freedom presented by the Ray, I was dismayed by a glaring inconsistency. In astronomical terms there is no reason to expect that the planets as a group are any more free of the Sun than is the planet Earth. The Earth is a captive of the Sun and all the other planets are likewise captives of the Sun. But because the insight into scale and relativity is so valuable to our understanding the different levels of human consciousness, I set aside this inconsistency as relatively unimportant. There were several occasions during the many years I facilitated Gurdjieff Study Groups when the matter of this inconsistency was presented to me by a pupil. I had to fudge my replies in defense of the Ray as presented, because I could find no valid rebuttal to the charge of inconsistency. My primary reply was that we should value the immensity of the concept of relativity and scale as it applies to the inner world of the psyche, as illustrated by the Ray when applied to cosmic entities.

~ Sy Ginsburg was born in Chicago in 1934 and currently resides in Florida. He was introduced to the Gurdjieff Work by Sri Madhava Ashish, an eminent theosophical scholar and Hindu monk, who became his mentor over a 19 year period. Ginsburg was a member of the Gurdjieff Society of Florida and later a cofounder of the Gurdjieff Institute of Florida. Currently, he is a Director of the Theosophical Society in Miami & South Florida and facilitator of the Gurdjieff Study Group at The Theosophical Society.

Paul Taylor
Beelzebub Alien

It is not unusual for a reader of *Beelzebub's Tales to His Grandson* to be so taken up with the story that he forgets the spatial point of view of the narrator, who is an alien, an extra-terrestrial, if you will, with non-human physical and mental characteristics, including narrative orders of action, place and time. Every word he relates to his grandson Hassein is spoken in outer space aboard an intergalactic vehicle, though most of what he relates concerns his experiences on Earth, where he is both listener and teller of tales. Although *The Tales* are stories related in space about space, as far as I have been able to discover, Gurdjieff's work seems not to merit more than cursory notice of the countless studies of the plurality of worlds and travels to and between them. Gurdjieff's readers are also likely not to care that Beelzebub, as an extra-terrestrial voyager observing the activities of humans on Earth, is just one of a legion of otherworldly beings who have been visited and engaged humans in recorded story. The striking difference, however, is that Beelzebub is a visitor to Earth rather than a receiver of visits from Earth. The stages in the development of stories of aliens in the western world develop from Aristotle's, Plato's and Heraclitus's scientific inquisitions into the shape and content of space. Following them, scientists and story-tellers consider possibilities of travel by inhabitants of the Earth into space in order where they find a fresh view of present, past, and future mortal activities of mankind from an extraterrestrial point of view. In more recent times, writers have portrayed aliens from superior cultures who, like Orson Welles' Martians, invade Earth, or like Swedenborg's angels, Gurdjieff's Beelzebub and Ashiata Shiemash, visit Earth for the good of mankind.

Gurdjieff had many models in the long history of extra-terrestrial travel to draw upon for the form and function of his protagonist Beelzebub. The science fiction and fantastic story of more recent times do not concern him. He is, rather, interested in delineating a historical trace of human civilizations and an "objective" criticism of man's behaviour. He accomplishes this by widening and deepening the genre of spatial travel by conjoining with it fresh ideas about human culture from a perspective that is reminiscent of the writings of Emmanuel Swedenborg.

~ Prof. Taylor lived for some years with Jean Toomer in New York and Pennsylvania as a young boy, studied with Gurdjieff in Paris after World War 2, before turning to a teaching career in Medieval Germanic languages and literature, first in Iceland and for the past thirty years in Geneva, where he lives with his wife and two teenage children.

Hotel Extol Inn, Prague, Czech Republic
Pristavni 2
Prague 7
170 00
Czech Republic

Reception tel./fax: +420 220 876 541, reservations tel.: +420 220 802 549, Reservations fax.: +420 220 806 752, contact email: info@extolinn.cz
Website: http://www.extolinn.cz/english.html

ADVISORY BOARD
Nick Bryce, Dr. Keith A. Buzzell, Seymour B. Ginsburg, Dimitri Peretzi, Prof. Paul Beekman Taylor

READING PANEL
Dr. Stephen Aronson, Rev. José Tirado, Terje Tonne
Music advisor: John Amaral

PLANNING COMMITTEE
Stephen Aronson, Paul Bakker, Marlena O. Buzzell, Farzin Deravi, Ian MacFarlane, Clare Mingins, Robert Ormiston, Bonnie Phillips, Arkady Rovner

Planning Committee

Paul Bakker - Netherlands
Marlena Buzzell - USA
Farzin Deravi - UK
Ian MacFarlane - UK
Clare Mingins - UK
Robert Ormiston - UK
Bonnie Phillips - USA
Arkady Rovner - Russia

Reading Panel

Stephen Aronson - USA
José Tirado - Iceland
Terje Tonne - Norway
John Amaral - USA (Music Advisor)

Advisory Board

Seymour B. Ginsburg - USA
Nick Bryce - Canada
Dr. Keith Buzzell - USA
Dimitri Peretzi - Greece
Prof. Paul Beekman Taylor - Switzerland

Speakers

John Amaral
John Amaral was born in Long Beach, California, raised by Catholic nuns, and trained in Electrical Engineering and Music. He has studied Gurdjieff with students of Mr. Nyland, Mrs. Staveley and Mrs. Popoff, and began to attend the A&E Conferences in 2003. "Perhaps the most useful aspect of the Conference for me has been that it has helped me to develop a more inclusive perspective about ways of Working. It has also opened for me new vistas of interesting inspiring contacts.

Seymour B. Ginsburg, J.D.
Sy Ginsburg was born in Chicago in 1934 and currently resides in Florida. He was introduced to the Gurdjieff Work by Sri Madhava Ashish, an eminent theosophical scholar and Hindu monk, who became his mentor over a 19 year period. Ginsburg was a member of the Gurdjieff Society of Florida and later a co-founder of the Gurdjieff Institute of Florida. Currently, he is a Director of The Theosophical Society in Miami & South Florida and facilitator of the Gurdjieff Study Group at The Theosophical Society.

Dimitri Peretzi
Mr. Peretzi is the president of the Gurdjieff Foundation of Greece. With reference to his personal contacts with eminent students of Gurdjieff, Lord Pentland, Madame de Salzmann, Dr. Welch and others, he has authored a number of books and articles that study the problem of consciousness, relating views from the esoteric traditions to those of the contemporary philosophy of mind. Mr. Peretzi did graduate work in Philosophy, at Yale, where he received his Master of Architecture. Having settled since 1974, he established his own Construction and Prefabrication Company.

Michael Readshaw
Mike Readshaw first read Beelzebub's Tales at University, where he obtained a degree in Mathematics, specialising in Mathematical Logic. A meeting with Rina Hands indirectly led to him producing a number of audio talks, the first of which, Reading Gurdjieff, exposed the difference between Gurdjieff's own writings and the established Gurdjieff canon of thought. This was much praised by Mrs Annie Staveley, but after a serious climbing accident in the Alps, Mike was distracted and had to re-learn to walk, married, and trained as a teacher. He lived in France for a number of years before family circumstances forced him back to England. Mike is a widower, with five children in his care, and teaches Mathematics in the north of England. Knowing that personality has ideas whilst essence has insights, his most recent work consists of devising 365 completely original sayings with the intention of raising the overall level of awareness of those in contact with him, based upon the principle that: A good saying stops all thought so that understanding can fill that vacuum.

Speakers

Arkady Rovner
Arkady Rovner was born in 1940 in Odessa, USSR and spent his youth in Tbilisi, Georgia. He studied at Moscow State University and Columbia University, New York. He taught numerous courses on world religions and contemporary mysticism at the New York University, the State University of New York, the New School for Social Research and the Moscow State Humanitarian University. He was introduced to Gurdjieff's ideas and practices in Moscow, Russia in 1965 and has been an adherent of the Gurdjieff Work ever since then. During the years 1975-1984 he was in constant communication with Lord Pentland, the head of the American branch of Gurdjieff Foundation. In the summer of 1980, with a letter of reference from Lord Pentland, he travelled to London and Paris where he met and interviewed a number of Ouspensky's and Gurdjieff's former disciples, including Mr. Tilley and P. L. Travers, as well as Michael de Salzmann.

Paul Beekman Taylor
Prof. Taylor lived for some years with Jean Toomer in New York and Pennsylvania as a young boy, studied with Gurdjieff in Paris after World War 2, before turning to a teaching career in Medieval Germanic languages and literature, first in Iceland and for the past thirty years in Geneva, where he lives with his wife.

Why is that Transformation, which Gurdjieff so wished for us with all his Being, and to achieve which he wrote Beelzebub's Tales to His Grandson, necessary, and how is it achieved?

Michael Readshaw

Abstract

As soon as he can, in *Beelzebub's Tales to His Grandson*, Gurdjieff makes the following claim: "Concerning all this it must be said that neither the organ Kundabuffer which their ancestors had is to blame, nor its consequences which, owing to a mistake on the part of certain Sacred Individuals, were crystallised in their ancestors and later began to pass by heredity from generation to generation."

"But they themselves were personally to blame for it and just on account of the abnormal conditions of external ordinary being-existence which they themselves have gradually established…" (Ch. 13. Why in Man's Reason Fantasy may be Perceived as Reality. p. 104/105)

And then this: "You yourself will very well understand that although the fundamental causes of the whole chaos that now reigns on that ill-fated planet Earth were certain 'unforseeingnesses,' coming from Above on the part of various Sacred Individuals, yet nevertheless the chief causes for the developing of further ills are only those abnormal conditions of ordinary being-existence which they themselves gradually established and which they continue to establish down to the present time." (Ch. 16 The Relative Understanding of Time. p.132/133)

In this talk, Mike analyses the expression 'the abnormal external conditions of ordinary being-existence established by them themselves,' - a phrase which Gurdjieff uses 153 times, in one form or another, in BT, to completely define the causes of our present sorry state - word for word, in order to find out what are these conditions, that is, what is wrong with us, how and why we establish these conditions ourselves, and hence he establishes why Gurdjieff wrote *Beelzebub's Tales* in order to transform us, and how that transformation is achieved.

Why is that transformation, which Gurdjieff so wished for us with all his Being, and to achieve which he wrote Beelzebub's Tales to His Grandson, necessary, and how is it achieved?

The more profound our reading of *Beelzebub's Tales to His Grandson* becomes, the less and less resemblance Gurdjieff's writings bear to the Gurdjieff Tradition.

Why is that Transformation…?

What I have done, therefore, is to choose four phrases, expressions, issues, which are in the Gurdjieff's writing, but which are not in the Gurdjieff Tradition.

And I would also like to add that there is one area of the Gurdjieff Tradition that I do agree with. From almost the very moment that it was written, the Gurdjieff Tradition has repeatedly maintained that the supposedly mysterious and incomprehensible book *Beelzebub's Tales to His Grandson* must be a legominism. I entirely agree with this.

And so, the four expressions, or ideas, are these: that Gurdjieff has written BT in order to transform us. Secondly, that he writes that he is going to do so by placing, what he calls, the essence of certain real notions, into our true consciousness. Thirdly, that he is transforming us out of the terrible state we are now in, which he calls the abnormal external conditions of ordinary being-existence established by us ourselves, and that finally, when the transformation is complete, then, and only then, do we have the possibility of creating conditions appropriate for, what Gurdjieff calls, being-partkdolg-duty, and developing in a real, genuine and objective sense.

I started teaching nearly forty years ago, as a teenager, teaching rock climbing. And when I learned to be a teacher, I learned the Army method of teaching. Now, the Army method of teaching is this: first of all, you tell them what you are going to tell them, then, you tell them it, and then, you tell them what you have told them.

Now, Gurdjieff's book is rather like this. In the first chapter, he tells us what he is going to do. In writing the book, and in us reading the book, he does it, and at the end, when the book is written, in the chapter on Form and Sequence, he tells us what he has done.

There are three stages.

On almost the first page of BT, Gurdjieff has written four paragraphs which constitute his 'statement of intent.' They are actually on pages 24 and 25. (My book is very small, and, if BT was only five times bigger, as we see, these paragraphs would be on the first page.)

Last year, I was privileged to be able to introduce the first of these four paragraphs, in Gurdjieff's statement of intent, for discussion. (see ref) This is it. I will read the shortened version here:

(… I wish to bring to the knowledge of your "pure waking consciousness" the fact that in the writings following … I shall expound my thoughts … that the essence of certain real notions may … of themselves automatically go … into … the subconscious, and there by themselves mechanically bring about that TRANSFORMATION which should proceed in … man and give him … the results he ought to have … proper to man.)

Now, you couldn't make this stuff up! As we see, Gurdjieff intends to transform us, to give us the results we ought to have, proper to man. Automatically, mechanically, just read the book, might be a bit of a surprise to you, on the first page of BT, as it were. But there you go: I didn't make this up, this is what Gurdjieff wrote.

Now, Gurdjieff is writing BT in order to transform us. It is not a textbook about the Universe out there, for example. Nor is it about self development, self study, work on oneself, nor is it about, for those more ambitious amongst us, self perfecting. A transformation is a change, not a development. If an egg become a chick, or, as Gurdjieff might put it, if an egg becomes an omelette, we would not say that the egg had developed itself, nor perfected itself.

Now, even at this early point in my talk, I can almost sense a member of the Gurdjieff Tradition walking over towards me. 'You know, Mike,' he says, 'BT is a legominism.' I smile at him. 'But what about the essence of certain real notions?' I ask him. 'Where are they in this Gurdjieff Tradition?'

Going back to his statement of intent, Gurdjieff says, quite clearly, that he is going to bring about that transformation by placing the essence of certain real notions into our true consciousness.

Not real notions, I note. Not even notions. Not ideas, not true ideas. But, the 'essence of certain real notions.'

In this first chapter of warning, Gurdjieff explains that man has two distinct forms of mentation. He calls these 'mentation by thought,' and 'mentation by form.' And so the more astute among us might suspect that there are, in BT, two distinct books, as it were, one within the other: one text, for the ordinary man, using this 'mentation by thought,' and another, inner text, awaiting discovery, using this 'mentation by form.'

Indeed, further, in these four paragraphs comprising his statement of intent, Gurdjieff points out, and maintains, likewise, throughout BT, as we shall see in the chapter on Hypnotism, this afternoon, that we have two relatively independent consciousnesses, having nothing in common. And our true consciousness - our true consciousness, he says, is our subconscious.

The transformation, Gurdjieff explains, will result in our true consciousness, that is, our subconscious, predominating in our common presence. Gurdjieff is not developing us in any way; the transformation is changing over our two consciousnesses, exchanging one for the other, that our true consciousness eventually predominates.

However, as we are, these two relatively independent consciousnesses, having nothing in common, are rather like the rails on a railway track, constantly moving in a parallel direction.

To our ordinary, false consciousness, - the outer text - Gurdjieff taught 'confrontative data.' That is, he took all the ideas that the ordinary man has about the world, and he confronted them, or contradicted them, to produce his novel. That is the purpose, he says, of our false consciousness, to provide confrontative data for our true consciousness.

Why is that Transformation…?

At the same time, as an inner text to this book, by means of this mentation by form, as he is doing this, he is placing into our other consciousness, our true consciousness, the other parallel track of the railway, the 'essence of certain real notions,' to, in fact, place into our subconscious, what to do, that is, what to do to transform ourselves, how to do it, and also of course, why we should do it. And then our true consciousness, the subconscious, according to its level of understanding, armed with this new knowledge, simply gets on and does it. This is his real teaching, as yet, perhaps, unrecognised.

And, thirdly, between the two consciousnesses, like the 'sleepers' on the railway track, keeping them apart, separating our self from our self, as it were, Gurdjieff created that friction necessary to release the energies we need for our true development.

At this point, again, the Gurdjieff Tradition tugs at my sleeve. 'It's a legominism you know.' It winks at me and I smile. 'Yes,' I say, 'but where are the abnormal conditions of external ordinary being-existence established by us ourselves? Where are they in the Gurdjieff Tradition?'

I first read BT many years ago now. And if you had asked me, after the first ten years, after the first fifteen years, even, I may say, perhaps, after the first twenty years, to tell you what, according to this book, was wrong with mankind, I would have answered, emphatically, and convinced I was right, that what was wrong with mankind was the 'crystallised consequences of the organ Kundabuffer.' In my mind, these were connected in some way with egoism, which, in turn, was connected with personality. This, of course, prevented essence from developing as it should. And this meant that I was not a true individual, and that I could not 'do,' and that I had not grown my own astral body, and that I risked being destroyed forever, such as I was, by the sacred Rascooarno. And so on. Complete nonsense of course. Just chains of thinking. Chains of association. What Gurdjieff calls: suggestibility.

It was only when I was able to read BT, going through the book more profoundly, that I came upon passages like the following.

This is from Chapter 13. Why in Man's Reason Fantasy may be Perceived as Reality:

"Concerning all this (why fantasy may be perceived as reality) it must be said that neither the organ Kundabuffer which their ancestors had is to blame, nor its consequences which, owing to a mistake on the part of certain Sacred Individuals, were crystallised in their ancestors and later began to pass by heredity from generation to generation.

"But they themselves were personally to blame for it, and just on account of the abnormal conditions of external ordinary being-existence which they themselves have gradually established…" (BT. Bk. 1. p. 104/105)

And then. It is from Chapter 16. The Relative Understanding of Time:

"And meanwhile remember, that although the fundamental motives for the diminution of the duration of the existence of the three-brained beings of this planet were from causes not depending on them, yet nevertheless, subsequently, the main grounds for all the sad results were - and particularly now continue to be - the abnormal conditions of external ordinary being-existence established by them themselves." (BT. Bk. 1. p. 131/132)

And then this, from the next page of the same chapter:

"You yourself will very well understand that although the fundamental causes of the whole chaos that now reigns on that ill-fated planet Earth were certain 'unforseeingnesses,' coming from Above on the part of various Sacred Individuals, yet nevertheless the chief causes for the developing of further ills are only those abnormal conditions of ordinary being-existence which they themselves gradually established and which they continue to establish down to the present time." (BT.Bk.1.p.132/133)

And it went on and on and on. Again and again, as I continued through the book, I found that this phrase, in one form or another, occurred again and again, over 100 times in all.

I like to imagine that there is, in BT, a sort of high level debate going on: what is wrong with Mankind? If we look at the great Messengers from Above, then what is wrong with Mankind, according to them, is clearly the 'crystallised consequences of the organ Kundabuffer,' and the battle against them. Saint Buddha says, in the book, that the best way to rid yourself of these consequences is to compel yourself to bear the displeasing manifestations of others towards oneself. Also, of course, for the great Ashiata Shiemash, the battle was against these crystallised consequences, using the divine impulse of Objective Conscience, still present in our subconscious.

Then, in complete and total contrast, as we have just seen, for Beelzebub himself, what is wrong with Mankind is the 'abnormal conditions of external ordinary being-existence established by us ourselves.'

And thirdly, of course, for Gurdjieff himself, as he says repeatedly, from almost the very first page of his book, and emphasises throughout the book, what is wrong with Mankind is that human beings are adapted to perceive the world only automatically. In consequence, we have been adapted so that certain exaggerated involuntary experiencings should proceed in us, so that we can at least automatically absorb and digest enough of the second and third being-foods, through impressions, to maintain merely our own physical existence. So for Gurdjieff, what is wrong with Mankind is that we are adapted to perceive the world only automatically.

And so, what are the abnormal conditions of external ordinary being-existence established by us ourselves, and how do we establish them? Clearly, we establish them ourselves.

Secondly, being-existence is the not the same thing as existence: it is not how we arrange our kitchen, or organise our day, or how we behave. What then is being-existence? It clearly refers to our inner existence, in some way, to which we are external.

More important here however, are two words in this expression. Gurdjieff is transforming us. From what and into what. Here we have the word ordinary, and so we are being transformed away from the ordinary. With the word ordinary, the beginning of the transformation, Gurdjieff associates the word abnormal. So, what is the end result of the transformation? What is the opposite of abnormal? Clearly, normal, and we are being transformed into normal men and women. The book, from the start to the finish, leads us through all the varied stages of this transformation.

Now, if we take a highlighter pen, as I have done, and highlight every time the words 'ordinary' and 'normal' occur, in BT, you will be amazed. The book suddenly makes sense as a constant comparison and a contrasting between the 'ordinary man' at the start of the transformation, with the 'normal man' at the end. The whole book weaves in and out, in and out, of these two conditions: man as he is, the 'ordinary man,' and man as he should be, the 'normal' man - usually situated in the past, since Mankind is pictured by Beelzebub as having degenerated, as confrontative data.

But, here, again, the Gurdjieff Tradition tugs at my sleeve. 'It's a legominism,' they say. 'I know,' I reply. But where,' I say, 'in the Gurdjieff Tradition, is there any understanding of the place of being-partkdolg-duty?

Gurdjieff says that he is writing BT in order to transform us. It is easy to assume, it is easy to assume that the transformation Gurdjieff speaks of involves being-partkdolg-duty. I have been through every mention, in BT, of being-partkdolg-duty, with my highlighter pen, - fortunately, when it comes to BT, I have seven different colours - and I have studied all these references, and I can say for sure that there is absolutely no suggestion anywhere in the book, at any time, that this transformation that Gurdjieff himself writes about, involves, in any way, being-partkdolg-duty.

Being-partkdolg-duty, it becomes clear, is a possibility for us only at the end of the transformation.

It is clear that we have failed, in some way, in the past, to create conditions in which being-partkdolg-duty takes place, as we should, as three-brained beings, and that we have, as a result fallen to the level of the ordinary man, and that, in consequence, Great Nature has been compelled to adapt herself, and us, to this fact. But, there is no suggestion, however, in BT, that we can simply begin again to create conditions for being-partkdolg-duty and hope that everything will be all right. The world is not like that. There are situations that are irreversible. The 'fall' from normal man to ordinary man is like this. To fall is easy. To climb back up is not, especially if we injure ourselves in the fall!

Being-partkdolg-duty is a possibility for the normal man, that is, the man as he should be, the man at the end of the transformation.

In this way, the various elements mentioned by me in this little talk, fall into place.

At this point the Gurdjieff Tradition tugs at my sleeve again. 'BT is a legominism,' it says. My patience snaps. 'I know it's a legominism! The Gurdjieff Tradition has been saying so for over sixty years. I know that *Beelzebub's Tales to His Grandson* is a legominism: but, what about? That is the key to it. It is a legominism, but what about? The term legominism originates in BT, but every time it is used there, every time there is a legominism, it is about something. The Terror of the Situation, the legominism of Ashiata Shiemash, for example, is about Objective Conscience. What is the legominism BT to His Grandson about?' I ask.

It is about this transformation. Everything in BT is about this transformation. The whole story, from start to finish, following the various stages of the transformation; the structure, comparing and contrasting constantly ordinary man with normal man, the division throughout of man into false consciousness and true consciousness with a view to changing these two consciousnesses over in man, everything in this book screams out that it is all about this transformation. I know that BT is a legominism, I say. 'And it is a legominism about this transformation!'

BT was published over sixty years ago. It then became, in a sense, public property. It is not a secret book. As a member of the public - I am not in any Gurdjieff group. I have never been in any Gurdjieff group. I do not have a Gurdjieff teacher - I read on the first page, as it were, of BT, that Gurdjieff is writing his book in order to transform us. He wrote this, not me. I couldn't make this stuff up. If Gurdjieff is writing this book in order to transform us, it seems to me to be a reasonable question, in response, to ask why is he transforming us, that is, why is this transformation necessary?

Gurdjieff writes that he is going to transform us. He wrote this, not me. I couldn't make this stuff up. And if he writes that he is going to transform us, it seems to me to be quite reasonable to ask, in response, how is he transforming us, that is, how is this transformation achieved?

Both these questions, asked here - Why is that transformation, which Gurdjieff so wished for us with all his Being, and to achieve which he *wrote Beelzebub's Tales to His Grandson*, necessary, and how is it achieved? - are intimately linked with the burning question that emerges from us all, at the heart of our reading of BT, mentioned here, and that is the question, what is wrong with mankind? What is wrong with us? What is wrong with me?

Why is this transformation necessary? Gurdjieff has given some answers.

We live in a false consciousness. We need our true consciousness to take over and predominate in our common presence, before we can develop.

We are living in the abnormal external conditions of ordinary being-existence established by us ourselves. We need to be transformed out of, and away from, these abnormal external ordinary conditions.

We have been adapted by Great Nature to perceive the world only automatically, and adapted so that certain exaggerated involuntary experiencings proceed in us. We need to be transformed out of this adaptation.

And there are other answers.

How is this transformation achieved? Gurdjieff says that he has written BT, and that he wants us to read it, in order to place into us, into our true consciousness, the essence of certain real notions.

The more profound our reading of BT becomes, the less and less resemblance Gurdjieff's writings bear to the Gurdjieff Tradition.

And so: Gurdjieff wrote BT in order to Transform us. He does so by placing into our true consciousness, what he calls 'the Essence of Certain Real Notions.' The Transformation takes us out of our present terrible state which he describes as 'the abnormal external conditions of ordinary being-existence established by us ourselves.' And that once this transformation is complete, we are then, and only then, able to create the appropriate conditions for genuine 'being-partkdolg-duty,' and to develop in a real, genuine, objective sense.

Now, bear with me for the last few minutes as I try to demonstrate clearly what this means.

Gurdjieff writes that we have two relatively independent consciousnesses having nothing in common. He writes that he is going to make our true consciousness - the subconscious - predominate in our common presence - predominate over our false consciousness, that which we are now in.

So here they are. Let us put our false consciousness here. And our true consciousness here. True, false. False, true.

Now, Gurdjieff writes that the main fault, as it were, of our false consciousness is that we are suggestible. So, our false consciousness here is suggestible.

Now, Gurdjieff does not say that in our false consciousness, we have a big red nose. Because, if, in our false consciousness we have a big red nose, we also have a big red nose in our true consciousness. Compare and contrast. Gurdjieff says that we are suggestible, in our false consciousness, to compare it with our true consciousness, where, we have the opposite of suggestible, namely, as he writes again and again, semooniranos, or impartiality. Impartiality.

And so, Gurdjieff does not write that, since the false consciousness is suggestible, that we must strive, struggle, tear ourselves apart, and make ourselves ill, working on ourselves, struggling with ourselves, trying not to be suggestible in our false consciousness. No. There is no suggestion of this.

The false consciousness, our false self, is suggestible. That is its nature. It always has been. Always will be, it is suggestible. We are not going to change it in any way. It is pointless to try.

Instead, Gurdjieff writes that he is going to transform us so that our true consciousness will predominate in our common presence. Then, we will no longer be suggestible, but impartial, because our true consciousness has the possibility of that quality of impartiality, and it will predominate.

Now, this was true even before BT was written. In the book *In Search of the Miraculous*, Ouspensky records, with ruthless accuracy, that Gurdjieff said to him that ordinary human being do not possess self-remembering. Ouspensky even put the word 'possess' into italics, in this book, to emphasise that self-remembering is a noun, something we either have, that is, possess, or do not have. It is not a verb. It is not something we do. It is a level of consciousness, or, at least, in the one mention of self-remembering in BT, the level of being in which we have the possibility of possessing this third level of consciousness, self-remembering. We cannot create self-remembering at will, we either have it or we don't. And Gurdjieff says that we don't.

And so, this ordinary, false consciousness, does not possess self-remembering.

Now, there is no suggestion anywhere that we should, in this false consciousness, struggle, strive, tear ourselves apart, make ourselves ill, trying to acquire self-remembering. No. We do not have it. This consciousness has never had it. It never will. It is not a property of this false consciousness to have self-remembering.

Now, Gurdjieff does not say that in this false consciousness we have beautiful blue eyes, because, if we have beautiful blue eyes in this consciousness, we also have them in this (our true consciousness.) Compare and contrast. Compare and contrast. He says we do not possess self-remembering, in this false consciousness, because we do possess it in this, our true consciousness.

The transformation that Gurdjieff wants for us is not to change this false consciousness in any way. We cannot do it. We cannot do. Instead, Gurdjieff is saying, in his writings, that we must make this true consciousness, the subconscious, predominate in our common presence, and when this true consciousness predominates, then, and only then, do we have the possibility of possessing self-remembering.

How do we make this true consciousness predominate in our common presence? BT is Gurdjieff's answer to this dilemma.

Gurdjieff says that he is going to do this by placing the essence of certain real notions into this true consciousness, telling it what to do, how to do it, and why it should do it. And then just let it get on and do it. All that we have to do is to read the book.

Gurdjieff's "Statement of Intent"

This is from Chapter 1. The Arousing of Thought. (BT. Bk.1. pgs 24/25/26)

"… I wish to bring to the knowledge of what is called your "pure waking consciousness" the fact that in the writings following this chapter of warning I shall expound my thoughts intentionally in such sequence and with such "logical confrontation," that the essence of certain real notions may of themselves automatically, so to say, go from this "waking consciousness" - which most people in their ignorance mistake for the real consciousness, but which I affirm and experimentally prove, is the fictitious one - into what you call the subconscious, which ought to be in my opinion the real human consciousness, and there by themselves mechanically bring about that TRANSFORMATION which should in general proceed in the entirety of a man and give him, from his own conscious mentation, the results he ought to have, which are proper to man and not merely to single- or double-brained animals.

"I decided to do this without fail so that this initial chapter of mine, predetermined as I have already said to awaken your consciousness, should fully justify its purpose, and reaching not only your, in my opinion, as yet only fictitious "consciousness," but also your real consciousness, that is to say, what you call your subconscious, might, for the first time, compel you to reflect actively…

"In the entirety of every man, irrespective of his heredity and education, there are formed two independent consciousnesses which in their functioning as well as in their manifestations have almost nothing in common. One consciousness is formed from the perceptions of all kinds of accidental, or on the part of others intentionally produced, mechanical impressions, among which must also be counted the "consonances" of various words which are indeed as is said empty; and the other consciousness is formed from the so to say, "already previously formed material results" transmitted to him by heredity, which have become blended with the corresponding parts of the entirety of a man, as well as from the data arising from his intentional evoking of the associative confrontations of these "materialised data" already in him.

"The whole totality of the formation as well as the manifestation of this second human consciousness, which is none other than what is called the "subconscious," and which is formed from the "materialised results" of heredity and the confrontations actualised by one's own intentions, should in my opinion, formed by many years of my experimental elucidations during exceptionally favourably arranged conditions, predominate in the common presence of a man."

© Copyright 2011 - Michael Readshaw - All Rights Reserved

Why is that Transformation...? - Questions & Answers

Questioner 1: I have two questions. The first is this: what do you understand by the term 'Gurdjieff Tradition,' - I ask this because we all have some idea of what this means, but I suspect that we all attribute a different meaning to this term that you have used; and secondly, you speak here of the subconscious. Is it possible for you to explain to me what you understand by the term subconscious?

I have thought much about this matter, and my conclusion after all this thought, is that the Gurdjieff Tradition consists of 'stories about Gurdjieff.' It is entirely that. The Gurdjieff Tradition consists of stories about Gurdjieff. These begin with Ouspensky's book, In Search of the Miraculous, which, although it does contain some very accurate statements made by Gurdjieff himself, actually consists mainly of just stories about Gurdjieff, and speculation by Ouspensky, to which he admits. And from then on, the Gurdjieff Tradition is just stories about Gurdjieff.

But many people find much of value in these stories and in this Tradition. It seems to me that you are rather like a medieval monk saying, simply, read the book. If it is in the book, it is true. If it is not, reject it. It is a rather primitive or retrograde step. I find much in this Gurdjieff Tradition that is valuable, and a help to understanding.

Michael Readshaw: I do not deny this. I am here at a conference about All and Everything, Gurdjieff's writing. And so I do say: just read the book.

However, I would like to add that I do not see any reason why the stories about Gurdjieff should have anything at all to do with what Gurdjieff was teaching. Why should they? This seems to me obvious. What Gurdjieff did and said during his life, where he went shopping and what clothes he wore, do not, it seems to me, have anything to do with what he was teaching. Many things that Gurdjieff did and said seem very strange and incomprehensible. So, to understand this, we must look at what he wrote to try to get a more complete picture. And when we do this, as I try to explain, we find a completely different picture from that presented of the Gurdjieff teaching by this Gurdjieff Tradition of stories.

As to you second question, I cannot say anything to you about the subconscious, other than what I have said in this short talk. Firstly, I have already presented a mass of ideas in the thirty minutes or so allotted to me. I can't explain, in that time, the whole of Gurdjieff's teaching. Even Gurdjieff had to write a book of a thousand pages to begin to do so.

Just read the book. Gurdjieff explains, from the first page of the book, everything you need to know about the subconscious. I cannot do so here. That is what the book is about.

Questioner 2: One thing I would like to say about Mike's presentation here, and that I personally am very pleased about, is that it is the first time I have ever heard anyone mention one of the most important aspects of Gurdjieff's writings, and that is this word 'impartial.' It is just such an important idea, and I have never heard it mentioned by anyone, at these conferences, before.

Michael Readshaw: Impartiality is the opposite of 'suggestibility.' It is the virtue to the vice, if you like. Compare and contrast. We are always going to be suggestible, in our false or fictitious consciousness. It is pointless to struggle with ourselves, beyond confirming this fact for ourselves. But gradually, as our true consciousness, this subconscious that Gurdjieff speaks of, begins to participate in us and to eventually predominate, then and only then do we acquire the possibility of 'impartiality.' Our false consciousness remains suggestible, but overall, we acquire impartiality.

It is worth mentioning also, that in the case of self-remembering, from the period before Beelzebub's Tales, we must not forget that Ouspensky struggled to 'remember himself' for two years, before Gurdjieff revealed to him that it was impossible, for the ordinary man, to remember himself, and that he could not do it, and would never be able to do it if he remained as he was. The task therefore, was not for Ouspensky to acquire self-remembering - we cannot and do not, until our true consciousness begins to participate and predominate in us - no, the task was to confirm, to come to a deep understanding, of this fact, that we do not remember ourselves, and cannot do so at will. This is what has become, in the Gurdjieff Tradition, 'work on oneself,' which is the work, not to acquire anything new - that can only come from our true consciousness, after this transformation - the work on oneself is to establish that we cannot do the things that we assume that we can do, such as, self-observation, self-remembering, not expressing negative emotions, acquiring knowledge of self, and so on. The list of things we cannot do is endless!

As I say here, Gurdjieff was, and is, transforming us, so that true consciousness predominates and we then, and only then, have the possibility of acquiring these qualities, and more.

Questioner 3: Is it not true that in Beelzebub's Tales, self-remembering is not mentioned at all?

Michael Readshaw: Self-remembering is mentioned in Beelzebub's Tales only once. (NB. Since then, I realise that it is mentioned three times! Still, not much, in a book of a 'thousand pages.' - Mike.) It is obviously, like many other things in the Gurdjieff Tradition, but not in Gurdjieff's writings, not an important part of Gurdjieff's teaching, although Ouspensky attached great importance to it as a philosophical revelation. Self-remembering, in Beelzebub's Tales, is mentioned as a level of being, that is, that level of being at which we possess self-remembering, or, at least, the possibility of possessing it.

Questioner 4: Can you give us, Mike, some idea of the way you personally have benefitted from reading Beelzebub's Tales?

Michael Readshaw: I think I have benefitted in so many ways that it is difficult to speak of this. If I speak however in terms of the Gurdjieff Tradition, then I would mention two things. Firstly, in terms of acquiring individuality, that is, my own 'I,' then I have made great progress in this, and acquired a certain confidence and force which I did not previously have. I think this comes across in all I do. Secondly, in terms of expressing negative emotions, or negativity in general, I think that I have acquired a very positive overall attitude, and an emotional robustness, as a result of my contact with Gurdjieff's writings and thought.

My personal opinion is that Gurdjieff's writings, if read correctly, lead in time to an overall unity and robustness, whereas the Gurdjieff Tradition seems to lead to increasing doubts, division and uncertainty. It is my opinion only, of course.

Questioner 5: I am finding it difficult, from your talk, to make clear to myself exactly what it is you are saying?

Michael Readshaw: I am in a vacuum as to why this should be so. I am saying that Gurdjieff has written Beelzebub's Tales in order to transform us. We are, as ordinary men and women, at too low a level to do anything to develop ourselves: we do not know what to do, nor in which direction to go. Gurdjieff says to us: stop, just read the book, and, by following the clues within it, you will be transformed, relatively automatically, mechanically, into normal men and women, in whom their true consciousness predominates, and who can hence begin, through their own intuition, to find their own, unique, way of working and develop.

It is a difficult thing to say to those in the Gurdjieff Tradition, as I call it: it seems too simple.

It is a question of becoming conscious of the other levels of meaning in Beelzebub's Tales, which, if you are concentrated on the mental ideas of the book and the theories of the Gurdjieff Tradition, is very difficult to do.

If you read Beelzebub's Tales, as Tales, that is, stories, or even, experience it as a piece of music, without thought or analysis, then it is much easier.

It is not so much what Gurdjieff says, that matters, rather, it is how he says it, and who - that is, which consciousness - he says it to. Gurdjieff speaks to the subconscious: the Gurdjieff Tradition tries to translate this into the language of our ordinary, 'fictitious,' consciousness, which rather misses the point.

Questioner 6: How would you advise people to read this book then?

Michael Readshaw: Read the book as phrases, like the notes in a piece of music, pausing each time there is a comma, or punctuation. It then flows easily. Once you have done this, listen to it again, this time pausing eighteen seconds every time there is a comma or piece of punctuation. This gives it time to sink in.

It is a kind of meditation. Inner silence, in which the meaning emerges. It is not an ordinary book!

Some Explorations of I Am, I Wish, I Can

John Amaral

Abstract

In the daily self-re-membering exercise "I am, I wish, I can," specific expressions are evoked. What are the meanings of these expressions? For example, if "I am" is an expression evocative of potential "Will-Being", what does this mean for me in the exercise, and what do the other expressions in the exercise mean to me? In this paper, I intend to give a sense of possibilities in the exercise, some of which may have been ordinarily missed.

An Exploration of I Am, I Wish, I Can

How many people here have done an I AM exercise? [show of hands]

Mr. Gurdjieff referred to the training offered by his Institute as "harmonic" or "harmonious." A sense of harmony may be experienced in the "I AM" exercise he describes in Life is Real. There is scarcely anything that one could add to this exquisite text (below) except by impressions having done it.

In the exercise, we intone words and simple sentences while sensing their resonances in unique areas of the physical body, feelings and thoughts. He says:

"For the correct understanding of the significance of this first assisting exercise, it is first of all necessary to know that when a normal man, that is, a man who already has his real I, his will, and all the other properties of a real man, pronounces aloud or to himself the words "I am," then there always proceeds in him, in his, as it is called, "solar plexus," a so to say "reverberation," that is, something like a vibration, a feeling, or something of the sort."

These reverberations can be "harmonious," that is, simultaneous with each other and having simple relationship with each other.

PART 1

1. The iconic word-sounds of the exercise are images which evoke a visceral understanding. These words function in a language simpler than that of ordinary exchanges and are understandable by all of us as three-brained beings because we have inner structures and experiences which resonate with them. On that level, the words are subject to less interpretation, fewer laws and contain

increased possibilities. But when we explain them with ordinary descriptions, they 'lose something in the translation' and become approximate (on a lower level). However, it IS possible to form sentence-thoughts without translating them downward. Demonstrating that is one of the aims of this paper.

2. The sounds of the words associate well with their locations: AM in the belly (almost the well-known OM), WISH in the chest (both "w" and "sh" have the sound of wind or breath), and CAN in the back of the head (the trailing consonant "-nnn" can be energized with the tongue touching the roof of the mouth and it vibrates in the back of the head. These can be considered to be three "musical notes" [demonstrates]

The exercise invites us to 'pop up a level'; to apply attention ('hydrogen 12') to these non-grammatical word-images ('hydrogen 24'*) and derive meaning from them directly. At this level, the Laws or Principles can be felt and understood with a minimum of interpretation. I feel therefore that this exercise embodies fundamental concepts and principles of the Gurdjieff Work, such as the Law of Three, Harnel Miatznel, Sacred Being Impulses, Worlds Three and Six, the resonant exchange of energy, self-remembering and self-observation, and so on. (It may be useful to note that it does not seem to embody the second conscious shock although it may be modified to do so. More about this later.)

At the level of I_Am... I_Wish... I_Can..., we may form sentences with the three words involving their entire sensation and meaning. With repetition, these sentences can begin to have meaning for us at that simpler level above our ordinary thinking. Sentences such as "I Can Am" begin to raise our level of Being according to the principle of Harnel Miatznel, "the higher blends with the lower to actualize the middle."

While interpretations in ordinary language are inadequate, it may be useful to suggest some possible meanings as preparation for direct understanding. I invite you to form your own impressions and notice whether they are the same or different than mine. It's particularly interesting to notice the role time plays in the forming of each impression:

1. THE SINGULARITY "I"

We begin with "I." How do we understand this word?

"I"   In language, "I" does not function alone; it works w/other words.

Gurdjieff defines "the genuine I of a man who has reached responsible age" as a concerted togetherness of three factors, notably "the entire sensing of the whole of oneself," the "I can" impulse and the "I wish" impulse. Only such a man, when he consciously says "I am" – he really is; "I can" – he really can; "I wish" – he really wishes.****

Some Explorations of I Am, I Wish, I Can

As demonstrated by JG Bennett's "This is not I" exercise, "I" is what is left when everything tangible is removed. It is not my body, not my feelings, not my thoughts, not my attention, not my will, not my degree of reason, not my actions, etc. Is it even "mine?"

[Plays recording]: Gurdjieff "Amen."

"I AM"   "Life is real only then when..." What do we make of the I AM part?

2. THREE NOTES

After the level of singularity, of "I," three new words represent three aspects of I. On this level, "I" can be sensed as composed of three parts: BEING is the capacity to remain in existence. WILL is the power to make choices. FUNCTION is the capacity to 'do'; to carry out those choices. Gurdjieff expressed these as the formulations I am, I wish, I can, which are both words and sentences.

I Am	My being exists
I Wish	I do wish
	I will (is there a difference?)
I Can	I am able to do
	I have potential to do.
	(contrary to "Man cannot do.")

3. SEPARATION

On this same level is the realization that there is both self and other. The task is to hold attention on both at once. This is the level where the possibility of CONSCIENCE appears. "HE" can be what you make of it: a particular other, all others, or even ENDLESSNESS HIMSELF. Each expression involves a separation from that which is "I".

HE IS
HE WISHES
HE DOES

4. INTERVAL HARMONIES

The Ray of Creation flows bidirectionally; downward automatically and upward by individual work. At the end of a location exercise transmitted by JG Bennett, the following formulations are given. One sense of them is as an exit-from and return-to the first level. Harmony restores the singularity and bridges the gap between God and Man, uncreation and creation, etc.

HE is I	Down the Ray- the "I" loaned to me is a particle of ENDLESSNESS
I Am HE	Up the Ray - the surrendering of "I" back to ENDLESSNESS

5. TIME ENTERS

The third level involves time. In his instructions in Life is Real, Gurdjieff introduces sequences. These sequences form and develop in us in linear time but they bring a kind of simultaneity we will look at:

"I am, I can, I am can.   BEING + FUNCTION = I am able to do.
I am, I wish, I am wish."   BEING + WILL = I am composed of wish.

MELODIC INTERVALS ("melody" means "sequence"; "interval" means "dimension")
IAm_Wish   I am entirely composed of my wish
      I am wishing
      That I am is the result of my wish
      That which I am is wish
IAm_Can   My being is entirely composed of doing
      I am doing (Gurdjieff said "I am canning.")
IWish_Am   I wish to be
IWish_Can   I wish that I can do
      I wish to be able to do
      I wish that I can
ICan_Am   I am able to be
ICan_WIsh   I am able to wish

6. MELODIC TRIADS

Now, we can have the full expression of sentences made with all three sounds (six simultaneous sequential relationships and subjective interpretations)
I Am Wish Can I am and I wish to be able to do I am wish(ing so that) I can
I Am Can Wish I am and I am able to do and to wish
I Wish Am Can I wish to be in order to do
I Wish Can Am I wish to do that I may be
I Can Am Wish I can do wishing for my being
I Can Wish Am I can do and wish to be

7. FAITH, HOPE AND LOVE

The words of the exercise can also be seen as expressions of sacred being impulses, forming a triad.

8.

At this point, we have examined the exercise as a horizontal (sequential) series in time, but we can remove the restriction of time and rise to a higher level; that of simultaneity.

PART 2 - INSIGHTS FROM MUSIC

By looking at the melodic possibilities of three musical tones, representing the three centers, we can expand our awareness of the meanings of the 'reverberations' which comprise the exercise and of the sentences we can make with them.

1. TONE RETENTION

We can understand and imagine a higher level, a world free of time, through musical insight concerning the cumulative simultaneity of events of a melody. In music, we call this the principle of "tone retention," which is the capacity of the memory to retain pitches heard in sequence (melodically) and to re-image pitches already heard and expected to be heard. It is the basis of the study of harmony. On account of this phenomenon, melodies can be heard as having a scalar-chordal-vertical-simultaneous-harmonic quality (which musicians call a "tonality." One recalls that Mr. Nyland, a good musician, described Work experiences as having "simultaneity" (in addition to "impartiality" and "objectivity").

On account of tone retention, melodies create what we call a "tonality;" a harmonic impression which may be identified by musicians in musical terms, such as "C major triad," "D melodic minor," F Phrygian Mode," etc.

For example, expectation may be easily demonstrated: it would be a surprise to hear a tune like Jingle Bells in a minor key. [demonstrates] We expect to hear a natural third step of the key. This fact makes us understand that an awful lot of synthesizing is going on in our brains to create inner impressions which are compared to outer impressions. The sounding of the unexpected exterior tonality with the expected internal tonality creates a clash in us, itself a new simultaneity.

Literature is another example of tone retention: words, such as this paper, ingested sequentially, whether heard or read, give us simultaneous re-evocable vertical impressions of story and style and meaning. We see from this that we are not talking merely of tone-retention but also of context and idea retention; the capacity we all have to follow the thread of a presentation or story or comprehend a book or master an entire academic discipline or solve a problem or build an invention or create a tool. We might go even further and describe the process of how we know that we are thinking; which is why our species is called "homo sapiens sapiens."

Gurdjieff's word poems in *All & Everything* are examples of tone retention:

"Faith of consciousness is freedom... etc."

"I AM THOU, THOU ART I, ... etc."

But once again, this kind of a simultaneity is lower than the one we seek, because it is composed of sequences, which are processes dependent on time.

2. CHOIR

For the musical experience we truly seek, we can experience a permanent higher level, a higher world free of time, through the vertical simultaneities produced by two or more melodies.

Gurdjieff trained in the choir at Kars Cathedral. Choir is a direct experience of self-other melodically. In choir, we sing while listening to ourself and others at once. To illustrate this principle using the building blocks of the exercise, let's sing.

We pay attention to the sensation of each note and 'place' that sensation in our bodies in the distinct locations 'belly', 'chest' and 'back of the head'.

(SING AS UNISON CHOIR)

Let's divide into three groups. Group A sings the bottom note I_AM first, then the middle, then the top and so on; Group B begins on the middle note I_WISH and Group C begins on the top note I_CAN.

(SING AS CHOIR)

We see from music that tempo is a major factor which changes our perception from time-based to infinite; the faster the tempo, the harder it is to catch the vertical coincidences.

Now that we have experienced melody and harmony (sequence and simultaneity), we can place the words in the same places. We pronounce the words "not only aloud, but even very distinctly and with a full, as the ancient Toulousites defined it, "wholly-manifested-intonation" - of course with that fullness which can arise in my entirety only from data already formed and thoroughly rooted in me for such a manifestation; data which are in general formed in the nature of man, by the way, during his preparatory age, and later, during his responsible life engender in him the ability for the manifestation of the nature and vivifyingness of such an intonation." (from *The Tales*, page 3)

(SPEAK AS CHORUS)

3. REGARDING THE SECOND SHOCK

In *Meetings*, at the end of "My Father," Gurdjieff requests that the following inscription be placed on his father's grave. The three couplets may be understood as expressions of the impulses FAITH, LOVE and HOPE in the context of self-other relationship:

I AM THOU, THOU ART I,   (FAITH)
HE IS OURS, WE BOTH ARE HIS,   (LOVE)

Some Explorations of I Am, I Wish, I Can

SO MAY ALL BE FOR OUR NEIGHBOUR.   (HOPE)

This may be taken on an ordinary level and has a value as referring to you and me, but suppose THOU and HE are actually ENDLESSNESS. We then see that the first two lines are similar to Bennett's formulations HE IS I and I AM HE.

Taking the choir experience of producing one part while imaging another, we might therefore have an expansion of the exercise which involves self-other relationship. This is CONSCIENCE - building and relates to the second conscious shock. In this approach, divide the attention and sense both poles of each line at once. Say and sense one pole while imaging the other:

I am   HE is
I wish HE wishes
I can   HE does

4. FURTHER CONSIDERATION

Christianity has added the possibly troubling Thou Art and Thy Will:

I am   He is   Thou art   You are
I wish   He wishes   Thy Will   You will
I can   He does   (be done)

These may be troubling because they seem to put us on a level where we are saying "I am" directly to God, a transgression which, in legend, ended Lucifer's angelic career (consider, for example, the Our Father).

5. FINAL NOTE

At first, one might think that I Am-I Wish-I Can must follow in a definite sequence, one dependent on the other. We now see that all the sequential possibilities are simultaneities.

References

*Prospectus of the Institute of Harmonic Development, G I Gurdjieff
**Beelzebub's Tales to His Grandson, G I Gurdjieff
***Meetings with Remarkable Men, G I Gurdjieff, Chapter One "My Father"
****Life Is Real Only Then When I Am, G I Gurdjieff
*****Perspectives on Beelzebub's Tales, Keith Buzzell, Ch 10, "Gurdjieff's 'hydrogens'"
******Image' has been identified by Buzzell as 'hydrogen 24', electromagnetic fields.

All & Everything Conference 2011

Gurdjieff's "I AM" Exercise

For the correct understanding of the significance of this first assisting exercise, it is first of all necessary to know that when a normal man, that is, a man who already has his real I, his will, and all the other properties of a real man, pronounces aloud or to himself the words "I am," then there always proceeds in him, in his, as it is called, "solar plexus," a so to say "reverberation," that is, something like a vibration, a feeling, or something of the sort.

This kind of reverberation can proceed also in other parts of his body in general, but only on the condition that, when pronouncing these words, his attention is intentionally concentrated on them.

If the ordinary man, not having as yet in himself data for the natural reverberation but knowing of the existence of this fact, will, with conscious striving for the formation in himself of the genuine data which should be in the common presence of a real man, correctly and frequently pronounce these same and for him as yet empty words, and will imagine that this same reverberation proceeds in him, he may thereby ultimately through frequent repetition gradually acquire in himself a so to say theoretical beginning for the possibility of a real practical forming in himself of these data.

He who is exercising himself with this must at the beginning, when pronouncing the words "I am," imagine that this same reverberation is already proceeding in his solar plexus.

Here, by the way, it is curious to notice that as a result of the intentional concentration of this reverberation on any part of his body, a man can stop any disharmony which has arisen in this said part of the body, that is to say, he can for example cure his headache by concentrating the reverberation on that part of the head where he has the sensation of pain.

At the beginning it is necessary to pronounce the words "I am" very often and to try always not to forget to have the said reverberation in one's solar plexus.

Without this even if only imagined experiencing of the reverberation, the pronouncing aloud or to oneself of the words "I am" will have no significance at all.

The result of the pronouncing of them without this reverberation will be the same as that which is obtained from the automatic associative mentation of man, namely, an increase of that in the atmosphere of our planet from our perception of which, and from its blending with our second food, there arises in us an irresistible urge to destroy the various tempos of our ordinary life somehow established through centuries.

This second exercise, as I have already said, is only preparatory; and when you have acquired the knack, as it were, of experiencing this process imagined in yourself, only then will I give you further definite real indications for the actualization in yourself of real results.

Some Explorations of I Am, I Wish, I Can

First of all, concentrate the greater part of your attention on the words themselves, "I am," and the lesser part concentrate on the solar plexus, and the reverberation should gradually proceed of itself.

At first it is necessary to acquire only, so to say, the "taste" of these impulses which you have not as yet in you, and which for the present you may designate merely by the words "I am," "I can," "I wish."

I am, I can, I am can.
I am, I wish, I am wish.

In concluding my elucidations of this assisting exercise, I will once more repeat, but in another formulation, what I have already said.

If "I am," only then "I can"; if "I can," only then do I deserve and have the objective right to wish.

Without the ability to "can" there is no possibility of having anything, nor the right to it.

First we must assimilate these expressions as external designations of these impulses in order ultimately to have the impulses themselves.

If you several times experience merely the sensation of what I have just called the "taste" of these impulses sacred for man, you will then already be indeed fortunate, because you will then feel the reality of the possibility of sometime acquiring in your presence data for these real Divine impulses proper only to man.

And on these Divine impulses there is based for humanity the entire sense of everything existing in the Universe, beginning from the atom, and ending with everything existing as a whole – and, among other things, even your dollars.

For an all-round assimilation of both these "assisting" or as they might otherwise be called "helping" exercises for the mastering of the chief exercise, I now, at the very beginning of the formation of this new group composed of various persons pursuing one and the same aim, find it necessary to warn you of an indispensable condition for the successful attainment of this common aim, and that is in your mutual relations to be sincere.

The unconditional requirement of such sincerity among all kinds of other conditions existed, as it happened to become known to me from various authentic sources, among people of all past times and of every degree of intellectuality, whenever they gathered together for the collective attainment of some common aim.

All & Everything Conference 2011

In my opinion, it is only by fulfilling this condition for the given proposed collective work that it is possible to attain a real result in this aim which one has set oneself, and which has already become for contemporary people almost impossible.

© Copyright 2011 - John Amaral - All Rights Reserved

Some Explorations of I Am, I Wish, I Can - Questions & Answers

Questioner 1: The notions of localization in the body of Am, Wish, Can, point to the direction of an alchemy of the body; some sort of alchemy in the body, yet to direct the utterance of such sentences, wilfully, here or there, points to an alchemy of attention. How would the two balance, in your way of thinking? Because these are two different directions. The one is there no matter what and the other one is there if I pay attention to it.

John Amaral: I would say that they are both going on at once. One of them is the directed Attention that sends something to the location and the other is something which reveals something already there. I don't think they are mutually exclusive.

Questioner 1: So in other words, I can say I Wish and direct it here (points to chest)?

John Amaral: Sure.

Questioner 1: OK

John Amaral: In fact, I think there is more to the exercise, in which you say I Am and sense all three at once.

Questioner 1: OK. Next question: You seem to identify Can with Do. Do you think this is good? One smells of potential and the other one smells of finality. Do is "I did it." "I Can" means I can do it, but then, I might not, and you seem to identify the two.

John Amaral: Well, I believe that one expression that I subjectively included was, as Gurdjieff expressed it, "I Am Canning." That is, it's happening now; that I am doing. And it's not something that has a finality, but something that continues.

Questioner 2: There's a problem here. Gurdjieff carefully says "can" in the Shakespearean sense. Does he not? He says "I can 'can' as Shakespeare meant it." How did Shakespeare mean it? He meant it as "ken." So then you have the understanding or the knowledge of what Dimitri means. It's interesting. Gurdjieff was very careful about localizing the direction of the meaning.

Questioner 1: You said "belly" and you were pointing here (points to gut). Why were you not pointing here (points to sternum)?

John Amaral: Musically or acoustically speaking, there is more movement here (points to gut).

Questioner 1: So you're searching for the key where there is light?

John Amaral: (laughs) Why not? Because this is not as fixed as, say, the genitals.

Questioner 1: No genitals. I wasn't pointing to the area of the stomach.

John Amaral: I think all of that (those locations) is open for exploration by the individual, but for me it's easier to sense below the diaphragm because it's not as 'fixed', so it can more easily vibrate. And if I'm teaching you to sing, I'm going to probably have you put your hand right here (belly) so that you can sense the vibration with your hand. The idea of resonance is that we have different parts of ourselves resonating at different frequencies, as in the world of sound. I think resonance and vibration is used in a very general way by Gurdjieff. He says "something of the sort."

Questioner 3: Unfortunately I have four questions. I am, I can, I wish resonates with my English language, but does that same resonance take place with the same words for somebody whose language is not English?

John Amaral: I hope someone will enlighten us about this.

Questioner 3: Because if I'm French, I say "je." I understand the vibration from "je." Or I'm Russian, I say "ya." And not the English "I."

John Amaral: Why don't we ask the question in general of the Russians? Is there any correspondence?

Questioner 4: There are two sounds: eeahh ayee.

John Amaral: So when you've come across this in Gurdjieff, has it created some dissonance with you for how this is supposed to work in Russian

Questioner 4: We didn't work with this technique but I like it very much.

Questioner 3: My second question concerns when you said that Mr. Nyland said objectivity, impartiality and simultaneity, he didn't mean it that way (the way you said). Mr. Nyland meant by simultaneity: at that moment, now, when I want self-observation by an I, means there must be no thoughts of the past or future. So that I know that there is a moment of timelessness, so it has nothing to do with music. And I would just like to say that my other comment is I don't have to go through all this very complicated exercise in order to have a direct and equally important result from music and I think that you can get exactly the same response from Rachmaninoff or Tchaikovsky or Beethoven or Mozart. And the actual vibration goes at that time to wherever it goes through Djartklom, so I don't decide where it goes. It enters me through my ears, which have a connection with my heart or it connects through my physical body or through my intellect, but I don't think I have a choice where it goes; I think it depends what my state is at that moment. So I think it's important for me, I do a lot of work with music; I think it's equally effective.

Some Explorations of I Am, I Wish, I Can - Questions & Answers

Questioner 1: If we see the connection between the alchemy of the body and the sound like the one you're describing, and leave the question open, that there is an affinity of the alchemy of the body with the one of attention, then there is a point of talking about directedness of the experience which could become independent of the particular sound.

Questioner 3: I know that we don't use the term "attention" because it means something quite different, I think. So I wouldn't ever use that word "attention," obviously what does it mean? Does it mean I'm more alert? Does it mean I'm concentrated? What exactly does "attention" mean? Because most descriptions of attention do not agree with what Gurdjieff says in the Third Series of what "attention" really is.

Questioner 1: I would not attempt to clarify these issues that you pose right now, but I am interested in what you (points to John) say about a body alchemy with that of directed attention alchemy.

Questioner 3: I don't know what "directed attention alchemy" is. My experience is that I create something, a real "I." If I can sustain that real I while the music is happening, then the I is a catalyst which converts impressions of the music into a substance and that's the alchemy of an I. I don't have experience of what directed attention is, but I do have an experience of what Gurdjieff calls an I and it comes from a separate part of the brain and that is the catalyst which converts the impressions, either from music, from opium (which is really fantasy), or from the white ray, as it's explained in that chapter "Heptaparaparshinok." He doesn't say anything about directed attention.

Questioner 5: When Nick speaks "that it moves free," in 1939, in one of the "I Am" exercises, he (Gurdjieff) actually says "what flows, where goes, none of your business." And I also wanted to say something about my attempts to work with this "I am, I wish, I can:" It has something similar in facing this question "who I am, where I am, what I am." And after certain experiences of mine, it seems that it has a quality of what can come out of these attempts is so much related to silence. It is as if even if I am having to reduce this experience of having a wish to work, I must not question if I'm doing it right. It must be operating from a very silent room in myself; a room which is completely separated from my mental apparatus. And that is why I find these attempts to be on the razor's edge. It has to be done in silence. One practical example is when Wim were with us not long ago, we had this during the weekend to have these questions in front of us: "Who am I?" "Where am I?" "What am I?" And I try to have them there and try to hold back mental activity; try to come up with a solution. And what came out of this for me was this: that to the question "who am I?" I am the one who is, that is as close as I can get and that was it for me. And "where am I?" Here. I could not 'find' any answer; that answer came to me when I tried not to find it. And "what am I?" This inner quest is the experience of This. So it's sort of a razor's edge; being on tiptoe.

Questioner 3: My fourth comment is, could you give, when you spoke about the second conscious shock, could you say more or less exactly what that means and at what stage does that take place?

John Amaral: I don't presume to be a teacher of this Work, but I believe the second conscious shock has something to do with ego, with self-other relationship, with conscience. And conscience is always operative in context with self and other, so in the spirit of experimentation that I believe Gurdjieff is inviting us to participate in, I'm looking for ways to 'push it' so that I can have an experience in the exercise that is related to self-other. Is that close to an answer (for you)?

Questioner 3: I think that one of the problems is that we have no common language, and I think Gurdjieff was begging us to have a common language and I think the second conscious shock is related to a precise period in the state of Work. The second conscious shock is Conscious Labor and Intentional Suffering but that must take place when the SI DO of the Kesdjan has been completed and I'm at the FA bridge of Soul, so then to cross the Fa bridge, so I have to now introduce Conscious Labor and Intentional Suffering, so it seems to me that it's a very specific and precise place where I am.

John Amaral: So I would ask you then, can you see Conscious Labor and Intentional Suffering existing without a self-other context.

Questioner 3: I don't know what that means.

John Amaral: In other words, can I do Conscious Labor and Intentional Suffering just with myself?

Questioner 3: With myself?

John Amaral: Only myself.

Questioner 3: Well, that's where it will take place. I intentionally go out to suffer but first I must prepare and then I select something I know I'm going to suffer (about). It could be "I hate going to a shoe shop," but I desperately need a new pair of shoes, but I hate confronting shoe salesmen, but I know I must do it, so I intentionally go out to the shoe shop to buy a pair of shoes but the emphasis is not on suffering; the emphasis must be on the awareness of me suffering. Then it's specific and precise attempt at Work.

John Amaral: I don't think we're talking at cross-purposes at all.

Questioner 3: But I have to be on a certain level to do that; I can't do that at the beginning of Work, because I don't know how to Work.

Questioner 1: One question: How many Rays of Creation are there?

John Amaral: I don't know.

Some Explorations of I Am, I Wish, I Can - Questions & Answers

Questioner 1: When we refer to a 'Ray of Creation', what exactly are we referring to? Experientially?

John Amaral: I think that some of the things I talked about in this are experientially related to that Ray on my level. Can I know about all the Rays of Creation (if there are more than one)? No.

Questioner 1: Is there a 'Ray' which passes through you and a 'Ray' that passes through me or are we in the same Ray, for example?

John Amaral: I don't know if you are going to like this answer, but I think it's both.

Questioner 1: I like the answer very much. But you see that the reason I put this question is that the self and the other, to have substance, they need to refer to this question.

Questioner 4: Dimitri, could you repeat the question?

Questioner 1: He used the expression: "the self and the other." How can there be a self and an other if I can only experience my Ray of Creation? If I can only experience my Ray of Creation, what *is* the other, exactly? Of course it's easy to consider the question in terms of directedness; attention directed away or toward what I perceive to be myself, which creates the 'other'; 'double-attention' or 'divided attention'. But is this division within the same Ray of Creation?

Questioner 4: I said, more profoundly, there is no 'I' and 'other'. There is no difference between them.

Questioner 1: It's experiential, though. Just to say the words doesn't mean anything.

Questioner 4: From the second level, there is no distinction between you and me.

Questioner 1: It's only me. (laughs)

Questioner 6: I'm still reverberating with the earlier exercise with the voice. This question about different languages then vibrated for a while. And it seemed to me that regardless of which part of the body vibrates, no matter how one says "I," what it draws us to is the experience of different vibrations of the body. Something becomes aware of those different qualities of vibrating. Something is now aware of a vibration here, here and here (points to belly, chest and head). There is then, from one angle, 'self-other'; the place of perception and what is perceived. And yet, the vibration is also in me, so it is one; and yet, it is separate. So then we come to the outside perhaps; how do I experience the vibration of, say, Dimitri? Well, in one sense, I experience Dimitri as different from me. And yet, if I try to experience the exercise simultaneously, I'm experiencing Dimitri, so I am 'me' and he is 'him', but he is also 'I' because I feel his vibration in me. And so, it's a matter of relativity, is it not? Being able to experience the different vertical qualities and horizontal qualities simultaneously. And if that is particularized from a certain angle, it seems 'self-other'. But experienced in a larger sphere of attention and noticing, it is all 'one'.

Questioner 4: Can I just add to what you said? Christ answering some questions that there are "no 'wives and husbands' in the kingdom of my father," so there is no separation and distinction in the "I Am;" there is no 'me' and 'you'. But it is actually not the final level, because Terje pointed to what he called "silence," that defies verbal description of everything, and this brings us to Buddhism, where there is no I; there is no "I;" where I dissolves into nothingness or silence. And even this is not the end, because Vedanta goes farther: It says that there is no 'I' and there is no 'no I'. There is reality. But I find this discussion and this exercise that we are experiencing now an extremely valuable example of "I Am." And it is on the edge of silence. It's the dearest thing to my heart.

Questioner 5: I think that what Stephen touches upon: outside and inside; he says that at some level of realization (this is how I understand it) there is a realization that when we use the terms "outside" and "inside" it is a mental activity. Now, I don't' think it is something opposing this that the true attempt to practice this "I Am" should exclude 'me' and 'others', because we have to start from where we ordinarily are. In my ordinary life, there is very much 'me' and then there are the 'others'. And I'm influenced that, so that the further I am away from myself, the more this is an actual reality: that I have to try to include the others also. It is only when I move away from 'me', my 'rights', my 'views', all that, that we can move in the direction of this unity. So if we start from where we are, I think that most of us will have to deal with it, in terms of 'the others', but hopefully we can have the experience of this unity.

Seminar 1: Chapter 32 - Beelzebub's Tales

Hypnotism

Facilitator: Steve Aronson

Introduction - Seminar Notes

Themes

The unnatural particular psychic property that permits entrance into a 'hypnotic' state.
The two system Zoostat. p559, 564
Necessity of a 'Wide Horizon'. p560
The Law of Typicality. p560
'Non-responsible-manifestations-of-personality. p560
Learned-of-new-formation and destruction of process of the Sacred Antkooano. p563
Egoaitoorassian-will. p564
Two-system Zoostat, sleep and hypnosis. p559, 564, 565
Logicnestarian-localizations, Education and Sacred data. p566, 567
Results of split-consciousness. p567
Influence of false consciousness on undeveloped sacred data of faith, hope, love. p568
Hanbledzion. p568
Aiessirittoorassnian-contemplation. p569
Hypnotic process explored in discovery by Pedrini and Bambin. p573-575
Sacred use and modern use of hypnosis compared. p578

Questions

Whom would I permit to see into my inner world? p558
How to understand 'Wide Horizon'. p560
How to understand 'Law of Typicality'. p560
How to understand 'Non-responsible-manifestations-of-personality'
Why is Science of 'Hypnotism' (non-responsible manifestations-of-personality) absolutely necessary to save three-brained beings from the consequences of the properties of the organ Kundabuffer. p562
What is relationship between Hypnotism? Learned-of-new-formation and destruction of growth of objective reason. p563
How do we distinguish 'artificial education about abnormal life from sacred data put in by Great Nature for forming real being-consciousness? p566
How do we understand 'Hanbledzion'? p568

All & Everything Conference 2011

How can we understand the nun, Ephrosinia's awareness of 'diabolical suggestions' in reference to the divided Zoostat. p574

Quotes

"I must tell you that formerly your favorites, like all the other three-brained beings of the whole Universe were without that particular psychic property which permits them to be brought into what is called a 'hypnotic state'. To get into that state became proper to your favorites, thanks to a certain combination obtained in their psyche and derived from the disharmony of the functioning of their common presence.

"This strange psychic property had its rise soon after the destruction of Atlantis and began to become finally fixed in the presence of every one of them from the time when their 'Zoostat', hat is the functioning of their 'being-consciousness' began to be divided in two and when two entirely different consciousnesses having nothing in common with each other were gradually formed in them, namely, those two different consciousnesses, the first of which was called by them simply consciousness' and the second -- when they finally noticed it in themselves - was called and still continues to be called 'subconsciousness'.

"If you try clearly to represent to yourself and to transubstantiate in the corresponding parts of your common presence all I am about to explain to you, you will perhaps then thoroughly understand 'nearly half of all the causes' why the psyche of these three-brained beings who have taken your fancy and who breed on the planet Earth has finally become such a unique phenomenon." p559

"…thanks to this strange property called suggestibility, which had only recently become fixed in their psyche, all the functionings in their common presences began gradually to change." p644

"Among the abnormal being-particularities or functions unbecoming to the essence of any three-brained being, the particularity of their psyche the most terrible for them personally is suggestibility." p107

"…thanks to that peculiar inherency called suggestibility all the surrounding beings believed this propaganda and there was gradually crystallized in each of them the periodically arising factor which actualizes in their common presences that strange and relatively prolonged psychic state, the 'loss of sensation of self'; in consequence of which they set about destroying everywhere, not only these wonder beds but also the existence of those beings who used them." p960

"You must without fail also know that when beings of the period of the Tikliamishian civilization constated for the first time about this particular psychic property of theirs, and soon made it clear that by its means they could destroy in each other certain properties particularly unbecoming to be in them, then the process itself of bringing someone into this state began to be regarded by them as a sacred process and was performed only in their temples before the congregation." p578

Seminar 1: Chapter 32 - Beelzebub's Tales

Seminar Discussion

Moderator: So a few quotes from this chapter to set the stage for our conversation:

"I must tell you that formerly your favorites, like all the other three-brained beings of the whole Universe, were without that particular psychic property which permits them to be brought into what is called a 'hypnotic state.' To get into that state be came proper to your favorites, thanks to a certain combination obtained in their psyche and derived from the disharmony of the functioning of their common presence.

"This strange psychic property had its rise soon after the destruction of Atlantis and began to become finally fixed in the presence of every one of them from the time when their 'Zoostat,' that is the functioning of their 'being-consciousness,' began to be divided in two and when two entirely different consciousnesses having nothing in common with each other were gradually formed in them, namely, those two different consciousnesses, the first of which was called by them simply 'consciousness' and the second—when they finally noticed it in themselves—was called and still continues to be called 'subconsciousness.'

"If you try clearly to represent to yourself and to transubstantiate in the corresponding parts of your common presence all I am about to explain to you, you will perhaps then thoroughly understand nearly half of all the causes why the psyche of these three-brained beings who have taken your fancy and who breed on the planet Earth has finally become such a unique phenomenon." p.558-9

***

"Thanks to this strange property which had only recently become fixed in their psyche, all the functionings in their common presences began gradually to change..." p.644

***

"...'suggestibility'.... [among] other properties quite abnormal and quite unbecoming to the essence of any three-brained beings..."

"...the particularity of their psyche the most terrible for them personally is....'suggestibility'." p.107

***

"Thanks to that peculiar inherency of theirs called 'suggestibility'....all the surrounding beings....believed this....'propaganda....there was gradually crystallized in each of them the periodically arising factor which actualizes in their common presences that strange and relatively prolonged 'psychic state'....the 'loss of sensation of self'; in consequence of which.... they set about destroying everywhere....the existence of those beings..." p.960-1

***

"You must without fail also know that when beings of the period of the Tikliamishian civilization constated for the first time about this particular psychic property of theirs, and soon made it clear that by its means they could destroy in each other certain properties particularly unbecoming to be in them, then the process itself of bringing someone into this state began to be regarded by them as a sacred process and was performed only in their temples before the congregation." p.578

Moderator: So we have a paradox - on the one hand, the hypnotic state seems to heighten suggestibility, is dependent on suggestibility, and leads to terrible unbecoming consequences; on the other hand, under certain circumstances it used to be considered a sacred state and was absolutely necessary for helping three-brained beings free each other from the consequences of suggestibility. So how can it be? Let's have a conversation.

Participant 1: I pose the question why Gurdjieff is referring to Mesmer as a person representing hypnotism and not referring to great teachers of humanity like Buddha, Mohammed and others, using this property with aim of liberation of human beings from hypnotism. So it's just a question.

Participant 2: Well perhaps I will begin, though I have not focussed enough on the subject. But Steven actually asked the same question which was repeated in Participant 1's question, namely of double use of hypnotism. So Gurdjieff several times in different texts refers to hypnotism as giving up responsibility. Responsibility is a quality that a human being develops in a responsible age. When the preparatory age is over, one takes on oneself responsibility for one's life. That is not a complete definition of hypnosis, but it is one of the definitions, giving up responsibility. Being irresponsible.

And the first question that arises is of what kind of responsibility Gurdjieff is talking about. Is not this responsibility connected with Partkdolg-duty, namely, the duty of everybody to do efforts towards awakening, towards becoming normal, from the original abnormal state?

What hypnosis does to a human being is it puts it into a sleep, in a state of trance where one perceives the world and oneself not as something that is real but perceives some imaginable features of the world and of oneself. So our sleep, our dreams, are a kind of hypnosis, and we are giving up responsibility when we sleep, when we dream, but in most cases we don't do bad things while dreaming, because we are immoveable. Then there is hypnosis that is imposed on us by education and upbringing, unconscious adopting of certain rules, values, that form our personality.

So actually hypnosis works with personality and it is capable of paralysing that personality, changing its stature and making some parts of personality inactive. So hypnosis can be used in order to disturb the world view of a person or of a group of people, and it can be used also to help a human being to get a sense of the essence of a human being. So it takes away that personality's activities by seizing these activities.

Also I can think of another use of hypnosis, to develop one's false personality, or disturb that personality, when a person has a certain system of values but he puts on another system of values that embellishes him, makes him think that he is different from what he is. You can think also of a conflict of personalities....... So it's a field where hypnotism can help and can harm, because it's a threshold to our essence.

Well now addressing question of Participant 1, I will say that Gurdjieff talks about hypnotism in general terms. He does not get into real techniques of hypnotism. He speaks of changing these blood pressures that can produce the hypnotic state but he does not reveal how he does it. He reached the same effect using his Hanbledzoin, but this was too expensive a price, and he gave it up. So I just give some preliminary thoughts on hypnosis.

Participant 3: I'd like to begin at the beginning of the chapter and to remind us that this is part of the sixth descent of Beelzebub to our planet. So what does that mean for me? What do I see that as? And for me, if I am in a state of work, it means the I comes closer to me to begin to help on a practical level with what the subject is. In this case I look in the dictionary and I look up hypnos – it means sleep, the signs of the phenomena of sleep, inducement of the hypnotic state, the thing that produces sleep. Persons under the influence of hypnotism only respond to external suggestion. But I think what he's saying is that we are desperately asleep, and are completely under the suggestion of all our thoughts and feelings, the media, newspapers, books we read, and everything in our ordinary life, which puts us into a deep hypnotic sleep. Two things that go on here are Beelzebub as a master can awaken us from this sleep through hypnosis, but only a master can do that, not an ordinary psychologist or psychiatrist or doctor, because he is completely unconscious, and how would he know what the trouble is if the subject is also completely asleep? So it has to be a separation that Gurdjieff or Beelzebub the master who can awaken me from my sleep.

And the reason for Mesmer I think was a man who had a tremendous insight and noticed that he was able to see the state of sleep in people and introduce some kind of a system, he doesn't explain, ... correct that statement. So I think that takes care on my perspective at the beginning of this chapter.

Moderator: But there's the implication then that to be suggestible means to be open. To be open to an input, a suggestion that might then take root and begin to produce a reorganisation that can lead to other manifestations. So then there's the question, open in what direction? So in your examples Nick, in terms of propaganda and politics......perhaps the influence of others, clearly the way we look at this is an involuntary opening to what comes in to us without an appropriate filter. There's also the question of actually an opening that comes from people inside. And perhaps this question of when would this kind of opening or suggestibility be sacred and when would it be profane might have to do with what direction it's coming from and for what purpose.

Let me say too that Beelzebub gives two reasons or two purposes for his sixth descent, and one of them is to gain entrée to all classes or castes, as such physician hypnotists enjoy great confidence and authority because ordinary beings are disposed to a sincerity towards them that convince them to penetrate their inner world. So in our own sixth descent there would be a suggestion that there needs to be sincerity and a wish to allow different parts of us to open to the search, perhaps. It might be related to Mike's presentation this morning. So there seems to be a relationship to openness and sincerity and directionality here.

Participant 4: Well there seems to be a paradox in that hypnosis seems to be presented here as both a curse and a cure, and when it is a curse it is obviously connected with the fact that there exists nothing, there are no parts in me, that can give directions, so I am open to anything, according to these suggestions. Then there is this possibility of being cured, and it presupposes that I have something in me that has to a certain degree recognised that something is not... and that would be an openness. And practically, this hypnosis works on the personality by me furnishing my intellect with new ideas. With these ideas, functions... I start questioning... that questioning that holds in me, that reacts to all these things. And through this questioning and through furnishing my intellectual centre with new furniture, new thoughts, I can gradually start hypnotising the personality. When I look at Bonnie, it looks like what I am saying is unclear.

And about Mesmer, I just wanted to add, it seems that he was chosen because he could see a connection between our ordinary life and there was something, I don't know whether he called it unconsciousness or what, but he could see those particular signs. And I don't know much about Buddha but I never heard that he was talking about the unconsciousness. What I am trying to say is that the hypnosis is my attempt that comes from refurnished intellect, new thoughts that can hypnotise my personality.

Participant 5: Just a couple of brief comments. It seems to me that the other messengers were involved in hypnosis. Jesus had his parables. We've heard about koans, Zen koans. And something simple to say about hypnosis from my point of view, the process is one in which we are put under, voluntarily or not, an influence. And in my experience I know that I'm quite gullible and perhaps some of the time the only choice I have is a little bit of choice about who or what is going to influence me, because I know that I'm experiencing hypnotic states quite often. So I just wanted to make the distinction between the process of hypnosis which is something we all do, and all experience, and then what happens when we're under that influence.

Participant 2: Well if we look at hypnosis as a certain openness to influences, then we have to ... what kind of influences we have in mind, mental influences, emotional, artistic, spiritual influences. Well, one of the universal systems of influences is the influence of a tradition. We know of quite a few traditions, Western, Oriental, such as Christianity, Judaism, and so on. These are universal systems, and they have a longer and stronger impact on us. We can instantly distinguish a person who is raised in Europe, in the Arabic World, in India, not only from the physical features but from their behaviour, reactions, rituals that we are involved in. And hypnosis in relation to the traditional impact can be seen as a way of imposing a certain tradition, deprogramming a person free from a tradition and imposing a new tradition, substituting one with the other. Pagan tradition versus Christianity. European modern paganism with Oriental traditions that are fashionable around here in the West.

And so we also must understand that the hypnosis that Mesmer and possibly Gurdjieff and other hypnotists worked with are based very often on a certain substance that Gurdjieff called Kesdjan body. They have different terms for that substance, prana ... many different words that describe this very gentle matter, substance. That hypnotist is addressing the hypnotised person. That substance is pooled from the hypnotist into the body of the hypnotised person. So it's not always ideas that hypnotise us, sometimes it's a pool of a special energy, of which Terje said, don't ask what is this and where it flows. It is. And that is well-known to everybody who works with hypnosis.

And we know how emotional exultation creates a field of hypnosis. When this has been studied in psychology of masses, in crowds, this was observed by many of us when we were witnessing hysterics of our friends, and the movements of these hysterics of other people. So there are many kinds of influences, emotional, pranic, intellectual, and so on.

Moderator: I want to make a suggestion that we strive as best we can to find a way to make this personally approachable today. And the other side of the question that for me is raised is what is it that flows in, the mystery of that, that I think Gurdjieff does address very specifically in a number of places in the chapter, is what makes us suggestible to it. It talks about the divided Zoostat, the divided consciousness, and how that develops. So although we may not understand what it is that flows, we can by studying ourselves understand more about our vulnerability to that flow, and feel that flow and begin to participate in a way that is useful to us and not subject to accident.

Participant 6: I feel that in order to come a little bit closer to maybe some understanding about this chapter, it is necessary at least for me to in a way use a magnifying glass. And that magnifying glass I have to put towards myself, because it is in that field of material I have the possibility to find something, and for me it is not far away in everything that it is somewhere in myself that I can try to find some understanding. And I have a simple example which just happened in the morning. I was having a rest upstairs and I fell asleep. It was very quiet, and I was together with a quiet place in myself and the time was coming when we were to be coming down here again, and then my husband came in through the door and he was quite firm in the way he acted, and I realised that I was short of time to come down here, and I could experience that there was some force coming towards my state that made me nervous and unquiet and out of sorts, and nothing to do with the situation, it was all related to the fact of somehow moving in the direction of getting identified with time. And that for me was an experience of being almost hypnotised, but I recognised it. It was a kind of hypnotic energy which was coming to put me to sleep. And I just wanted to bring this in as a practical example. I think it is very important to also in order that everyone else can take heart in the process that one tries to relate that what we talk about towards ourselves and that we don't get lost in all kinds of philosophical ideas.

Participant 7: Well I want to point out that we're definitely beginning with a question here. A question has been put that how is it that, what do we mean that, there's a situation of hypnosis, a situation by which certain aspects of man's psyche are put down, at least that are open to influences that keep you bonded to false reality. And at the same time, it is this hypnotic state that will free all aspects of this hypnotic situation of his, that will free him from this state. I would like to point out and explain that this is related to the second conscious shock.

If we can imagine an enneagram, and we remember the enneagram that Ouspensky describes, he puts at number 3 the first conscious shock, and he puts at number 6 the second conscious shock. At the same time, in man's work, his position, his desires, his wish to work, is the active force which has to go to point number 3. And at point number 6 is the negative force which is human mechanicality. So what we're dealing with here is that on 6 we have the negative force that opposes the effort to work, the effort to awaken, and at the same time we have the second conscious shock which awakens. So we're talking about some sort of a mystery here. How is it that at point number 6 we have both the negative and the positive aspect of awakening? The negative in the sense of what keeps man asleep, and the positive of what wakes him up to another reality. And I think that this is what we are dealing with when we're talking about hypnosis. We are dealing with our attempt to detect the factor that is responsible for sleep, and at the same time could awaken.

The mechanism we can understand. When I'm asleep, to awaken to my reality of being asleep, my consciousness of being asleep has to give in somehow. My egoism that keeps my world in the state I imagine it to be has somehow to subside, to go back, so it can open up to another kind of reality, which in my own state, my egoism, is what keeps being fed by the image of the world, and my logic keeps coming back to creating the world of false images of false consciousness that I have.

So what we are looking at here is really the mystery, I believe, of the second conscious shock. There is more that could be said about that; I just wanted to point out the similarity which I think is the very basis of this picture, of this structure we are presented with in this chapter, of the same factors being the negative points that keep us asleep, and the positive that can be the opportunity to shock into a new reality.

Why is it that we are not receiving the second shock right now? What do we need to have to be able to receive it? Something has to change, and I believe that the work of change is, and always is, that of the transubstantiation of the negative emotions into positive.

Participant 3: I think that one of the interesting things about this book is that some of the answers are not given in the chapter we are studying. Some of the answers are given in previous chapters or chapters ahead of us. So I think that's one of the problems that I have to bear in mind when I'm thinking about this subject. And if we go back to the chapter on the Genesis of the Moon where he says that Anulios was known in Atlantis as 'Kimespai', in other words 'Never-Allowing-One-to-Sleep-in-Peace.' [p.85]. So for me this process of work is first to awaken conscience. Once I've awakened conscience this conscience will not allow me to sleep in peace, and it will tell me and draw my attention to the fact that I'm asleep and completely unconscious. And it wakes me up, not exactly wakes me up but draws my attention to the fact that I am asleep, and from there I can change direction. So I think it's conscience that reminds me that I'm asleep... And that's a very practical result of what we're talking about.

Moderator: So the question of the vision is right there at the beginning of the Tales with the collision of the comet. So let me ask this question: How do we understand the 'two-system-Zoostat'? How do we understand for ourselves this division into two consciousnesses, one of which we tend not to notice, but which Gurdjieff says should be our true consciousness? How is this related to Itoklanoz, the Foolasnitamnian principle, and education? He gives many examples in here that we could relate to our own personal lives to study our own vulnerability to being open in the wrong way.

Participant 3: Well I think, maybe Dimitri can correct me, but I looked up in the dictionary, what does 'zoo' mean? And it comes from the Greek, 'living,' or 'animal life'. Is that right? So where does that put it, I mean what's the connection? Zoostat – does that mean it's the status of my animal life?

Participant 7: Yes

Participant 3: I struggled with that for a long time. I still haven't found what, because he never mentions Zoostat again in the book. It's the only time he mentions it. So it's a very difficult term he uses, and having it placed, here, I mean really he does define it as our unconscious existence and our real consciousness which is buried in our subconsciousness, and as he says, at the time of Atlantis, the destruction of Atlantis, when essence began to be covered over, what does that mean to me? It means that when I was a child I was not asleep. It means that I was more conscious when I was a child than what I am now. So it's only when people begin to influence me that essence, real essence, of consciousness, gets buried deeper and deeper.

Moderator: The definition on p.559 is "'Zoostat'....the functioning-of-their-'being-consciousness'."

Participant 8: I want to tell some words, maybe not about Zoostat.

[Translated] Well before we go to some aspects of our discussion is the questioning of the possibility of hypnosis to free human beings from false presence and lead human beings to the discovery of some real treasure in oneself. So where is the guarantee that we will reach liberation through hypnosis? It looks like a fairy tale.

In some places in the book, Gurdjieff writes about the highest degrees of human achievement, compares it with the microcosm. In the microcosm, the ultimate source of all activities of the subject is absolute.

In a human being, if we try to compare human beings with the microcosm, the profound layers, levels, of us are not active, are not involved in, they are not conscious of them. And since we don't have clear perception of our death we are subjected to hypnosis.

Once again the same question: If in deep hypnosis, if we go deep inside the layers of ourselves, will we find there shining substance of absolute or layers of swamp and thickness and darkness?

Participant 7: Well, first I would like to say something about 'Zoostat'. Well the word, the meaning exactly, in Greek, could be level of being an animal or level of being alive, either of those two meanings. So what I think it says in there is that there are two levels of being alive – because I think it is about being alive not about being an animal. And he says that this is two levels of being-consciousness which is again the idea of two consciousnesses existing. In other words he wants to say that people who live in their personality, that's how I understand it, can be very alive, but it's one level, one way of being alive, and they can be alive on different levels. But there's another kind of consciousness as well.

Now I will be talking tomorrow about consciousness, and that's exactly the point I will be analysing, but just to wrap it up as fast as I can, we're talking about not being conscious of sensation, which is personality, and being conscious of sensation. And these are the two kinds of consciousness I think that he is talking about.

Participant 2: What kind of sensations?

Participant 7: Sensation in the body. The energy of the body. The life of the body. I think that's what he's talking about. So what is happening here is that the Zoostat, if you're very intensely alive but in personality you have to lower this level, or you have to be hypnotised so to speak for another thing to become possible, so that you can listen to sensation, you can become aware of sensation in the body. You have to learn how to become aware of sensation. And this in a way you have to be hypnotised to begin into believing that there is such a thing as sensation.

So I do not see what Participant 8 says as a contradiction, or as a fairy tale, not as a fairy tale. But you make it difficult by putting the concept of certainty in it. How can I be certain that it is not a fairy tale? Well certainty cannot be because, well you can walk out and something can fall from the sky, like a stone from a building, we can't be certain that this will not happen, you know what I mean. So there is one thing about certainty, one we really have, and another thing, what the laws are. And I think that one can become certain of the laws, that certain effort will bring him into contact with sensation and that there is work to be done with sensation, with the second Zoostat, the second way of being alive, of understanding of being alive, and there you can form the changes so that you can apply certainty of the laws that you are under. And then work toward freedom through the second kind of real consciousness, of one with sensation, not with the real one which leads us from the work.

Seminar 1: Chapter 32 - Beelzebub's Tales

Participant 3: I'd like to address what you said, but first I think we have to be very clear, this word hypnos or hypnotism means sleep. So I can't by introducing sleep awaken myself, and only a master can hypnotise me so that I can awaken. That is only one acceptable way of hypnotism which is permitted in work, and that is music. That I can put myself in a certain state, which requires a lot of practice, and I can put myself in a certain state of trance whilst allowing the music to happen to me. The only way I can describe it is having two tuning forks. So I tap a fork, ping, this tuning fork is alive, so that's the music, and it's vibrating. This tuning fork is dead, that's me. So I've completely effaced the manifestations of myself, all thoughts, all feelings, all liking, disliking, categorisation and interpretation, and I sit there like a lump of meat. But then the music happens to me, then something can begin to vibrate in me in response to the music which is happening to me. And from there I can find a treasure which will come alive in me.

And the second one is, hypnotism, sleep from other people, not you. I am awake, I go to a store, a shopping centre, hundreds of people, all asleep, all radiating energy from wanting, desiring and eating, and wishing, and all this hypnotic state they're in is radiating out energy. If I am awake at that time I can suck all that energy from those people into me. They're in the hypnotic state, I'm not, I'm awake, but I have to be awake in order to do it. So I absorb all the energy from them. Gurdjieff in Heptaparaparshinokh calls it opium, the same thing, opium puts me into sleep, it means sleep, it means fantasy. But I use your fantasy to prepare for my energy.

Participant 4: There is something that Dimitri spoke of that triggered something in me. Change. In order to break out of this hypnotism there has to be a change. Where is that change? Where can it come from? If we look at the nature of change, it's very different from the nature of a circle. A circle is just a circle. So I get hypnotised, and I keep getting hypnotised, and I keep getting hypnotised. So the nature of change implies an alternative. And this alternative can be found in ideas, and they can be very nourishing. But they can only really nourish me if those ideas bring me to an experience where I can verify what they are saying.

I have a situation: at the airport when I was coming here, there was a queue and we were not really late, but something in me started to get identified with time. Well this identification was recognised in my head, certain thoughts. I also recognised in my emotional centre in terms of specific sensations. The distance between that which could see that and what happened in it was like two different worlds. And that kind of experience gradually builds up new material for associations. And I need associations in order to be able to see when I am on my way into a situation where I am getting identified, where these associations in one way of another tell me, Ah, I have to work. And that's what happened at the airport.

Then we can talk about, and have all kinds of ideas about this, and they can be nourishing. But when it comes to a real change, when this alternative is going to have some kind of substance that makes me feel alive. Having the freedom at that airport to just with my head, I used my head. I did it like this: I looked away and then I could look back again. And I had the experience of freedom, and this freedom was: I don't have to go with it. I have to accept that it was there, but I didn't have to go with it. And it is this kind of experience that makes me feel alive and which is a real alternative, and is material for new opportunities. New opportunities to associate that kind of situation with an opportunity. That is the real alternative, as I see it.

(Coffee Break)

Moderator: I now want to suggest that we also consider in our conversation examining our own personal vulnerability to this phenomenon, so that we can decrease our susceptibility when it is inappropriate, and have more of a sense of how to open ourselves in a way that will be useful to our work.

So:

> "...during the last twenty centuries almost the entire process of the ordinary waking existence of most of the three-brained beings....particularly of the beings of contemporary times, flows under the influence of this inherency of theirs, nevertheless they themselves give the name hypnotic state only to that state of theirs during which the processes of this particular property flow in them acceleratedly and the results of which are obtained concentratedly. And they fail to notice, or, as they would say, they are not struck by irregular results of this inherency which has recently become fixed in the ordinary process of their existences, because, on the one hand, in the absence in them in general of normal self-perfecting, they have not what is called a 'wide horizon,' and on the other hand, arising and existing according to the principle Itoklanoz, it has already become inherent in them 'quickly-to-forget' what they perceive. But when the said results of this inherency of theirs are obtained 'acceleratedly-concentratedly,' then every kind of irregular manifestation, their own and those of others, become real to such a degree that they become acutely obvious even to their bobtailed reason and therefore unavoidably perceptible.
>
> "But even if certain of them should by chance notice something illogical in their manifestations or in the manifestations of others, then, thanks to the absence in them of the knowledge of the law of 'typicality', they at best ascribe it to the particularities of the character of the given beings.
>
> "This 'abnormal' particular property of their psyche was first constated by the learned beings of the city Gob of the country Maralpleicie; and even then they made it a serious and detailed branch of science which spread over the whole of the planet under the name of 'non-responsible-manifestations-of-personality'." (Beelzebub's Tales p.559-560)

Participant 9: Now regarding this 'quickly-to-forget', I must say I have observed this. But it is not possible, or it is actually possible to reconnect. I have been in a class called...., and one of our tools used there is that we pick up some sense impressions, and we pick for instance whistles....sensation, body sensation....and making the story of what we went through, it is possible to reconnect these different sense impressions. So everything is not lost. It is possible to reconnect.

Participant 4: This 'quickly-to-forget' seems somehow to be connected with the storing of the impressions, and as each centre has its own number, it is limited when they operate as he says on p.565 he speaks of two independent blood circulations, and he says...what he called the two....that the artificial perceptions acquire its own independent functions....automatic function. When he on the next page speaks of the senses, he says that they are isolated, and it seems to me that there is a connection between the isolated operation of senses, and independent functions of centres, that these limitations, that they are connected.

And one practical example I have: I came home...and we move on to ....I sit down and have dinner.....and then suddenly I see my food. And that was such a shock. And I found it quite interesting, and I started tasting and smelling, and I become active in the process of eating. And also adding listening to what was going on.

And when he speaks of the senses, the six senses, he says that they count them as five. And for me this experience of bringing all these senses acting together was as if I had the sixth. I know there are many different variations of what the sixth can be, but the totality of that was very different. And I'm not surprised that one can use the method that one's speaking because I myself can very vividly remember that meal.

Participant 10: It seems to me that when the personality changes, I remember other things, when I am with my family, I remember other things when I am in a state of awareness, more force of remembering.... I think when I am in the situation of awareness I can receive the impressions. These impressions are more valuable because I remember with my body.... This situation must be very common to every human being. If we are in this situation we can't communicate, that if we talk with personality we can't communicate because everybody has different associations. This is something that came to me very clearly here, because there are many persons with different languages and different associations....

Participant 2: I remember what John Godolphin Bennett wrote about the Law of Three, Triamazikamno, he said that there is a law that is in the foundation of the second law of thermodynamics. Everything slows down, falls down, in cosmos everywhere. And our perceptions also slow down, and the frequency of our life vibrations is getting slower, thicker, heavier. Actually, hypnosis can be useful when we deal with personality, with the frequencies of the personality, of the ordinary man. And we cannot hypnotise normal man. Hypnosis can help in the Work, in the task of bringing ordinary person to normal person, working with ordinary person. And it can work....

One of the strongest hypnosis that we know is the hypnosis of a tradition. Every tradition is based on a myth. There is a Christian myth, Buddhist myth, Muslim myth, and there is a range of esoteric myth - there is a myth of Madame Blavatsky, of Ayurveda, of Gurdjieff. And all those myths are very obscure and fragmentary. But the difference between them, the essential difference, is the frequency of vibrations. Every myth that influences people, that wakes them up, is of a very high frequency. But it cools down, and it becomes irrelevant to those who were formally excited by Secret Doctrine of Helen Blavatsky, or by Krishnamurti, or by Paracelsus, are now pretty indifferent.

They react to Gurdjieff's teaching because of the high frequency of his teaching and of his myth. It's a universal myth. And the myth is not just a story. It is a story that is connected with a value system in us. It is a story according to which we live our lives. We feel, we act, and we think.

Participant 11: I was speaking to a couple of you earlier, and I have a question about how Ouspensky reports about our identification in In Search, and how Gurdjieff finally put not so much about identification in the Tales but really went into hypnosis. And my question is I would like to understand that more, if anyone had any ideas about it, because for me hypnosis has maybe a wider horizon - I'm just using that because it came up earlier.

Moderator: Inclusive?

Participant 11: Yes. It's much more inclusive of both the problem and the solution. So if hypnosis is used in their temples, in front of the congregation, it seems much more serious and sincere than the way Gurdjieff talked about it in the earlier years as identification. Do any of you see a parallel there and could help me understand that more?

Moderator: Coming back to what Bonnie said earlier, there is an extensive discussion here about the role of education, appropriate education, and inappropriate, for placing in us data that can either put us further into sleep or begin to wake us up in perhaps the sacred process that Bonnie's alluding to.

Participant 12: Gurdjieff said that he want to be doctor, hypnotise doctor. I need to find my own doctor inside... Now I can find this way. My doctor is above me. He can help me. In this moment he will be connected with it, with myself, inside me.

Moderator: So Great Nature has placed within us sacred data to help awaken us. It's already in us, but buried in our subconscious. So how to find something to lead me to the suggestions already placed in me by Endlessness and Nature waiting, for me to listen.

Participant 9: I think that for me it is easier to take this identification thing on a more spiritual level. It is easier to speak about this identification and that nothing happens. So there's a situation where this hypnosis is more serious. And it functions on so many levels that I cannot speak myself out of it. It is more serious.

Participant 13: I agree that identification is a common case of hypnosis in general, and I wanted to add what I think how because it would be useful because I didn't understand it for me what it was.

But I always thought that it was with the corrupted state of man when the connections between centres are broken. And so how can we use this state, to live as a man, to awaken? So I think that as far as I understood it, this idea, I probably took from Arkady, that there is useful hypnosis, for example, we influence our children to keep their room in order, to make exercise. We make, we insist on this. They want for example to run away to eat a lot of sweets, but we hypnotise them, we put our ideas on them and they have to accept it. So there can be better and worse kinds of hypnosis. And I think that such famous people named here, Mesmer and Buddha, I think that they offered a better kind of hypnosis, of myth, like good parents give their children a better kind of hypnosis than for example....of the same children.

Participant 14: When I am thinking about this process... that we could influence by education, by our parents, later by our teachers, the process of getting hypnotised which develop our personality with all its consequences... the same, I ask myself this could be, and I also think what Bonnie said about the influence of ceremonies, of priests, of rituals, of tradition, so there is a lot of this in the chapter 'Art', a lot of influences are described, for which I think they could be very helpful for us if we can connect to this.

And I also think....what is the placebo? Because I heard a presentation I went to two weeks ago about treatments with placebos and with real substances and that they had the results that the placebo was as strong or effective or sometimes more effective than the substance by itself. So what happens by the placebo? I believe I get the treatment and my immune system or my body system starts the process of healing. So this could be a kind of, has something to do, I think, with our belief, and this is what happens also in education, our parents, our school....what is developing, and that we have a strong influence on ourself, when we change our attitude, or when we think, when we can.... What is the placebo and why the same do the same? So it means that we can get by with certain help, reconnected to our.....

Participant 13: How can hypnosis help everything? I didn't finish. I knew that one hypnosis better than the other from point of view of the Way because there are such dreams, such states, where man has no chance even to learn about this opportunity, and when man has experience of self-discipline, he reads books, he is seeking for something, at least he is not being corrupted by his way of life. He has chance. His personal state of dream can give him opportunity to find his way. And there are a lot of kinds of dreams which don't give opportunity to their owners to get away somewhere, that's the difference. There are dreams which have a way out and there are dreams which have no such. A good hypnotiser gives his audience this dream which has a way out.

Participant 7: I would like to talk about an issue which I think came up with the most recent remarks, starting with Bonnie's, and which I think also touched upon even the initial remarks of Nick's in the morning when he said that we are looking for a common language to communicate amongst ourselves. We have expressions such as identification, hypnosis, personality, existence of two consciousnesses, existence of two Zoostats, the Itoklanoz and Foolasnitamnian way of living. They all seem to be referring to the same problem of man, of not being normal but being ordinary. Are they all the same thing? I don't think they are. What does the difference consist of? I think that Gurdjieff's ideas and the way he presented his teaching defines an image for the human mind. Gurdjieff says it's good for you to awaken, that awakening means such and such and such a thing for you to do, because your brain is formed in such and such a way, it has three centres, and this thing happens and the other thing happens. So the differences between identification and hypnosis and personality etc are I think different ways, different angles of seeing the human condition from these different aspects of how the mind is structured. Hypnosis is a general state. Personality refers most, to my understanding, and maybe we can communicate on that, eventually we might be able to communicate fully, personality has more to do with the fact that man presents an image to his fellow men. I know it's George, I know it's whoever is there, because it has common traits. These traits I call personality. By identification, I mean that this man, or me, at a particular moment, think of myself as such, as a speaker, I identify with this. By hypnosis we're talking about a state in my Zoostat as Gurdjieff explains, that there are two ways of explaining how people are, sometimes their level of being alive has to do with intensity in their personality way of expressing and other times it has to do with intensity of the way we are in touch with the inner energy.

So I believe that these discussions, these terms, and the way we use them contributes substantially to our communicating, which Nick mentioned as one of the aims of these conferences, and which I realise now, after I said my remarks yesterday that it is the most important reason why I'm here, that we build together this kind of communication and understand these terms that sometimes seem to be identical and yet they refer to different image of the mind that Gurdjieff gave. And I think that it is important that we understand the image of the mind that Gurdjieff gave, in all its aspects. And again Nick mentioned something about Gurdjieff insisting that all these terms have to apply a very specific meaning for us, and not be hazy and general when we talk about self-remembering to talk about this or that, but seeing and understanding it in the context of all the relationship of all the terms to the image that Gurdjieff gave us of the mind. And I think it is important. My experience with the work is that this is an important thing to have.

Participant 6: I would like us to look a little bit closer on something which also Steve alluded now. How do we understand Hanbledzoin? Because he says here 'I find it necessary before speaking further to inform you just now about this cosmic substance.' He says you must know more in detail concerning this cosmic substance. And for me personally I would be very glad to hear something about what this blood of the Kesdjan body is and how it could be possible to have a bit more practical understanding about it so that it can be useful in a practical way for myself, for my work.

Participant 3: I think it covers all the subjects we're talking about: hypnotism, sleep, identification, mechanicality, the whole thing. This is my ordinary life. So it's like Mike was saying this morning, running parallel to my ordinary life, if I know and have the skill to do it, is I'm creating something separate, in a separate place from my ordinary life. And when this separate objective faculty is activated and is running parallel to my ordinary unconscious existence, that when Terje was talking about the sense apparatus, the sense apparatus is completely and utterly unconscious. But when I activate this objective faculty, it means to me that the sense apparatus inside is shut down; otherwise the objective faculty can't work. If I can operate the objective faculty which is observing, participating, in my ordinary unconscious existence, it converts the energy from that unconscious existence and converts it into a substance called Hanbledzoin, which comes down a certain part of my head - he explains it in the chapter Purgatory - and down my neck and down into my heart. And that substance Hanbledzoin can only be created as a result of the objective faculty, because all the energy without that objective faculty goes into my cerebellum and is lost forever. But the objective faculty converts it in the cerebellum to Hanbledzoin, and it goes down my spine into my heart and down my neck into the front of the chest and into my heart. And that's how I understand how it works. He says that in the chapter on Purgatory.

Moderator: We'll have to leave a more extensive discussion of that later. Let me conclude with just two brief impressions. On p.565, Gurdjieff further states the Zoostat refers to our spiritualised part. We could have gotten into a discussion of what that could mean, but he often speaks of spiritualised parts, if we perhaps consider the possibility that here we're talking about not only that it would bring a conscious awareness of those parts, but wherever we go at that discussion, if the Zoostat refers to our spiritualised part and it is divided, it is split in two, then the book has many instances of this splitting, such that part of it is focussed through the senses on the outside world, and the influences or suggestions from the world as hypnotist then come in unopposed by these sacred data that have already been placed in our spiritualised part and which is now not accessible to us because we're so focussed on the outside, from our education, the necessity from the body of survival, so that the potentially sacred something that we are is turned upside down or that the horizontal is pointed outwards instead of in. So how to awaken that? We could then see the hypnotist, whether it's life or a person or a sensation or an impulse, we can see that if it comes from level horizontal or beneath our spiritual potential then that suggestion will put us further into sleep. If the suggestion or the impulse comes from something higher or deeper then we begin to wake up. So there is a criticism of how hypnosis has become used in contemporary life, and even by most psychotherapists and physicians, which at best bring a person to an adjustment to the horizontal world, or even worse to indulge their senses or their issues where it strengthens Kundabuffer. But if the hypnotist is conscience, or the book, or the wish to awaken, then that begins to move us into another direction.

So if we really are something that encompasses three cosmoses and are open to the flow of energy coming down all the way, coming up all the way through the entire ray or rays of creation, then we must also be open at both ends. So being open only at the end that flows down could put us into sleep. Being open at the end that wakes us could wake us up. So what is our greatest vulnerability may also be the greatest potential. So the sacred hypnotist I would think is that influence which seeks us to awaken and become masters of ourselves and conscious participants in the cosmic drama. The Black Magician would be that which wishes to put us deeper into the service of life and personality.

End of Session

Conscience and Consciousness in the Tales

Dimitri Peretzi

Abstract

The talk traces the way the author applies these two terms, "Conscience" and "Consciousness", in the text of "Beelzebub's Tales to his Grandson" and compares the connotations of their use with the meaning given to them by contemporary Science and Philosophy of Mind. The importance of the philosophical study of Consciousness over the last two decades has rendered the concept a key for the formation of any theory about the Mind and the operation of the brain. The way the two terms are used in the Tales gives clues about the way Gurdjieff views the Mind and point toward a coherent and quite advanced theory proposed for its structure.

Conscience and Consciousness

To unfold his ideas about Man's possible evolution, Gurdjieff employed extensively the concept of "Consciousness"

The word *"Consciousness"* appears in the "Tales" right from the start, from Chapter One. In *"The Arousing of Thought"* the author announces the important role that this notion will play in the structure of whatever it is that he is about to write:

"…before continuing this first chapter, which is by way of an introduction to all my further predetermined writings, I wish to bring to the knowledge of what is called your "pure waking consciousness" the fact that in the writings following this chapter of warning I shall expound my thoughts intentionally in such a sequence and with such "logical confrontation", that the essence of certain real notions may of themselves automatically, so to say, go from this "waking consciousness"- which most people in their ignorance mistake for their real consciousness, but which I affirm and experimentally prove is the fictitious one- into what you call your subconscious, which ought to be in my opinion the real human consciousness, and there by themselves mechanically bring about that transformation which should in general proceed in the entirety of a man and give him, from his own conscious mentation, the results he ought to have, which are proper to man and not merely to single- or double-brained animals".

With this statement Gurdjieff,

- precedes the introduction to all his further "predetermined writings"
- declares the goal and the method of the Work he proposes

- places the notion of Consciousness at the centre of this method

His clear distinction between two "kinds of Consciousness" - the *"fictitious waking consciousness"* and the *"real human consciousness"* - is echoed throughout the *Tales*. It is explicitly mentioned in a number of chapters:

- The Arousing of Thought
- The Terror of the Situation
- Organization by Ashiata Shiemash
- The Sixth Descent
- Hypnotism
- Mutual Destruction
- Author's Conclusions

In other words, this is a point that appears from the very begging to the very end of the text.

As had been recorded by Ouspensky, Gurdjieff introduced the idea of Developing Consciousness as an integral part of his teaching right from the beginning, as early as nineteen twelve (1912). This is an issue in itself. Today such talk may sound self evident – anyone who follows some sort of spiritual discipline may refer to his goal as "Developing Consciousness". But for that time this expression must have been rather unusual.

Using the notion of "Developing Consciousness" to describe the aims of spiritual effort has a taste from the social wave that we associate with the New Age movement, with Esalen Institute and the California, post-LSD crowd of the sixties and the seventies. In fact this idea was articulated clearly in Ouspensky's *In Search of the Miraculous* and in the *Tales*, both of which were already published and had been made accessible to the public a few years earlier, since 1950.

Contemporary study of "Consciousness"

During the last three decades, the study of Consciousness has acquired great prominence in contemporary Science and in academic Philosophy. This is a relatively recent trend. The topic of Consciousness had remained in some sort of limbo for more than a hundred years, since the German philosopher Husserl wrote extensively on it at the end of the nineteenth century. His work was crucial for the development of twentieth century Existentialism, but the idea of investigating Consciousness further was subsequently put aside, as it was thought that everything about Consciousness was obvious and that there was nothing to add to what every person intuitively understands about the concept.

The study of Consciousness acquired new impetus in the nineteen eighties. Conclusive experiments that were mostly conducted by neurophysiologist Benjamin Libet showed that we, humans, cannot possibly be aware of most our reactions to external stimuli, the ones that we routinely believe we are conscious of. These observations were based on the timing of the activity of neurons, of the cells of the nervous system that trigger human responses. Neurons fire messages and information to each other, and scientists showed that, contrary to all expectations, it actually takes longer for the mind to become aware of an external stimulus than to react to it. This means that our reactions are quicker than our realizing, what it is exactly that we are reacting to. We are constantly shooting from the hip, so to speak. What we believe we are "conscious of" seems to consist of inventing subsequent stories to explain why we did this or that. In other words, according to the date accumulated by scientific observation, it seems that we are reacting to the world mechanically and automatically.

Such observations run contrary to what was believed about consciousness, so they awakened the question of what Consciousness is. And the debate that begun at that point made everything that was taken for granted in this matter to be thoroughly revised. For the last thirty years this field keeps expanding, and the number of books published on the topic has made the bibliography on Consciousness the fasted growing of all fields.

Today the investigation of the nature of Consciousness can be seen both

- as the direction that academic science and philosophy are converging, but also
- as the point of bridging between the domains of academic philosophy and esoteric (or mystical) thought, since both realms seem to consider Consciousness the concept by which they can best describe the goal they hope to reach by their efforts

Since Gurdjieff based all his explanations about spiritual advancement on the detailed images he gave of the Mind, the question is whether his ideas provide a consistent model, a full and accurate image of the Mind and of mental operation. Besides, if his concept of the possibility for Consciousness to develop has a real basis, any academic theory about Consciousness that does not incorporate a comparable feature will be inadequate to describe the true essence of the Mind's activities.

Gurdjieff called the Fourth Way "an exact science". If one is to take this literally and not accept it just as a metaphor, there has to be a way by which the possibility of working on one's self and the physiological results that come with such an effort can be described in scientific terms.

The problem with attempting this is that the formal science of Consciousness is still developing and it is far from being able to provide clear images about Consciousness and about the way the Mind functions. So, if one wishes for any reason to express Gurdjieff's thought in strict scientific formulation, his efforts have to cover two fronts. He has to develop a clear understanding of what the terms that both Gurdjieff and contemporary Philosophy of Mind refer to, while he also has to show that Gurdjieff's assumptions are compatible with the data which have been accumulating about the ways the nervous system operates.

Conscience and Consciousness in the Tales

What did Gurdjieff exactly mean by "Consciousness", by "Conscience" and by "the Subconscious"?

If Gurdjieff's ideas can indeed form a model of the Mind that is acceptable in scientific terms, a question to be asked would be, what did he exactly mean by "Consciousness", by "Conscience" and by "the Subconscious"? The everyday general understanding that people have about this term has proven to be inadequate for exact scientific exchanges.

In the passage from the "Tales" noted before, Gurdjieff seems to be proposing in no uncertain terms that, to achieve spiritual progress, the Subconscious has to come into Consciousness:

"...to achieve spiritual progress, the Subconscious has to be become Consciousness, as it is in the Subconscious that true Conscience lies buried..."

Does this make any sense in terms of the known physiology of the nervous system? And beyond this, in what way does it relate to what we know to be "the Work" as we know it being practiced in the Groups?

By assessing the instances where he uses the word, one may come to the conclusion that by "Consciousness" Gurdjieff refers to *"the way a person is present to the world"*, to *"the way he interprets what he perceives"*, and, in general, to *"the image he has of reality and of what goes on around him"*. In this way, by "usual Consciousness" he means, of course, *"our usual reality"* or *"our usual way of interpreting the world"*.

The idea that our interpretation of reality incorporates faulty features is encountered in many traditions, each tradition referring to these faults in its own way.

- The Christian and the Jewish traditions incorporate the idea of man having fallen from divine grace, having lost Paradise, and of human life being lived in the state of sin.
- In Hinduism we find the concept of "Maya", the idea that our image of the world is an illusion fabricated by the senses.
- Plato gives the allegory of the cave, where he describes that all that ordinary people see is the shadows of reality, not reality itself.
- As was mentioned, even contemporary philosophers like Heidegger claim that man's usual way of being present to the world is problematic.

Questions that arise in reference to a strict, scientific approach to investigate the physiological nature of such "faults" would include,

- Does this idea of "faulty Consciousness" cover all such instances of man's "faulty interpretation of the world"? And can it be used to describe it in scientific terms that are compatible with the findings of contemporary science?

- Is it possible that a "path of salvation" from these faults can be described in ways that are compatible with contemporary science, that are in accordance with scientific knowledge and scientific observation?
- In fact, is there a "way to salvation"? Is there something to be done to avoid the pitfalls of faulty interpretations and live a life of "being present to genuine reality"? Is there such a practical path, one that can be followed in life?
- What would a possible "change in one's Consciousness" consist of in physiological terms?

The "System", of course, is precisely this. It is a coherent way of describing the way toward freedom from the slavery of the state that our usual "Consciousness" operates in, from the artificial images that make our everyday reality. But, it could be asked, does all this make any sense for the contemporary scientific approach to consciousness?

This is not an easy question to answer. The reason is that, contrary to what many may believe, it is not at all clear what each scientist who studies "consciousness" refers to by this word. Each seems to be using it in his own subjective manner. Scientists in this field definitely do not adhere to common assumptions. Wikipedia, for one, variously defines Consciousness as *subjective experience*, as *awareness*, as *the ability to experience feeling*, as *the understanding of the concept of the self*, and notes that this *is an umbrella term that may refer to a variety of mental phenomena*. This confusion causes misunderstandings and nurtures the problems that contemporary Philosophy of the Mind is faced with.

No matter how things are with the academic community though, there is an important way in which Gurdjieff's approach differs from all the others, and in fact stands quite apart from them. Gurdjieff regards human Consciousness not as something fixed, but as a faculty of the mind the quality of which may fluctuate from one moment to the next, and which in fact has the possibility of dramatically developing.

By making the distinction between the *"waking Consciousness"* and the *"real human Consciousness"* Gurdjieff underlines his point that the very nature of human Consciousness may develop by, what he calls, man's fulfilling in his life *"his being-Partkdolg duty"*.

Even if one does not readily understand Gurdjieff's formulation about Consciousness here, the possibility of the quality of Consciousness fluctuating and its possible development is quite dramatic. It definitely differs from that of the other points of view on consciousness. And if it does reflect accurately data that are overlooked by the usual approaches of academic Philosophy, it surely brings a completely new outlook to the study of Consciousness.

Something "Subconscious becoming part of Consciousness"

When Gurdjieff says, that in order to achieve spiritual progress, *"the Subconscious has to become Consciousness, as it is in the Subconscious that true Conscience lies buried"*, he is giving a most condensed practical description of the Work which is related to man's "*Partkdolg duty*". Only one has to be careful, to avoid a superficial or frivolous interpretation of what he proposes to be done.

In general, one cannot understand what it is that Gurdjieff means about anything merely by "*thinking associatively*". To understand him one has to "*actively mentate*". To understand him presupposes to investigate the way he expresses himself in many different cases. His phrases should not be taken out of context; each should be compared with the meaning of Gurdjieff's other statements, and, most importantly, with the actual practice of the Work.

Though Gurdjieff's approach to natural phenomena is rigorous and thoroughly scientific, yet in his life he made no effort to express himself in strict scientific terms, at least not by using the contemporary scientific jargon. Besides, especially in expressing ideas about the functioning of the Mind, it has to be stressed that this "jargon" and the descriptions of formal science given by its employment are, still, quite inadequate.

When referring to the Subconscious, it is crucial that the distinction is made between Gurdjieff's "Subconscious" and what contemporary Psychology calls "the Subconscious".

In Gurdjieff's terms, for example, we cannot think of "dreams" as being a part of the Subconscious's usual function. Dreams according to Gurdjieff would be thought of as the result of the mechanical and uncontrolled activity of the "formatory apparatus", of which activity we may become aware during sleep, when the connections between the centres have been suspended. When we "have a dream" during sleep, something in our mind is mistaking that dream's content for "reality". This is the only "reality" the mind is aware of at that moment. This is no Subconscious functioning of the mind. It is simply poor quality consciousness; it is the quality of consciousness there is during sleep, which results in perceiving inadequately some automatic, uncontrolled associations of the mind.

The Subconscious according to Gurdjieff is to be thought of as, simply, all mental activity that we are not conscious of. This is the reason why, instead of the word "Subconscious", he often uses the term "Subconsciousness" (*Tales*, p. 365, 377).

In that sense, dreams, which are formed not only during sleep but also during the waking state and cause absent-mindedness and fantasies, are part of the Subconscious, not when we are aware of them, but only when they proceed without us realizing they are there. It is the dreams of our waking state that go on subconsciously, the ones that we do not realize their presence. The dreams that one "has in his sleep" and happens to remember when he wakes up, they are part of a function of his mind that something in him was conscious of, albeit in an incomplete way.

For something *Subconscious to become part of Consciousness*, this for Gurdjieff would mean for the mind to become aware of some mental activity which is there, but which, for one or another reason, nothing in him has been able to focus his attention on until that point.

All & Everything Conference 2011

How are we to understand Gurdjieff's "Conscience"?

By "Conscience" we usually mean something like an internal a voice, some kind of mental whisper that is supposed to be telling us what is wrong and what is right for us to do in each occasion. According to Wikipedia, *"commonly used metaphors for Conscience include the 'voice within' and the 'inner light'."*

In that same article, in Wikipedia, Conscience is defined as *"an aptitude, faculty, intuition or judgement of the intellect that distinguishes right from wrong"*, a judgement that has to do with *"moral evaluations"*. The text goes on to say that *"in psychological terms Conscience is often described as leading to feelings of remorse when a human does things that go against his/her moral values, and to feelings of rectitude or integrity when actions conform to such norms. The extent to which Conscience informs moral judgement before an action and whether such moral judgements are, or should be, based wholly in reason has occasioned debate through much of the history of Western Philosophy"*

Is this, or something such, what Gurdjieff means by "Conscience"? Could he be referring to a *"faculty of the intellect"* that has to do with *"moral values"*, the kind of values which, invariably, have been learned and acquired during one's formatory years, and which are *"based wholly in reason"*, the usual reason that humans employ when they live by personality's standards? Of course, Gurdjieff could not have meant this by "Conscience".

The Wikipedia article continues by saying that, *"religious views of conscience usually see it as linked to a morally inherent in all humans, to a beneficent universe and/or to divinity. The diverse ritualistic, mythical, doctrinal, legal, institutional and material features of religion may not necessarily cohere with experiential, emotive, spiritual or contemplative considerations about the origin and operation of Conscience."*

In practical terms, what this tries to convey is that by following his Conscience man may find himself in moral conflict. And, the article says, this may happen when ritualistic, doctrinal, legal, institutional etc. features of social morality are incoherent, when they clash with what one may feel inside him as being right, as being the right thing for him to do.

This passage is quite straightforward. These *"incoherent mythical, doctrinal, institutional etc. features"* of contemporary life are formalized ways of thinking which at some moment may come into conflict with a deeper voice, with a deeper sense of what is to be done.

In other words here we are talking about conflict, pain, about the pain that comes with remorse of conscience.

And, of course, this is precisely the kind of internal experience that Gurdjieff is referring to with the word he fabricated, "Aieioiuoa". This "Aieioiuoa" he defined in Chapter 17 of the *Tales*, as *"remorse of Conscience"*. About this same concept he proceeded in Chapter 22 to give the allegory of "*Aieioiuoa*" being the "*light of day*". In other words, by this "lawful inexactitude", of defining "Aieioiuoa" in two different ways, Gurdjieff seems to be indicating that the true light in one's life, "Aieioiuoa", the one that will light his way and show him the direction he should follow, is "Aieioiuoa", the remorse of his Conscience.

Ashiata Shiemash and the Voice of Conscience

According to Gurdjieff, abnormally formalized patterns of thinking of contemporary "three brained beings", humans, block behaviour and direct our actions away from what is the right thing to do. Mental features that we are not aware of, features that are related to Conscience and which exist in the Subconscious, must be brought into Consciousness, into our reality. We are to become conscious of the voice of Conscience. And Gurdjieff underlines the point that the "inner voice" of Conscience has not atrophied in us, that it remains intact.

Questions that may arise at this point include,

- Is there a way that we can come into conscious contact with this inner voice?
- How will this "inner voice" talk to us?
- In what language, for one?
- How can we be sure that such a "voice" is a not thought, part of yet another fantasy?
- In which practical way can it influence us in the right direction?
- Do people in the Work know about this and do they follow such a practice?

In the chapters on Ashiata Shiemash, which deal with these issues extensively, Gurdjieff gives important clues to help with the clarification of what he wishes to convey. In the last paragraph of "The Terror of the Situation" he writes, "*these ponderings of [Ashiata Shiemash] then first of all fully convinced Him that though it were indeed possible to save [terrestrial three brained beings] by means of the data which survived in their common presences for engendering this sacred being impulse (conscience), nevertheless, it would only be possible if the manifestations of these data which survived in their Subconsciousness were to participate without fail in the functioning of that consciousness of theirs, under the direction of which their daily-waking existence flows, and furthermore if this being-impulse were to be manifested over a long period through every aspect of this consciousness of theirs*".

Many who have studied the Tales believe that Gurdjieff gives yet another allegory here and that in some way he identifies himself with Ashiata Shiemash, and the Work with Ashiata Shiemash's "labours". This makes sense if we realize that Gurdjieff speaks about this relationship between Consciousness, the Subconscious and Conscience throughout the text of the Tales. Right from the start, from the first paragraphs in chapter one, the statement by which he presents a condensed form of his own teaching reads as if it refers to the teaching of Ashiata Shiemash, as well.

Ashiata Shiemash says in his legominism[1],

"...*it was just then that I indubitably understood with all the separate ruminating parts representing the whole of my "I", that if the functioning of that being-factor still surviving in their common-presences were to participate in the general functioning of that consciousness of theirs in which they pass their daily "waking-existence", only then would it still be possible to save the contemporary three-brained beings here from the consequences of the properties of [Kundabuffer]*".

About that being-factor, Gurdjieff has Ashiata Shiemash say,

"...*I made it categorically clear to myself that although the factors for engendering in their presences the sacred being-impulses of Faith, Hope, and Love are already quite degenerated in the beings of this planet, nevertheless, the factor which ought to engender that being-impulse on which the whole psyche of beings of a three-brained system is in general based, and which impulse exists under the name of Objective-Conscience, is not yet atrophied in them, but remains in their presences almost in its primordial state*".

Which is this being-factor that may cause Conscience to surface into Consciousness? Why is Gurdjieff not defining clearly what this factor is? Is this some kind of "secret"?

If it is not a secret, then everyone sincerely interested in the Work should know about it. If on the other hand this being-factor is some sort of secret, some fact that is hidden in one way or in another, a factor which can help people find their way to salvation, then only those who have been in authentic groups for some years should know about it.

If this idea of "*something in the Subconsciousness that must come into Consciousness to engender Conscience*" is of any real importance, then, certainly, people who have been seriously involved in the Work must have worked with it. Otherwise, the work in the traditional Gurdjieff groups would be ineffectual and even worst, meaningless, since *only when this factor participates in the general functioning of their ordinary consciousness would it still be possible to save them from the consequences of the properties of Kundabuffer*. So, if their work is not useless, traditional groups must understand the kind of practice that goes with this "something".

And since Gurdjieff, at least in terms of the way he describes the "labours of Ashiata Shiemash", wishes to point out that this element is novel and special and that it is not to be found in previous traditions, which attempt to utilized the atrophied factors that should engender "Faith, Hope and Love", then, people that have not been involved with authentic groups could not know about it, as they never received "influences C", that is, direct transmission of the teaching.

---

[1] By the word "Legominism" Gurdjieff refers to a condensed form of an important message or teaching.

Conscience and Consciousness in the Tales

The factor that may lead to Conscience

The being-factor that engenders the being-impulse of Conscience, which must rise from the Subconscious into Consciousness, is becoming aware of the sensation of the body and working with it. Working, in other words, until one becomes conscious of the light of Aieioiuoa in him. And this can happen only through influences C, under the direct guidance of a leader of traditional group Work.

Sensation is always there, unnoticeable to the way attention usually operates. Self observation may refine attention, to the point that the observer can become aware and conscious of body sensation and its complex manifestations. Sensation may thus lead to a full sensing of Conscience, to the voice that can direct one's actions.

In other words, through Work on oneself, the organic need that eventually arises, to be in touch with sensation, dictates the adjustment of one's actions in the way that is proper for attention not to be severed from the possibility of sensing.

The moral dimension in these relations consists of the fact that the actions carried out when following the sensation in the body are sanctified. They belong to *"living in the 'second river' of life"*. One, simply, cannot act wrongly and at the same time preserve the sensation of the body within the field of his perception. This is a fact that has to be verified, and the verification of which leads to the understanding of its true meaning.

The internal effort one has to apply against the distractions that the external world exerts on his personality to remain in touch with sensation is by itself the Work that will awaken Conscience in him.

This factor, working with body sensation, is what differentiates the Work from all other teachings that have used as motives factors for divine impulses that have atrophied, and more specifically the ones that engender in three-brained beings the sacred being-impulses of Faith, Hope and Love.

We are talking about the very core of the Work here, about the way that the sly man can avoid ineffectual techniques and teachings that are based on factors in the Mind that have atrophied because of the abnormal way social life has proceeded for the last centuries.

Organization by Ashiata Shiemash

In the "Organization by Ashiata Shiemash", starting at page 377, Gurdjieff writes extensively about this factor. What he mentions there leave no doubt that what he is writing about is Work with sensation:

"...*the mentioned duality (i.e. <u>split</u>)*² *of their general psyche proceeded because on the one hand various what are called "individual-initiatives" (i.e. <u>reactions of individuals</u>) began to issue from that localization arising in their presences, which is always predominant during their walking existence (i.e. <u>their personality</u>) and which localization is nothing else but only the result of the accidental perceptions of impressions coming from without (i.e. <u>from accidental external stimuli</u>), and engendered by their abnormal environment, which perceptions in totality are called by them their "consciousness" (i.e. <u>their usual way of interpreting what is going on in the world</u>); and on the other hand, similar individual-initiatives also began to issue in them, as it is proper to them, from that normal localization existing in the presences of every kind of being and which they called their Subconsciousness (i.e. <u>actions which are the direct result of "essence", which come from the way they feel, which they can sense only when they learn how to become conscious of sensing the body</u>)*".

"*And because the mentioned individual-initiatives issue from such different localizations during their waking existence, each of them, during the process of his daily existence is, as it were, divided into two independent personalities*".

"*Here it must be remarked that just this said duality was also the cause that there was gradually lost from their presences that impulse necessary to three-brained beings, which is called "Sincerity"*".

© Copyright 2011 - Dimitri Peretzi - All Rights Reserved

---

[2] The underlined text in the parentheses is there to expound on the interpretation given.

Conscience and Consciousness in the Tales - Questions & Answers

Participant 1: What if it is not a question, but a comment? Well, I was up taking with great interest to the presentation of Dimitri, who touched on extremely important issues, problems that all of us have pondered about. I found a lot of conformity with what was said here, but I should confess that during my lifetime development, I have developed for myself a completely different attitude to major statements made by Dimitri and with your permission I will take three-four minutes of your time to elucidate this. Well, we all know, that modern thought, 20th century thought, worked comparing to the ancient philosophy, medieval philosophy or in the direction of reductions, we all know of the phenomenological reduction by Husserl, we know how economical he was in his thinking, Whitehead, Wittgenstein, everybody brought to the great Baroque constructions of thought, brought to the minimal level, to the limits, and Gurdjieff who was undoubtedly a traditional thinker and Gurdjieff's teaching is a traditional teaching. He also worked all of his life; he was developing certain reductionalist mysticism. Instead of saying that we are normal human beings and we aspire to be angels, saints and strive towards becoming God and so being as perfect as God is, Gurdjieff said no, we are handicapped, we are ordinary, we must be normal. And this is just one example of Gurdjieff's reductions, he lowered our position and he suggested that we first become normal. And that's a very refreshing, very attractive way of presenting traditional mysticism. It is interesting that Dimitri discussed such terms as consciousness, conscience and un-conscience and he never mentioned the word super consciousness. Now, it is interesting that in the Russian language consciousness is … (word unclear). This is co-knowledge, when I say co-knowledge it means aggregated knowledge or total knowledge. Now, conscience is … (word unclear), which is co-message or total message, this is how it sounds in Russian. And un-conscience is in Russian … (word unclear), or co-knowledge less, or absence of this special kind of knowledge, co-knowledge, co-conscience. Actually I am opposed to the Western way that was adopted by Christianity, by Judaism. I don't possibly buy this lamp of trying each time to apply science to religious and mystical knowledge. Religious knowledge, mystical knowledge are not the knowledge of science, they are different knowledge. It must be another word, not the word knowledge when we speak of religious or mystical knowledge. It's completely different level of perception, of understanding, of interpretation, and they are not compatible, the mystical knowledge and the scientific knowledge. That's my conviction, contrary to what you say. When you speak of the sub conscience you say that these mental features must be brought to reality or to light, no, sub conscience, in reality super conscience mental features, cannot be reduced to scientific knowledge, scientific knowledge cannot prove and support mystical experience. Both require verification, both, but scientific verification is on one level and mystical verification can be done not by everybody, which is a requirement of science. The experience of Ramakrishna, of Patanjali, of Buddha, of Christ, could be, if it could be verified at all, can be verified only by those who reach that level of experience, that level of co-knowledge or consciousness. So, in my understanding super-consciousness is part of what Gurdjieff calls un-conscience. Super-consciousness is, as you said, atrophied parts of our sub-conscience. Yes, it is in us, but it is practically dead and our task is, first of all, of vivifying it and then bringing it to life, not in terms of modern knowledge. When I say modern I mean knowledge of the 21st century, of the 18th century, of the 16th century. Subsequently, every century, every period has things of itself as modern, so it should not be reduced to the level of modern science, and consciousness. Modern science should aspire through mystical exercises, through striving towards higher levels of understanding, should strive to near, to approach the mystical science. But I support, with all my heart, all my conscience, your appeal that Gurdjieff groups must Work with consciousness and super-consciousness. I disagree with the notion of body sensations as typical of reaching something very serious, it's one of the hindrances in Gurdjieff's Work, this fixation on Gurdjieff movements, on body sensation and on many other productive exercises, productive means. But they direct the attention of most of the Forth Way practitioners from what you, yourself, said Work with consciousness, with sub consciousness, with super consciousness, that is the focal point in my opinion. Thank you very much.

Dimitri Peretzi: I think you misunderstood what is there. It is already in writing, so I could go over it phrase by phrase. I never said most of the things that you attributed to me. I never said it has to aspire to science at all, I said it has to conform to the data accumulated by science. Now this conforming is quite obvious, I mean, one can say: *people who are meditating said they can levitate*; and it is true that some people said that, but it is not true, they cannot levitate. They can be put into a meditation mat and they will not rise. This is data accumulated by scientific observation and whatever people who meditate do, has to conform to this data. That's one. The idea of two different kinds of consciousness, two different approaches to consciousness this is the Holy Grail to the academics. To maintain different academic faculties they have to say, that "this is a different topic", that "what we chemists are studying as natural science, say, is different than what physicists are studying as natural science"; and of course what philosophers study as natural science is yet something else. But it is not. I study the world as one thing. I am one; unity is what I work for. I am the scientist, I am the metaphysician. What I just said in this talk could adapt to an audience of scientists, or to an audience of metaphysicians. But it has to stand from the same central point, and it has to conform to scientific observations. It does not have to revere specific scientific theories and follow their interpretations, but it has to conform to the results of their observations. If it contradicts them, it is nonsense. So there are many points like that in what you said and you juxtaposed your position with some of the things, it was like you to attribute to me things that I did not say, and definitely things I did not mean. The Work is about unity and the question is how to be practical about Work. To work with the sensation of the body is being practical 'par excellence'. Now it has difficulties and pitfalls. We can see such difficulties when we use expressions like, for example, "the opening of the chakra". What would it mean, for the "chakra to open"? Is it sensual awakening, or is it intellectual awakening? Or is it emotional awakening? Such subtle differentiations are very difficult to approach and to explain. This is why work with sensation is needed and this is what it means. It means precisely to be able to read the voice of sensation inside you. The voice of sensation is something objective. It is not subjective, it is not what I think, it is not what I believe, it is what I see in front of me. But it still needs to be interpreted. What is emotion? What is intellectual? What is a body reaction? The understanding we usually have of all these is mixed, and this is what the work on the groups is about. Because there is like a spirit of understanding that has to be given, how to differentiate such aspects of

Conscience and Consciousness in the Tales - Questions & Answers

sensation. Sensation is everything, attention is everything, consciousness is everything, but you cannot work with consciousness, if you are unconscious. You work in consciousness; you describe your work as work in consciousness from the distance, but how we can get to that distance? We can only intellectualize about that distance, we cannot be practical. Practically, objectively, means it is there, I am here and this is there. Only then is there observation. This is the basis of observation. It is there, I am here, there is a distance between us. To effectuate this distance, to make it real, you need to work with sensation. There is no other way, to effectuate the distance. Of course it could have been other ways, we can speak about the drama of Jesus Christ and we could have been influenced and we could have love emerge into our being - but this possibility (according to Ashiata Sheimash) is atrophied. You hear about Jesus Christ and we think about vacation in Christmas and Easter. It has atrophied the possibility of it being a concrete influence; it has become thinking by association. All of the factors that engender, Love, Faith and Hope, have become thinking by associations. The only real thing that exists is sensation. But one has to work and understand what it means to work with sensation. Sensation is not just to feel your body; sensation is to be able to differentiate the depth where reading emotion. Where the depth is of and the difference between reading emotion and reading something I feel from touch. I touch this, is what I feel here emotion? Or is the sense of the skin? How I can be sure that I can see deep enough to know what I am looking at is a result of emotion? I have to learn this and I have to work to learn it and this is very hard work. This is bringing the unconscious factor into consciousness. Living by such practice creates consciousness, in the sense that you realise that our life is wasted, that your life is being wasted, that my life is being wasted. This is remorse of conscience, this is what you need the profoundly negative emotion and the pain that comes from the realization of having wasted one's life. This is what I need to work. Otherwise work is words. If it doesn't pain me, if I see work like a luxury and not as a need, then it is useless, then it is thinking by associations, it becomes atrophied once again. It has to pain, it has to be Aieioiuoa, to be real and I can read this reality only through the study and work with sensation. We have to look to this only factor. What is the only factor that we know of? Our idea of consciousness is theoretical; I speak about consciousness, then a professor of philosophy can start talking to me about consciousness, he has read Husserl, he has read all these big names, so he knows everything about consciousness and he knows nothing. This is the point of sensation and this is the place it has. The strange thing is that I agree with what you said, I agree but I did not say that.

Participant 2: You promised to say something about the biological, physiological manifestation of this changing consciousness; this is what I have got, one of the questions that you raised. In fact I was looking forward to that bit, because I have some sympathy for your project, of making all these teachings related to science. At the same time I also have sympathy for Arcady's perspectives there. Science maybe is not the right vehicle for exploring all of these. I felt that the last quotation you had about there is two independent, it seems to be, two independent personalities and divided into two independent personalities. I was wondering if you could say something about that. What are these two independent personalities? What is the anatomic correspondence?

Dimitri Peretzi: I will try to be very quick and to the point. The two different personalities or two different entities, I'd rather say, is the one that has taken over when my reactions to external stimuli are dictated by my education (as for example, when you see a red light you do not cross the street, and things like that), and the other one is when they are dictated by the impulses that are coming from inside from the body, from the real agitation in the body. These latter are probably caused, to a large extent, by concentrations of adrenaline in different parts of the body.

Participant 3: Are these independent?

Dimitri Peretzi: Yes, this is what Gurdjieff says, exactly, they are independent. For example a person can have a brave personality and a weak essence. This means that he may learn to be brave in his life but he may lack the structure of the anatomy to be brave. He doesn't have the muscular power or whatever it takes to be brave by nature. So he could behave like a brave man outside, but inside he would be a very weak person. This is the same differentiation Gurdjieff says about essence and personality, two different people living inside me. Now the question is, does this have a physiological basis? Yes it does, one that describes these physiological differentiations in at least two ways. One way is essence and personality that a body can be a strong body and he can be a very timid person because he was beaten by his parents when he was child, so he is very timid and he does not want to move to any direction though his body is very strong and we have a weak giant or vice versa etc. This is one way to talk about it, but there is another as well. The learned behavior is the way neurons have learned to bind with each other. Different new structures, different new entities, different I's are not theoretical they can be traced anatomically, so to speak, and there is a question of uniting the reactions of these neurons to larger formations. This is the quest for unity until reaction can be from a unified nervous system and not a fragmented nervous system which takes into account the reality of what is happening in terms of reading this reality on the moment, authentically, not by associations of what I think is happening right now but what is really happening. I do not take a comment as an attack, in other words, somebody else could have done it or I could have done it at a different moment, this would be reacting in one way but the unity of my understanding my life puts things in a better perspective.

Gurdjieff's Beelzebub's Tales - A Landmark in the Spiritual History of Humanity

Arkady Rovner

Abstract

One of the most important books written in the last century, "Beelzebub's Tales" is, according to its genre an epic poem comparable with the number of works pertaining to the same genre, such as: the Hebrew Bible, the New Testament, the Koran, the Upanishads, the Mahayana Sutras, the Ramayana, the Mahabharata, Homer's Iliad and Odyssey, Dante's Divine Comedy, François Rabelais' Gargantua and Pantagruel, Nietzsche's Also Sprach Zarathustra, Helen Blavatsky's The Secret Doctrine and some others. Most of these works are considered to be landmarks of the spiritual history of humanity, albeit in different degrees.

These works often carry in themselves new metaphysical principles, new cosmological and historical concepts, new codes of behavior and ideals of human existence, predictions and prophecies said to be obtained through spiritual revelation. The authorship of or inspiration for many of these works has been ascribed to Almighty God or to the Spirits closest to Him, as well as to Archangels, Angels, prophets or legendary beings.

A special kind of sacredness has been attributed to these works, and they have been made objects of exclusive reverence and worship as well as of systematic study and commentary, the latter sometimes leading to creation of special kinds of disciplines, e.g. Christian theology, midrashim, kalam, etc. Special rituals for handling these books and special manners of recitation have been created and particular schedules and orders of their private and communal recitation have been established. Many of these works have been considered to contain special secret content, a "bone" or "a dog" buried in them which the devoted reader is supposed to dig out. Some of these works have been engaged in the process of enculturation, i.e. incorporation of their content and style into the various layers of existing culture. As a result of constant recitations, quoting and references, some of these poems acquire the character of a warrant of objective Truth, as they have solidified in an inert culture and their ideas have ceased to develop and grow, thus becoming an infallible dogmas.

The aim of this presentation is to pose and to make attempt of answering the following question: How could we avoid the danger of pitfalls contained in the uncritical attitude towards Gurdjieff's main work?

All & Everything Conference 2011

Gurdjieff's Beelzebub's Tales – A Landmark in the Spiritual History of Humanity

Various attitudes to Gurdjieff's book Beelzebub's Tales and different contrasting approaches to ways of its treatment can be seen among its readers. Four of those are the most widespread in the groups of its admirers and critics:

(a.) Reading with the aspiration to dig up the "bone" or the "dog" buried in the book.

(b.) Reading as a form of "work on oneself" upon overcoming the difficulties of reading and understanding.

(c.) Development of technologies of reading for obtaining the best results, for instance, reading the book three times, following the method proposed by Gurdjieff; reading it 30 or more times, following the recommendation of some of Gurdjieff's pupils (A. L. Staveley[1]); continuous reading of the entire book from the beginning to the end, according to the method of J.G. Bennett[2]; reading it with pauses after each comma, following the method of Mike Readshaw, etc.

(d.) A harsh rejection of this book as something alien and adverse.

As a philosopher in my education and a literary man by my calling, in my approach to *Beelzebub's Tales* I utilized an appreciative perception of it as a literary product with a definite form and content. This approach is a traditional one, applicable to any text, large or small, trivial or profound. At the same time I have also not rejected the first three approaches, namely: digging up the "dog", reading in the manner of "Work" and testing various technologies, particularly applying the technology of reading without any definite sequence, according to an intuitive principle.

I shall begin with the question of the genre of this work. Next will follow the issues related to its language, composition, conception, significance, its novelty and similarity to other analogous works, etc. I plan to conclude with the consideration of this work's possible future.

Genre of Beelzebub's Tales.

Those who have written about *Beelzebub's Tales* placed this book in various categories or genres – they saw this work as being a fairy tale, a work of science fiction, a cosmological or alchemical treatise, a piece of social satire etc.

Just to give an example, I would like to mention Reijo Oksanen's *Comments of Beelzebub's Tales* where he writes about the "fairy tale" character of the book. I quote Reijo Oksanen: "After translating the first 50 pages of Beelzebub I saw much more of the "fairy tale" character of the

---

[1] "Gurdjieff advised us to read, reread and then read this Book again many, many times. Read it aloud with others and read it to yourself. Even if you read it thirty, even fifty times, you will always find something you missed before - a sentence which gives with great precision the answer to a question you have had for years." From the dust jacket note for the Two Rivers Press reprint of the first English edition of *Beelzebub's Tales,* 1993.

[2] J.G. Bennett and Elizabeth Bennett *Idiots in Paris*, Santa Fe 2008, p. 21.

Gurdjieff's Beelzebub's Tales – A Landmark in the Spiritual History of Humanity

book. In fact it now looks surprising that I was not so much aware of this before. Why I did not see it? Is it that I get this sense of the fairy tale when I read what I have translated into Finnish? It seems to be connected with reading it in my own language. How do I know what is true and what is 'airy fairy'? It actually means that the translating and reading the book becomes much more a kind of an adventure in itself!" [3]

I perceive this work as a long epic poem which maintains its rightful position among the other prominent works in the same genre, such as *Gilgamesh, Ramayana, Pistis Sophia, the Old Testament, the New Testament, the Holy Koran,* Homer's *Iliad* and *Odyssey,* the *Theogony* of Hesiod, Dante's *Divine Comedy,* John Milton's *Paradise Lost* and *Paradise Regained,* Nietzsche's *Also Sprach Zarathustra,* Helena Blavatsky's *The Secret Doctrine* and many others.

Most of these epic poems are considered landmarks in the spiritual history of humanity, albeit to different degrees. Some of them carry new metaphysical principles, new cosmological and historical concepts, new codes of human behavior and ideals, new answers to the question of the meaning of human existence as well as predictions and prophecies, said to be obtained through spiritual revelation or artistic inspiration. Due to its magnitude and universal importance, Gurdjieff's *Beelzebub's Tales* can be considered to belong to the same category as all of those works.

What makes this work an epic poem?

Actually we have here two questions: what makes it an epic and what makes it a poem? I take a definition of "epic" from the *Poetry Handbook* by Babette Deutsch: "An epic is a narrative poem, noble in conception and style, which treats of a series of heroic exploits or supernatural events and usually centers upon the adventures and accomplishments of one hero, such as Odysseus in the *Odyssey*.[4]"

In the same *Handbook* the term "poem" is defined as "a composition that partakes of the nature of both speech and song". Developing this definition farther, the author continues as follows: "It is chiefly distinguished by the feeling that dictates it and that which it communicates, the economy and resonance of the language, an imaginative power that integrates, influences, and enhances experience.[5]"

I would also like to refer the listener and the reader of this text to the American poet William Carlos Williams (1883–1963), who, much like Gurdjieff himself would have done it, defined the word "poem" as "a small (or large) machine made of words" adding that "there can be no parts, as in any other machine, that are redundant". Similarly, the Anglo-American poet W.H. Auden

---

[3] http://www.gurdjieff-internet.com/article_details.php?ID=123&W=4
[4] Babette Deutsch *Poetry Handbook. A Dictionary of Terms,* Funk & Wagnalls, New York 1974, p. 50.
[5] Ibid. p. 122

(1907–1973) remarked that "… whatsoever else it may be, a poem is a verbal artifact which must be as skillfully and solidly constructed as a table or a motorcycle.[6]"

This work by Gurdjieff possesses a unique style, a slow and sublime pace and a poetic cadence, all of which make it indeed a narrative poem, skillfully constructed, noble in conception, displaying an imaginative power that integrates, influences, and enhances reader's experience.

What kind of epic poem is Beelzebub's Tales?

The following questions could be asked: what makes an epic poem a landmark in human history? And another question: what is similar and what is different in Gurdjieff's epic and in analogous works? We believe that some epics, such as *the Hebrew Bible, the New Testament, the Holy Koran,* are books of a sacred knowledge given to humankind by God, while others, such as Virgil's *Aeneid*, Homer's *Iliad* and *Odyssey*, Dante's *Divine Comedy* and Nietzsche's *Also Sprach Zarathustra* are man's creations that reflect the national spirit or the spirit of a particular civilization. Still others, like *Poimander*, *Pistis Sophia* or *The Secret Doctrine* are sources of wisdom and spiritual inspiration for smaller and often dispersed spiritual communities. In a historical perspective, *the Hebrew Bible and the New Testament*, even following a long series of editorial alterations which have emasculated their profound and mighty spiritual impulse, nevertheless have preserved the stable status of the canonical books of the major Western religions, while the books belonging to the third category have lost and keep losing the attention and appreciation of their readers. The works of the second category have become legitimate elements of world culture and have a general albeit a weaker inspirational effect on their readers. Some of the poems belonging to either category may have had a rich past, but possess no future, since they have exhausted their inspirational resource, while others, possibly unknown today or known only to a small groups of adherents, may have a great future.

During the last several decades we have observed a growing interest on the part of readers and publishers toward *Beelzebub's Tales*. Three months ago the original Russian version of that book was republished in Moscow, Russia, following its first publication in Canada in 2000. Today it is a "topical" book for those who are capable and willing to decipher its secrets and extract the precious kernel from its shell, as well as for those who are intrigued by the scandalous reputation of its author. But will this book be as important within the next decade or two? Will it attract the attention of new generations of spiritual seekers? Does it have a linguistic and stylistic perfection and rich content that distinguishes other great works of humanity, and would it really attract readers for centuries to come? Could it eventually become a canonical book of a new religion, or will it remain an inspirational source for a small group of admirers? Might it happen that the book would simply be forgotten by future generations? I shall discuss all of these possibilities in the latter part of my paper.

---

[6] Ibid. p. 122

Gurdjieff's Beelzebub's Tales – A Landmark in the Spiritual History of Humanity

The main narrator of Beelzebub's Tales.

The authorship of some of the epic poems or their inspirational source has often been ascribed either to God Almighty or to prophets and various legendary or semi-legendary individuals. Sometimes these beings are seen as the heroes of a narrative or their main narrators. In Beelzebub's Tales we see as the central character and the chief narrator the fallen Archangel Beelzebub, who had repented of the transgressions of his youth and was pardoned by the Holy Creator of the Universe. Beelzebub is travelling to the centre of the Universe and en route educating his inexperienced but sincere and goodhearted grandson Hassein. Beelzebub's status of one of the closest Spirits to God adds to the weight of the poem's message. However in Beelzebub's Tales the fictional narrator is essentially merged with the author of the poem, creating a double effect of both a human and superhuman being acting on the part of the history of humanity more as a benevolent observer and experimenter, rather than a reformer of life on planet Earth.

A special kind of sacredness has been attributed to some of the epic poems

A special kind of sacredness has been attributed to some of the epic poems, and they have been made objects of exclusive reverence and worship as well as of systematic study and commentaries, the latter sometimes leading to creation of special disciplines, e.g. theology. Special rituals for handling these books, special manners of recitation, as well as particular schedules, sequences and quantities for private and communal recitation have been established. Many of these works were believed to possess a deeply hidden secret content, which the devoted reader was obligated to dig out. Some of these works were involved in the process of enculturation, i.e. the dissemination of their ideas and incorporation of their content and style into various layers of existing culture. As a result of continuous reciting, quoting and referencing, some of these poems have acquired a status of a warrant of the Objective Truth, as they have been solidified into an inert culture and their ideas have ceased to develop and grow, hence becoming dogmas. A critical approach towards the ideas, style, composition, language and rituals of a particular teaching instantly generates the reaction of a backlash from the group that draws its self-importance from it. Such a community would not tolerate criticism of the source of its inspiration. In Gurdjieff's community, as dispersed as it is nowadays, such a person or group would be ostracized for being a wiseacre, a hairsplitter and a "know-it-all," instead of developing any "real understanding". And that alleged "real understanding" is claimed today by a various contending parties.

The language and style of Beelzebub's Tales require special attention

It has been said that Gurdjieff wrote and dictated his book in two languages, – namely, Russian and Armenian. The Armenian copy of *Beelzebub's Tales* is thought to have been transported to Armenia by Lilly Galumian, but as rumors tell us, this book has been taken to Russia and today nobody knows where to find it. The only currently available original is the Russian one, and it has never been critically examined from the point of view of its language, style and structure.

The Anglo-French scholar Denis Saurat writes: "Beyond some excusable mannerism and the peculiarities which give charm to every author, I see nothing in that book that could be objected to.[7]" I wish I could agree with that assessment concerning this book's particularities.

The language of some pages of Gurdjieff's book is indeed fascinatingly sharp and precise. The readers of *Beelzebub's Tales* must mark the spontaneity and improvisational energy in some sections of the book, as well as the exactness of formulation of some of the conceptions, albeit most part of the book has a cumbersome and verbose style creating an unfortunate type of dragging of the narration which hardly enhances its perception. Those viscid pages of the book which Gurdjieff devoted to the vices of Russians, Americans, Englishmen, Germans and Frenchmen presently arouse only annoyance and disappointment; nonetheless they amount to almost half of the book's length.

It has also been said that Gurdjieff in *Beelzebub's Tales* had deliberately obscured and complicated his language, the way it has been done by the authors of some of the alchemical treatises of previous times, who intended to conceal their secrets from the uninitiated readers so that the latter would toil and labor, overcoming the difficulties of deciphering them. The instigation of this effort of deciphering those books, provoked by Gurdjieff, must have been aimed at enhancing the readers' vigor and persistence in their efforts in digging out the "bone" or the "dog" buried in the text.

Similarly, the language of *Beelzebub's Tales* is in most instances awkward, heavy, verbose and monotonous. Especially monotonous is the language of Beelzebub himself, being abound in lengthy periods, full of artificial constructions, as well as stylistic and grammatical flaws. The language of Beelzebub's grandson Hassein is likewise inanimate, dull and lifeless. There are no fresh dialogues, no vivid intonations and no really adequate idiomatic expressions brought in to enliven the story. All the aphorisms by Hodja Nasruddin incorporated by Gurdjieff into his book are banal and stylistically tarnished. The Russian language of the original version is full of bureaucratic terms, presumably aimed at hampering the reading process and at provoking the reader's resistance and even protest.

In the introductory chapter of his book, Gurdjieff wrote about the "*bon ton* literary language" as the common requirement in the literature of his time. However, he himself had serious problems with concise Russian language. Growing up in the outskirts of Russia and spending over twenty years in the Orient, Gurdjieff spoke Russian the way many of the inhabitants of the Caucasus and Central Asia speak up to the present day, being often unaware of the stylistic and grammatical incorrectness of their speech.

Among the numerous irregularities of language I must mention the following, frequently used by Gurdjieff: «обяснить о чем-то или о ком-то» (i.e. "to explain about something or about somebody"), while the Russian language requires the expression «обяснить что-то и кому-то»

---

[7] Denis Saurat's letter to S.C. Nott: www.duversity.org/PDF/DenisSaurat.pdf

Gurdjieff's Beelzebub's Tales – A Landmark in the Spiritual History of Humanity

(i.e. "to explain something and to somebody"). Also I must mention the unreadable words «функционизация» (i.e. "functionization") used instead of «функционирование» (i.e. "functioning"); «трехмозгный» − instead of «трехмозглый» or «трехмозговой» (i.e. "three-brained"); «облекание» (i.e. "shaping" or "clothing") (p. 797)[8] − instead of «облик» (i.e. "image"), such as, for instance, in the phrase «все трехмозгные существа нашего Мегалакосмоса без различия в их облекании», i.e. "all three-brained beings of our Megalocosmos without distinction of exterior coating;" «трансформировываются» instead of «трансформируются» (i.e. "transform themselves"); «образовываются» instead of «образуются» (i.e. "educate themselves"), etc.

Among other obvious flaws in the original text one should mention the following: «не переставая смотреть на *сказанную статую*» (p. 615), i.e. "And not ceasing to look at the said figure"; "адьютант имел очень заметную ту *специфическую типность*" (p. 616), i.e. "This adjutant of his who came had the very marked specific type"; "я *объясню* тебе о каждом из них в отдельности" (p. 621) "I will explain to you about each of them separately"; "*оформливается*" (p. 631) "their strange Reason proper to them alone is formed there"; "я тебе *расскажу* сейчас *пару картинок*" (p. 637), i.e. "I will now give you a couple of little scenes from former history"; Хассейн: «*Дедушка! Дорогой дедушка! Прояви, пожалуйста, вслух имеющиеся в твоем, особенно для меня дорогом, общем наличии такие, тобой узнанные за время твоего долгого существования, сведения...*» (p. 641), "Grandfather! Dear Grandfather! Manifest please aloud those informations (!) which you have in your common presence, particularly dear to me, and which you have learned during your long existence"; "следует *отметить и о том*" (p. 651) "It must be remarked that"; "*водящиеся существа* на этой местности" (p. 651), i.e. "The beings dwelling in this locality", etc.

Many of those irregularities of the Russian original were corrected by the translators into English and other languages and now sound like regular English, so the English version of the book has smooth and proper language, although the oppressive awkwardness and heaviness of style, not to mention the uncountable unutterable neologisms, have remained and could not be eliminated in those translations. And if I were asked whether the irregularities of the Russian language in *Beelzebub's Tales* have resulted from Gurdjieff's limited command of the Russian language or were a product of an intentional hampering and complicating the language and style, I would in all honesty answer: it was both.

While the Russian text of the original suggests the idea that it is a translation from an unknown language into Russian, the English translation of the book has more right to be treated as the original because of the tidiness of language and style, and for the reason that the book was translated into English in the author's presence and under his supervision and, hence, reflected the collective linguistic atmosphere of Gurdjieff's circle of the time, in which the simultaneous process of writing and translation was on the way.

---

[8] The following group of page numbers is referring to Russian edition of *Beelzebub Tales*, Triangle Editions, Inc. Canada, 2000.

I have found an unexpected support of this attitude from Reijo Oksanen, a translator of *Beelzebub's Tales* into Finnish, a person who runs a well-known website *Gurdjieff Internet Guide*. Reijo Oksanen writes: "Gurdjieff wrote and dictated Beelzebub's Tales in Armenian and Russian. From these was rendered the English version with which Gurdjieff worked from when he began writing in 1924 until 1949. There were many changes made to the English text. Therefore it can be considered to have in it what Gurdjieff wanted to put into it – it is his final version."[9]

We may remember that the New Testament has become known in its Greek version, notwithstanding the fact that Jesus himself and his disciples spoke Aramaic, which was the vernacular language in Palestine of their time. Similarly Buddha's teaching became universally known thanks to translations from the language Buddha and his disciples used into numerous other languages. Incidentally, it has still not been established which language Buddha used for his preaching.

Richness of the content of Beelzebub Tales

Many men and women of great repute have left highly impressive statements regarding the importance of *Beelzebub's Tales* as well as the richness of its content. One can bring many examples of Gurdjieff's ideas influencing the newest trends in philosophy, psychology and sociology, as well as exerting a direct personal influence on many remarkable men and women. This fact was obvious since the time he presented his teaching to a group of Russian intellectuals in 1914-1917.

In his book *Gurdjieff's Teaching* (*The Journal of a Pupil*) Ch. S. Nott[10] recalls A. R. Orage saying that *Beelzebub's Tales* can be compared to an onion that has an infinite number of layers. After having peeled several layers, one realizes that there is still much more to peel, because each new layer reveals a new meaning, thus making the process seemingly endless. Orage continued to say: "The book is an objective piece of art. The objective art consists of the conscious variations of the original in accordance with the plan of an artist or writer, striving to make a certain impression on his audience".

In his Introduction to *Beelzebub's Tales* A.G. Blake makes the following statement: "In its complex and complicated character, as a text about alchemy, in its acuity and judiciousness, similarly to chronicles by Rabelais in its scope, as a monumental work of historical analysis, in its passionate character, as something almost sacred, the Beelzebub's Tales surpasses the boundaries of all ordinary works. This book is a manifestation of a new and, at the same time, an ancient way of thinking, stemming from the utmost depths of our nature.[11]"

---

[9] http://www.gurdjieff-internet.com/article_details.php?ID=123&W=4
[10] C.S. Nott *Teachings of Gurdjieff: The Journal of a Pupil.*
[11] J. G. Bennett *Talks on Gurdjieff's 'Beelzebub's Tales to His Grandson'*, 1988. A.G. Blake, Introduction.

Gurdjieff's Beelzebub's Tales – A Landmark in the Spiritual History of Humanity

Denis Saurat calls *Beelzebub's Tales* an astonishing book and makes a number of observations which, as he believes, denote its supernatural, super-terrestrial source. However he thinks that "its allegorical and philosophical meaning which is easy enough to someone who has studied the traditions would be completely beyond the public.[12]"

What is new in the Beelzebub's Tales according to J.G. Bennett?

Beelzebub's Tales is indeed an unusual book. But what is really new in this book? J. G. Bennett writes: "In detail, there is little new in *the Beelzebub Tales*. Not much research is needed to discover the affinity of Gurdjieff's cosmology with Neo-Platonism in the West and Sankhya and the Abhidharma in the East. It is easy to show where he has drawn upon Christian (especially Greek Orthodox), Buddhist (chiefly Mahayana and Zen), Moslem (particularly Dervish and Sufi), and Ancient Egyptian and Assyrian sources. The originality of his teaching does not lie in its raw material but in the use to which it is put.[13]"

Turning to the specifics Bennett writes that the outstanding elements of Gurdjieff's book are his theogonic and cosmogonic myths.[14] Gurdjieff's myth is undoubtedly a Mediterranean myth belonging to the Judeo-Christian family of myths. However, according to Gurdjieff's Creation myth, the very existence of the Universe is subject to numerous overriding and determining conditions, which make the complete realization of the Divine Purpose inherently impossible. The fact of a successive actualization in Time imposes on every process the price of incompleteness and imperfection. Time, the Merciless Heropass, which has no source from which its arising should depend, always flows independently by itself. For Gurdjieff Time simultaneously possesses an absolute character and holds the supreme position among the forces of the Cosmos. Nevertheless, the Heropass is vanquished by the infinite wisdom of the Creator, not as an enemy or opposing principle, but rather as an ineluctable fact, the very condition of the possibility of existence.

This statement does not give an exhaustive evaluation of Time. Time is not only an ineluctable fact and a condition for the possibility of existence, but it is a Force that rules over the Universe. God has to consider and bypass it, so that He Himself and His Creation are safe from its destructive effect. God creates the Trogoautoegocratic principle, according to which the permanent harmony of the Universe is assured by the reciprocal feeding of everything that exists. According to Gurdjieff's myth, the Trogoautoegocratic principle is absolutely necessary for the understanding of human destiny. Everything that lives must serve the "all-universal purposes". Gurdjieff says: man is not exempt from this necessity, and must, either by his life or by this death,

---

[12] Denis Saurat's letter to S.C. Nott: www.duversity.org/PDF/DenisSaurat.pdf

[13] J. G. Bennett Gurdjieff's *All and Everything. Gurdjieff International Review.*

[14] Many societies have two categories of traditional narrative, "true stories" or myths, and "false stories" or fables. Myths generally take place in a primordial age, when the world had not yet achieved its current form, and explain how the world gained its current form and how customs, institutions and taboos were established. *Wikipedia*

contribute his quota to the transformation of energy upon which the reciprocal maintenance of all existence depends. This way God has solved the problem of Time, and Time has ceased to be His adversary, however the sad result of this invention is that everything in the Universe becomes a prey to Devouring Time.

Great Nature has given man the possibility of being not merely a blind tool of the full service to these All-Universal objective purposes but, while serving Her and actualizing what has been foreordained for him – which is the destiny of every breathing creature – of working at the same time also for himself, for his own individuality. Man has thus a two-fold destiny, either to live only as the unconscious slave of the All-Universal purpose, or to pay the debt of his own existence, thus attain independent individuality and work towards his self-perfection.

However, according to Gurdjieff's myth, we inhabit a Universe ruled not by the Law of Love, as it is asserted by the Christian teaching, but by the principle of total devouring. If we accept this assumption, then we will have to admit that there is nothing wrong with people's mutual destruction in wars and revolutions, as well as the habit of blood sacrifices so passionately condemned by Gurdjieff in his poem.

Gurdjieff writes of the ultimate regulating principle of universal validity, a sacred unspoiled impulse dwelling deep within the human psyche. This is the Sacred Impulse of Conscience, which cannot be destroyed, since it is implanted by Divine Grace. But does not this Sacred Impulse of Conscience contradict the Trogoautoegocratic principle or the Universal Chain of Feeding?

A further look at Gurdjieff's book

According to Bennett, Western thought remains encased within the dualism of good and evil, of conflicting wills, of antithetical purposes. This conflict is inherent in all our myths, from the Chinese Yin-Yang and *The Book of Job* to Goethe's *Faust,* as Bennett notes. Dualism is embedded into our mind. Throughout the Universe there reigns the union of opposites, which provides the ground for dualism.

In concurrence with Bennett, we can see that Gurdjieff specifically rejects the myth of the opposition between good and evil. After his repentance Beelzebub is not God's adversary anymore; on the contrary he is God's faithful ally, and this element in Gurdjieff's myth seemingly eliminates any kind of dualism in the Cosmos. However this dualism reemerges in the relation of Time (Heropass) with the rest of the world, including God Himself; God the Creator has been put into strained circumstances under the pressure of Time that forced Him to take extraordinary measures to straighten His position. Time is working against everything in the Universe, and the Trogoautoegocratic principle of reciprocal feeding saves the Whole of the Universe trough sacrificing every single part of it.

Indeed Gurdjieff's God the Creator is not the Absolute God. Adjacent to God the Creator, even prior to the Act of Creation, we can observe other forces and entities, actually, other gods, some of them more powerful than God and others subservient to Him, such as Time, Space, and Primordial Matter (Etherokrilno), an equivalent of "ein-sof" of the Cabbalists. After the Act of Creation more entities – including the stars and the planets – have been generated without God's direct involvement in the process; all of them are undoubtedly gods in relation to the human scale. The very Act of Creation of the Cosmos is compulsory in its character, enacted out of pressing necessity. Thus, Gurdjieff's God the Creator is not the Sole Monarch of the Universe, but rather a Demiurge, who has been compelled to invent a method of protecting the Sun-Absolute, which was the dwelling abode for Him and his Seraphs and Cherubs. God had generated only the Creative Impulse, the Logos or Theomertmalogos, and the subsequent process went automatically by itself, without the participation of the Divine Will, as the result of the operation of two basic laws, the Triamazikamno and the Heptaparaparshinokh.

This story reminds of the myth conceived by Valentine the Gnostic (2nd century AD), in which God the Creator is actually a Demiurge (Ialdabaoth), i.e. a lesser god, who creates an imperfect World out of necessity with numerous shortcomings in it that have to be later corrected by the Messengers of the True God. In Gurdjieff's myth the supremacy could be ascribed to Heropass, who could be associated with the Zoroastrian god Zurvan Akarana, the father of twin sons Ahuramazda and Angro Maniu, one representing quantative time, while the other representing quantative space. Zurvan or "Boundless Time" represents endlessness, which corresponds to the title by which Beelzebub is referring to God the Creator, His Endlessness. According to Avesta, Zurvan Akarana (Zeroana Akerne) has always existed, his glory is exalted, his light is resplendent; he is beyond human intellect and comprehension. Everything that has ever existed emanated from Zurvan Akarana.

Gurdjieff's God can be also seen as Ishvara of Advaita-Vedanta and the Upanishads. Ishvara is merely the lowest aspect of God, perceived from a lower viewpoint. The full Truth is revealed on the highest stage of spiritual progress, when the practitioner realizes that God is a transcendent pure Being, a Reality that can be approached only by means of negation of all qualities.

Another point of reference is the famous Arian controversy, which took place at the time of early Christianity. Arian, a priest who taught in Alexandria declared that the Logos is no more than a power or a quality of the Father. Before time began, the Father had created the Son by the power of the Word to be His agent in creation. Arian's myth was rejected by the three Cappadocian Fathers of the 4th century AD: Saint Basil, Gregory of Nyssa and Gregory of Nazianzus, who argued that the Godhead is the entire Trinity: God the Father, God the Son and God the Holy Ghost. In their writings they made extensive use of the formula "three persons (*hypostases*) in one substance (*ousia*)," and thus explicitly acknowledged the distinction between the Father and the Son, but at the same time insisted on their essential unity. This formulation has been accepted by the mainstream Western and Eastern Christianity, while Arianism has been declared to be the worst of all the heresies. It must be noted that Gurdjieff's myth bears resemblance to both the Arian theology of the Logos (or the TheomertmaLOGOS), who is no more than a power or a quality of the Father and whom God made an agent in the Creation of the Cosmos, and the

Cappadocian concept of the Trinity, which presents the idea of the distinction and unity of these three forces.

Gurdjieff writes of the resistance to insurrection against God's creative plan by one of the Highest Spirits, which was supported by this Spirit's entire clan. This rebellion was a highly dramatic event on the primeval stage of the history of Creation, for had that Spirit won (which is what he counted on, when he started the rebellion), then the process of Creation would have gone in a totally different direction. That again proves the idea that His Endlessness is a Demiurge, and that Gurdjieff's myth of Creation is a demiurgic myth.

A special part of the creation myth is Gurdjieff's teaching about Okidanokh, the universal principle of three forces existing in every phenomenon, acting in the way of involution. Okidanokh produces Self-Criticism and Self-Accusation in all phenomena; when one part of a phenomenon feels dissatisfied with another part, it experiences remorse. This brings us to the concept of Conscience, which is hidden in the deepest parts of a human soul, playing the role of Christ living in the heart of every man.

Another important myth introduced by Gurdjieff is the myth of the Moon's origin and its role in human destiny. Once again, we find here the force of pressing necessity that forces the Great Commission of Sacred Individuals headed by the Archangel Sakaki to decide on the creation in an instrument that would stabilize the situation after the occurrence of a cosmic accident in the solar system Ors, namely to create the human race on this "unfortunate planet" with the sole purpose of sustaining the Moon in its orbit. Among other purposes, this myth underlines the small importance of the human race which is destined to fulfill a limited cosmic task. This book clearly states that humanity has a much lesser value than that of the stars and planets. In regard to this myth of Gurdjieff, I would like to make a reference to Helen Blavatsky who wrote: "The Moon plays the greatest and the most important role both in formatting of the Earth itself and in populating it (the Earth – *A.R.*) with the human beings"[15]. These words from the *Secret Doctrine* give an additional demonstration of the affinity of Gurdjieff's concepts with the ideas of his predecessors.

Judaism and Islam are more consistent than Christianity in putting the monotheistic principle through, leaving all the dubious Gnostic ideas to their mystics. However, both the strictly monotheistic and the demiurgic myths continued their disputes, presenting their claims as being fully justified and condemning the opposing ones.

All these myths deal with matters that are beyond possible human grasp or communication. None of them is essentially better or worse, none depict reality as it is; each myth reflects a vision of a mystic, intended by him to be shared with others. However such a vision can reflect the profound levels of reality and give way to the myths, which ultimately end up contradicting each other.

---

[15] Helen Blavatsky *The Secret Doctrine,* volume 1, Part 1, Stanza VI, p.235 (Е.П. Блаватская *Тайная доктрина*, т. 1, с. 235).

Gurdjieff's Beelzebub's Tales – A Landmark in the Spiritual History of Humanity

I am convinced that Gurdjieff wrote his book from his great integrity and on the basis of his own mystical experience which was embodied into a mythical form. Many elements of Gurdjieff's teaching appear to me as being self-evident and do not call for any rational confirmation. His teaching is topical and strikingly realistic, merciless in regard to sentimentality and intellectual inertia.

Like many, if not all universal myths, Gurdjieff's myth is fragmentary and obscure in many ways. Attempting to give the answers to the ultimate questions, all these myths, however, cannot be proven by reason or verified by personal experience. P.D. Ouspensky, J.G. Bennett, Rodney Collin and Rene Daumall, all of whom can be seen as belonging to the tradition of the Fourth Way, have created their own myths, inspired by Gurdjieff's original myth. Other spiritualists, such as Helen Blavatsky, Vladimir Soloviev, Rudolph Steiner, Aurobindo Ghosh and Ramana Maharshi, also came up with myths rooted in the great ancient traditions of the West or East. Each of those myths carries in itself the seeds of what intuitively is being perceived by us as the Truth, and these myths do not contradict but complement one another.

Christianity attempted to improve and upgrade the Judaic myth, while Islam claimed a development and an improvement of both the Christian and the Judaic myths. Origen, the Christian Gnostics, Jacob Boehme, Vladimir Soloviev, Rudolph Steiner, Teilhard de Chardin and many others believed that they were developing the Christian myth. Gurdjieff's mythology was a further step in that direction.

Gurdjieff's myth was a direct response to two most influential myths of his time – the Christian and the Theosophical. Towards the beginning of the 20th century, the Christian myth has reached a peak in terms of fossilization. It lacked the spiritual dynamics as well as realism, proper to the requirements of the epoch. The Theosophical myth, as rich and elaborate in details as it was, could not satisfy the intellectual expectations of the time, and became outdated, especially after Krishnamurti's dismissal of the Theosophical movement in his famous speech of 1929. In that context, Gurdjieff's myth seemed to carry the essential answers to these requirements.

At the foundation of Gurdjieff's myth one can see a categorical imperative expressed in a condensed way by means of a formula made from one concept repeated three times in three languages: Armenian, Russian and English languages: partk-dolg-duty. This term refers to the obligation of every human being to work consciously towards being capable to take a responsible part in the maintenance of our cosmic home and, simultaneously, to work towards one's own self-perfection.

Gurdjieff has created a great universal myth, which incorporated together with this ethical teaching a well developed cosmogony, cosmology and philosophy of history. Similarly to many of the ancient and modern myths, this myth contained many maladjustments and equivocations. All universal myths, including Gurdjieff's, are doomed to be fragmentary and inconsistent and carry equivocation in themselves. That happens because mystical experience in its pure form surpasses all rationally conceived human concepts and cannot be reduced to any rational form. The content of mystical experience is in principle not describable by philosophical and even mythological language.

Mystics assert that Ultimate Reality is beyond the scope of all myths and philosophies and beyond any representation, as it is stated in the words of the ancient Greek philosopher Gorgius (483-375 B. C), who said: Reality cannot be perceived, if perceived it cannot be cognized, if cognized it cannot be expressed, if expressed it cannot be communicated. The great Advaita-Vedanta thinker Shankara stated this same idea in a simple and precise manner: "His (God's – *A.R.*) true nature cannot be known by the senses or the mind".[16]

Christ lifted from the shoulder of mankind the weight of original sin and took it on Himself. Gurdjieff placed a great part of the responsibility for the catastrophic human condition on the Sacred Individuals who acted as they did for a higher purpose. However, most of that responsibility was placed by him on human beings, who, according to Gurdjieff, have all that is necessary for them to liberate themselves from the mechanical laws by following their Partk-dolg-duty.

The dethronement of old myths and the development of new ones often present one and the same process. Krishnamurti in 1929 was preoccupied with the dethronement of Theosophy and the formation of his own teaching. German philosophy, Marxism and Positivism criticized Christianity and defended their own causes. P.D. Ouspensky, J. G. Bennett and Rodney Collin were distorting and simultaneously developing Gurdjieff's myth with varying degrees of success.

Concluding remarks

From this brief overview of historical parallels we can see that Gurdjieff's cosmology and especially his myth of Creation as they are represented in *Beelzebub Tales* stand next to the great classical Western cosmologies which have inspired humanity throughout its history. Myths have an enormous power over human beings. Most people are reassured by myths in their actions and thoughts, but at the same time they may frequently get caught into the myth's pitfall. Only very few are capable of developing their own myth. P.D. Ouspensky, J. G. Bennett and Rodney Collin being nourished by Gurdjieff's myth were not capable of developing myths that were entirely independent of Gurdjieff's. Even more stuck in that myth is the A&E Conference from the year of its emergence.

Early Christianity was enriched and straightened on the way of assimilating Hellenistic wisdom in the melting pot of Alexandrian pluralism. St. Paul and the early Christian practitioners and thinkers (in most instances they were both) refined the teaching of Jesus and sharpened it in open controversy. This ongoing process of mythical creativity made Christianity a solid and lasting instrument of spiritual progress, whereas the cessation of that process caused a continuous necrosis in a formerly flourishing religion.

---

[16] Paul G. van Oyen *The Crown of Reason. 'Vivekacudamani' of Shri Adi Shankara,* Conversion Production, p. 21

Gurdjieff's Beelzebub's Tales – A Landmark in the Spiritual History of Humanity

What was the role of the Gurdjieff Foundation in the Gurdjieff community? From the time of Gurdjieff's death it tried to maintain a commanding position by condemning and suppressing any dissent. Gurdjieff Foundation has "excommunicated" Ouspensky and Bennett, two most brilliant disciples of Gurdjieff, and insisted on a blind acceptance of its exclusive interpretation of Gurdjieff's teaching instead of encouraging an intelligent and independent approach towards the teaching among its members.

Myths are tools but these tools are aimed at different purposes. Some are meant to impose a slumber on groups of people. Others are meant to serve as alarm clocks, to wake them up from an illusion. Those myths carry in themselves a conflict. Gurdjieff's myth was supposed to work as an alarm clock. And to a certain extend it worked so.

But watch: suddenly people become deaf and blind to the merits of other myths and no less sophisticated concepts. They say: we came here to worship this myth and to occupy ourselves with this book and if somebody is not satisfied with that he or she can go and look for another company. And again as it was numerous times in the past, we have created an idol – a book that, as some say, has an extra-terrestrial origin. Why don't we kiss this book each time we take it in our hands and why don't we declare all other books irrelevant?

The A & E Conference resembles Church Councils of the first Christian centuries. Those Councils had authority and power and they confidently used that power, while our Conference deliberately reduces its role to merely illustrating and confirming of the old schemes. Gurdjieff's alarm clock has been successfully silenced. The A & E Conference might have become the unbearable Cayenne pepper of a Kurd from Gurdjieff's story. It could have but it did not.

Gurdjieff's myth as a traditional myth must be developed further in order to have future, or it will be extinguished and forgotten, as it happened to many ancient and more recent myths. Instead of stimulating mythical consciousness in their members, some Gurdjieff communities of today direct their members chiefly towards body-oriented practices that frequently deprive them of creative intellectual initiative. Intellect per se is often renounced by them as a dangerous toy for wiseacres.

Wiseacring indeed is a serious problem for many types of minds and characters however that is not a sufficient reason for addressing intellect in pejorative terms. Different spiritual seekers need different types of practices corresponding to their inner state and inner resources. My conviction is that mythical and metaphysical thinking should be not reserved only for participants of A&E Conference but must be justified and encouraged as a legitimate type of spiritual practices at least for those who have suitable capabilities and who have raised their overall being to a proper level.

Gurdjieff's teaching was instrumental in vivifying and temporarily dispelling the stagnation in the spiritual atmosphere of the West in the first half of the previous century. In the brutal epoch of wars and revolutions he brought a "breath of hope" to the despaired spiritual seekers of Russia, Western Europe and United States; however the cumbersome and unwieldy form of his major literary work precludes it from becoming a source of inspiration to many people or, in the words of Denis Saurat, puts it "completely beyond the public"[17]. One should take into consideration that during almost seventy years since *Beelzebub's Tales* were written, humanity has moved further along the path of spiritual degradation and is currently even less ready to accept a teaching that requires spiritual effort. If the question of a new teaching should ever arise, humanity would prefer a spiritual discipline that does not demand any effort whatsoever but gives a straightforward direction for actions.

The influence of Gurdjieff's ideas is steadily growing among groups of intellectuals worldwide, and this accounts to the richness of its ideas; however Gurdjieff's epic poem has little chance of becoming a canonic book of a new extensive spiritual movement and even lesser chance of becoming a cultural monument of humanity. There is a great probability that it will preserve its current status of an inspirational source for a limited community. Gurdjieff's myth contains in itself certain features of novelty which have been discussed earlier and which make it so attractive. However no myth today can claim a conclusive explanation of the origin and means of functioning of the Universe; each can be only an approximation of such knowledge. Furthermore, Gurdjieff's myth has been embedded in too bulky a shape and expressed in an excessively awkward style and viscous language. Rephrasing the words of the American poet William Carlos Williams, we can say that Gurdjieff's long poem is a cumbersome machine that has many extra parts, and those parts do not enhance its functioning. Taking into consideration the stylistic, linguistic and compositional shortcomings of the original (Russian) version, we cannot expect that this book would ever become an example of style and language for poetry or philosophy of the future, as it was the case of the *Old* and *New Testaments,* the *Holy Koran*, Homer's *Iliad* and *Odyssey*, Virgil's *Aeneid,* etc. Of course this assumption is essentially hypothetical, since nobody can give the final verdict in such a delicate question.

© Copyright 2011 - Arkady Rovner - All Rights Reserved

---

[17] Denis Saurat's letter to S.C. Nott: http://www.duversity.org/PDF/DenisSaurat.pdf

Gurdjieff's Beelzebub's Tales - A Landmark in the Spiritual History of Humanity - Questions & Answers

Questioner 1: …the other reason I am stepping out – this is a footnote – your literary perception is very good. There was never a Russian original. I know this history very well. My mother spent every day with Gurdjieff, translating and editing in the four weeks, first four weeks of 1928, when a version that we have was put into some form.

Arkady: You mean, English?

Questioner 1: Yes, from the beginning. The Armenian notes, I know very well, were thrown away. The Russian notes were stacked and saved in a package that Gurdjieff had in a safe at Rue Colonel Renard for some years for various reasons I do not know. But the point is that when the original was rewritten – there was original English – rewritten – decidedly in November 1927 – rewritten in the first weeks of 1928, then reedited, worked out to Gurdjieff's satisfaction and printed in 1931. When Gurdjieff saw that, he then took it and he gave Jeanne de Salzmann the responsibility of turning it into French, Louise Goepfert – of turning it into German and Lili Galumnian of turning it into Russian. And that was the Russian text that was printed in Toronto that you ran into.

The text that you call the original came from scraps, and this is a terrible story, and when Gurdjieff died, within twenty-four hours his apartment was raided, robbed, his safe was emptied, and all of his notes were taken, the Russian notes were taken, and those notes ended up in the south of France and stayed there for some years and then reemerged when Madame de Salzmann and Michel de Salzmann decided to save the copyright in 1991, so that that they would have a new copyright. They said: "this is a translation of the original". It is a lie. That is it. And if anyone wants more details, I know it all. I have been close to the whole Gurdjieff family for all my years. And for my work with Ordail (ordeal?), people will say, I heard something about All & Everything for 40 years – 80 years, those are my years.

Arkady: Just one remark. The so-called Russian version was published in 2000 in Canada with an introduction by Michel de Salzmann. He states that this is the Russian version from which everything was translated into all languages, and he explains some particularities of it, so we take it for granted that the Russian version existed and was the source for the translations.

Questioner 1: When you say "the original," which version are you talking about?

Arkady: I am talking about that version with the Michel de Salzmann introduction.

Questioner 1: Well, then. The one that was the translation from English was the one that Gurdjieff himself authorized.
Arkady: And this is what I and some other people say – that the English version is the original.

Questioner 1: It is.

Arkady: So we agree on this completely.

Questioner 2: I'd like to make a comment first. The book as you described it, Arkady, has absolutely nothing to do with the literature or pompous language or anything like that. For me, when you buy a car, the car comes with a manual. All & Everything is a manual for work on yourself. I see myself on every page of that book. That's the whole purpose of the book – to see yourself as you are. What's the Russian version? What's the German version? What's the French version? What's the American version? It has an absolutely practical purpose, like when I have to repair my car, I look in the manual. And when I want to repair myself, I look in All & Everything. And that's the whole purpose of the book.

Arkady: Nick, it does not illuminate the question of the genre. Some believe it is a social satire, some believe it is an alchemic treatise. I believe it is an epic poem. You think and you state that it is a manual for the work on oneself. All of us have a right to see it this way or that way.

Questioner 2: But to say that it has almost no value…

Arkady: Who said that?

Questioner 2: You're saying that the language itself, when he explains…

Arkady: I talked about the so-called Russian original. I always added this expression; "so-called" because I was not sure that it is the original. And I said that the English language version is the original, and Paul confirmed this. So I don't like the Russian "original" presented and published by Michel de Salzmann, and I recommend that all of us stick to the English version. That's the only thing I have said.

Questioner 3: I have one more question – a very short one. I have a special interest in Rodney Collin. You said that Rodney Collin distorted Gurdjieff's work. Could you talk a little about it?

Arkady: Well, I read two of his works: "The Celestial Influence" and the second thick book – I forgot the title.

Questioner 3: "The Conscious Harmony?"

Arkady: Yes, I think it's this one.

Questioner 3: There is only one thick book.

A Landmark in the Spiritual History of Humanity - Questions & Answers

Arkady: Yes, "The Celestial Influence." I have it at home. Well, he was one of a few people who gave not only his own interpretation of Gurdjieff's and Ouspensky's concepts, he created his own concept. He was very charismatic, very convincing, and at the same time to my taste I found in him very mechanical in his thinking. For instance, he follows a familiar method of philosophizing, speaking of different ages – childhood, youth, mature age, old age. Each time he connects it with a certain mystical realizations. I think that is a little superficial, because there are old children, and there are young grown-ups. The count of years is not really as important as some believe it is. Rodney Collin's cosmological ideas are not convincing. But, nevertheless, he worked with Gurdjieff's and Ouspensky's heritage and he created an independent teaching. So he distorted the source concept and created something new.

Questioner 3: And this is what I want to know – how he distorted? What do you mean by "distorted"?

Arkady: By distortion I mean…

Questioner 3: Don't give the definition of "distortion. I know the definition of "distortion." You said: "Rodney Collin distorted the Gurdjieff work.

Arkady: I would say that Ouspensky and Bennett also distorted the Gurdjieff work, and therefore we have to refer to the original, to the "Beelzebub's Tales" and other works by Gurdjieff in order to straighten our understanding of what was the source.

Questioner 3: Could you say it, I would appreciate it, how did Collin, by what means did he distort Gurdjieff? That was my question. How did he do it? You didn't say whether he was right.

Arkady: He created his own cosmology, he created his own great cosmic teaching, that was different and that was in a way a development of Gurdjieff's teaching. In my view he went astray, he went his own way, and that why in my evaluation was not productive. This is why I think he has distorted it, the way St. Paul distorted the teaching of Christ and the way the three closest disciples of Buddha, Ananda, Kasiapa and Shariputra distorted Buddha's original teaching. Every interpretation is a development and a distortion. This is terminology that is clear to me.

Questioner 3: I am left with this, but I don't think I have time to say it.

Questioner 2: Now we have run out of time, so I would appreciate it if we stop now.

Seminar 2: Chapter 7 - Meetings with Remarkable Men

Prince Yuri Lubovedsky

Facilitator: Dimitri Peretzi

Introduction

Gurdjieff names Prince Lubovedsky "the man I loved the most in life". They first met at the pyramids, where Gurdjieff worked as an aid to professor Skridlov an old acquaintance of the Prince. Both Gurdjieff and the Prince had copies of pre-sand Egypt made from an old parchment owned by a priest, whom Gurdjieff had met when working for an Armenian secret organization. The relationship lasted for thirty-five years. The Prince helped Gurdjieff's search by introducing him to appropriate people.

At some point in Istanbul the Prince asked Gurdjieff to escort Vitvitskaia to Russia and he left for a voyage to the Far East. All contacts between them having stopped for long, Gurdjieff came to believe him dead.

In the meantime Gurdjieff had met Soloviev in Bukhara, where he was looking for the dervish Bogga-Eddin, the one who told him about the Sarmoung brotherhood, which eventually Gurdjieff joined in a monastery in central Asia. The trip to the monastery began along the river Amu Darya and lasted for twelve days. At the monastery Gurdjieff found again Prince Lubovedsky and was introduced to the sacred dances that were practiced there. Eventually the Prince learned that he had only three years left to live and decided to move on to another monastery at the brotherhood to finished his days. The chapter on Prince Lubovedsky ends with Gurdjieff's description of the circumstances of the death of Soloviev.

This is the chapter where Gurdjieff talks about Vitvitskaia the only woman member of the Seekers of Truth. She was Polish just like Gurdjieff's own wife.

The chapter includes the story of Soloviev and the circumstances of his death, the story of his dog Philos, the story of the painted canary, visits to Tibet, the secrets of the Gobi desert, the Sarmoung brotherhood, sacred dances.

The name "Lubovedsky" derives from the Russian word for love. Gurdjieff's other attributes for Lubovedsky include, friend of my being, an ideal to follow, close and respected friend, long term friendship, a real bond and idealist, remarkable and true saint.

Was Prince Lubovedsky a real person? There is no easy answer to that, as Gurdjieff always seems to be creating some sort of haze around his characters. Suggestions that Lubovedsky was the known Prince Oktomsky do not lead to anything conclusive. Nevertheless the writings of Oktomsky himself reveal that the Czar's upper class in Russia had a deep interest in things and the ideas of the East, something that can be seen today at the Moscow museum of Eastern art, some of the most important collections of which were formed around that period.

The idea of death in Lubovedsky: His search started with the death of his young wife, he follows the advice of the old Tamil, who urged him to follow the true path of spirituality by dying to what he has been that far. After they separated in Istanbul, Gurdjieff considered Lubovedsky to be dead. At the monastery where they met again, they were ultimately separated when Lubovedsky decided to go to the old man monastery to die. The chapter is concluded by the description of the death of Soloviev.

Further questions that the Lubovedsky story may give rise to:

- There are nine chapters and nine characters around which meetings revolve. Did they represent nine aspects of Gurdjieff himself or types of man in general?

- Does the approach to Work and to the idea of esoteric ethics of these nine characters represents nine aspects or types of Work?

- Do the shortcomings represent nine types of archetypal chief features? Lubovedsky's chief feature, as is pointed out by the old Tamil, appears to be curiosity.

- Why are the stories of Soloviev and Vitvitskaia not narrated in separate chapters, but they are part of Lubovedsky?

- Who were the Sarmoung and does this brotherhood in a monastery like the one that Gurdjieff describes really exist?

- Who was the dervish Bogga-Eddin?

Bukhara, where Gurdjieff met Bogga-Eddin, is the place where the order of Naqshbandi Sufis originated at the fourteenth century and it is still the center of Islamic mysticism. Bennett believes that Bogga-Eddin refers to Baha-ud-Din the founder of the Naqshbandis. Naqshbandis themselves believe that the Gurdjieff teaching stems from their dogmas.

Is the Sarmoung the Naqshbandis? Features that collaborated to this are related to the Naqshbandis believing that Work is to be carried out in life, importance they give to the study of the energies in the body; the fact that a Naqshbandi will never reveal who his teachers were.

Seminar 2: Chapter 7 - Meetings with Remarkable Men

Seminar Discussion

Participant 1: My feeling is that the whole book and also this chapter is very cleverly picked up, so for me the question about reality is not so important as the structure of the book and the walk through, to tell us both to the structure and to the different aspects.

Facilitator: Would you mind to say something about this structure, please?

Participant 1: Well, I could give as an example this story of Vitvitskaia. She is very absorbed by the question of music, but does not get the information she seeks from music and there she is led to answers by probations and there it seems to me that it is very condense form of exposition of some of thoughts about probations, about intervals, about … music, the whole thing is in a very condensed form.

Participant 2: The purity that it seems to be described seems to be reason why something at all could happen to her including almost this terrible accident…

Facilitator: I am sure that we are talking about Vitvitskaia, actually?

Participant 2: Yes, he also described … never met a woman … refers to the purity, which could be dangerous…

Facilitator: It might seem a pedantic question yet, since Lubovedsky is such a big long chapter and Vitvitskaia seems to be an independent description within it, why would not need a special chapter, or the reason why the chapter on Vitvitskaia is a joined, is being made a part of?

Participant 2: There is a special function in that part.

Facilitator: Which is?

Participant 2: (laughs)…

Participant 3: So, he hated her very much, it's such a formulation, cause later on he developed that she was a most respective woman but in the first part of the beginning he hated her so much, so when Lubovedsky asked him to bring her, so there is some change in the perception.

Participant 4: There are several initial impressions for beyond free willingness this afternoon. I have stroked by the different expositions of love, they mentioned both, but it was the love of the dog, the love of the man, the overcoming of initial conditioning, this is a dog that is not allowed into certain places, and yet it was a great friend and … Not to mention that for Vitvitskaia initially he had a conditioned prejudice against her without known her ... The desire of the mind should become the desire of the heart.

Participant 5: I being forward, I ask people to speak a little louder because sometimes we can't hear and you have to speak a little clearly…

Participant 6: I think this chapter is very sentimental; it shows the way of the desire of the mind becoming the desire of the heart. It includes the proposition that you have to die to everything… The energy that comes out of this chapter leaves a very strong impression…, like the images in the desert. What is the symbolism of the desert, what is the symbolism of Gurdjieff crossing the bridge? They may show deliverance to a new level of conscience. You feel the risk when you try to pass the bridge, it's a risk which is different and this keeps you from the mechanicality

Participant 7: I don't want to annoy you but I am afraid I will. Gurdjieff wrote a letter in 1931 saying that: it is the thirty seventh year since I have founded the foundation, now I am sitting here writing the last chapter of *Meetings with Remarkable Men* … The ten chapters appear to be father and son, he is the tenth person. He says, I can't help it, the introduction to the text says that it was added, from where? No, Gurdjieff says he wrote it for years.

Facilitator: Mea culpa.

Participant 7: The problem is that anyone who has read the text assumes something which is not true. Because in one of my books … It bothers me because, ten is good, I think because to begin with Father and end with Son, this is the ten Remarkable Men, I think fits perfectly.

Facilitator: I find nothing objectionable with this and it doesn't offend in anyway … of the fact that there are nine personages that are not Gurdjieff that he stands in front of nine personages and the question of what they represent is still valid. Actually I did not know that detail of yours, and I personally excluded this chapter from putting them altogether in one list, for the very simple reason because it says in the book that it was added by Madame De Salzmann. But I don't think it alters the kind of approach that it was presented today.

Participant 7: No, no. I don't say that, I just like the ten that fits and the story with Father and ending with Son…

Participant 8: Quick supplementary question. Is there someone aware he writes ten books in three series? And which are these ten books?

Participant 7: That's another one. You can't count it. He talks about another one which he never got into it…

Participant 8: May I ask a question for something, I was assumed that 'ved' in Lubovedsky is the carrier of love, or not?

Participant 1: The knowledge of love. Love and knowledge are the two words both created the name Lubovedsky…

Seminar 2: Chapter 7 - Meetings with Remarkable Men

Participant 9: And what kind of love is it? (Laughs)

Participant 1: Just love …

Facilitator: So, we have the first book *'Beelzebub's Tales to His Grandson'* which aims *to destroy, mercilessly* etc. and now we have these *Meetings* which aim at providing the material for a better world, any comments on that? Has it worked for anybody in this way?

Participant 1: I would like to quote from the introduction; also he says that he writes this book to answer nine questions:

1. What remarkable men have I met?
2. What marvels have I seen in the East?
3. Has man a soul and is it immortal?
4. Is the will of man free?
5. What is life, and why does suffering exist?
6. Do I believe in the occult and spiritualistic sciences?
7. What are hypnotism, magnetism, and telepathy?
8. How did I become interested in these questions?
9. What led me to my system, practiced in the Institute bearing my name?

So that is a follow-up, a special conception, of this book and its content.

Participant 10: I find this book even much more difficult to understand than the first series, because I think there is a tremendous amount of information in there and I can't take account of some of it… and it also repeats certain things which are for me very important and … and it appears in this chapter and in many chapters in the first series and that is what are the deserts and what they represent in me, because it has to mean something to me and also why and what are they looking for this map of pre-sand Egypt? Why they want a map of pre-sand Egypt and went to a lot of trouble both Lubovedsky and Gurdjieff to steal a copy of this pre-sand Egypt. And I can't remember the exact description; the deserts represent the absolute colors, so all are real essence, uses sand of the desert as a metaphor of recovering of our real essence and our real knowledge. Every time Egypt is mentioned it's for me a source of historic knowledge. So when I discover a map of pre-sand Egypt it means I discover the method, so anything to do with Egypt of pre-sand it means that the method is revealed. In the first series he talks about many countries and this country in the second transapalnian perturbation is now covered in sand. In the first transapalnian perturbation happens men and children and most children remain in essence completely uninhibited and truthful. It's only when the child begins to say, I want and I like, that is the first transapalnian perturbation and all the other transapalnian perturbations arrived in sand or in water.

So I think this ... in the desert seems to me a very important part of this book and this particular chapter because of this...

Participant 1: I want to make two remarks. First regarding the manuscript, I don't know if it is the Russian the original or more likely it is these translations... Nevertheless it is a beautiful nineteenth century style, style of Tolstoy's childhood ... very graphical of other Russian classical writers. Language is exquisite, beautiful style, brilliant... Prince Lubovedsky is presented to us as a spiritual seeker and a person who actually wasted his life, but he was searching all his life then decided to go to another monastery to die, as Gurdjieff says.

Participant 10: I'll pass it to you guys, I'm sorry doing that, but I would just like to say – refer to something that Arcady brought up really the sorry condition of these people in the chapter and we do want him to go on because they have seen remarkable …well, and were essentially remarkable, and I think that is the point at least that I understand their early lives, that all of us, that there is hope no matter what kind of drop-out I've been all my life. So, I just wanted to say that.

Participant 11: No just to fill in something new. This book was started before "All and Everything", started in April 1924 and then it was continued in 1926 - 27 finished in '28. That is one thing. The interesting coincidence that I find is in 1924 in New York City, Gurdjieff was in contact with this man from Saint Petersburg called Nicola Gurtig(?). And Gurtig had already been in Tibet, and had been in Mongolia, and Gurtig had found a grass that grows under sand, it's called loafgrass in English and it was imported in 1935 in Mexico which is close. And this goes along with what Nick said, among others, that there is life under guts, and of course Erasmus the one who introduced the roik (?) to Gurdjieff. So that is just one more nice piece.

Participant 12: Thank you for that. A couple of things came to my mind. One was in response to what Ron Said about these nine things that Mr. Gurdjieff promises to cover, and I just looked up in "The Herald of Coming Good", there is a mention of the second series being three books under the common title of "Meetings with Remarkable Men". So it could be that the book we have now is only one of the series, there are two other books... What are those books? Where are those books? That could be one question.

Participant 14: What's interesting in what Alan said, I'm just interested in... But I think it is also very interesting this question of the fullness of the early narrative and the sparseness. I don't know, I think that my responses that grow the confusion…

Facilitator: Let me add something to that, a personal comment. In the case of the Prince and of Vitvitskaia, although there is this misery of their early years, some sort of dissatisfaction of their lives, it is absolutely clear that they move-on to better realities. Even when they go to the monastery, that you say up in Tibet, he goes there because B. made his years most fruitful. So it's not just going at the... And Vitvitskaia of course, we have no notion of her perishing in bad circumstances. But it is different with Soloviev. And I remember ever since reading this book for the first time, which was many years ago, it was one of the characters that stood up mostly in his

Seminar 2: Chapter 7 - Meetings with Remarkable Men

dramatic implications, like he has some short of negative Karma to live through, heavy Karma. The man who was forger of bills and was stealing from his mother, he wishes to become a good man, he finds the way to join up with the seekers of truth, and he dies bitten by a wild camel...I don't know, I find this thing heavy, like there was something there...you cannot escape fate... And I think there is a differentiation there. I don't know, this is a question of mine. Did anybody feel that there is a very dark shadow following Soloviev?

Participant 15: Yes, but he died in the Gobi Desert. And Gurdjieff says to another book that this city has everything to know how to be a real man, to "All and Everything" chapter on "Hypnotism", I think that says this.

Facilitator: About the Gobi Desert?

Participant 15: Yes. And he died in this place! You can see it with another way.

Participant 16: It seems that there are all kinds of questions popping up and very few threads on which tie or strain, tie on a way out of the labyrinth, but just a couple other comments of Dimitri pointed out a death theme, and if you look at what we have been talking about just so far in the last few minutes, there is a ...lot of love theme. "Philos" is the name of the dog. So, other people smarter than me know something about Love and Death, there is some theme somewhere else in Russian? Love and Death? I don't know. Second thing I like to point out is in those nine questions, now ...going to answer. As I heard you read, I didn't notice this before but six of those nine questions are addressed in Bogachevsky. And they are maybe addressed in other places as well but they are definitely strong in Bogachevsky, which is two chapters back. So this makes me ask, wow, what are the other chapters all about, if he has already covered all those matters and is raising the questions. And the one that are left of, "What remarkable men have I met", that's the whole book supposedly, "What marvels have I seen in the East?", and the last one, "What led me to my System?" So finally let's not forget the placement of this chapter that is also pointed out, that is at 6, maybe that has some significance here too ... in this puzzling, it's a mishmash, many different things it seems.

Participant 1: Speaking for the "confused" and "dissatisfied", I probably didn't find the right word, the third word which was "I wanted more" when reading this book, I wanted to know more about Soloviev, about Vitvitskaia, about Prince. And in this way I think the book is a certain instrument, a certain way of creating this desire for more, going deeper, and building in myself what I could not find in this book, and in this way this book is very provocative and very helpful.

Participant 16: That's going inside, it is the nature of the point 6 of enneagram...

Participant 17: This book is all about relationship. The first series was to destroy all beliefs and understandings, our relationship with the world outside. This book is all about the essence of real relationship between self and others, and self and self.

This chapter has several examples of ... service, even an issue of persistence, themes of surrender. And I also know that the dog Philos was with him for nine years, and the Prince has three years left, and so there seems to be an issue of some numbers.

I am just also curious, and also distract, by the death in the desert. Was death by camel, a more common occurrence? How does one gets killed by camel? I wonder if there is any significance...

Participant 18: I suppose we could look at the three characters, as Lubovedsky is intellectual (subject), Vitvitskaia with the emotional (something), and Soloviev is the physical (something) which dies.

I think for me the sparseness of the book is not a matter. What I am looking for is what the real life in this is. I am not interested in style, or this or that. I want to know what is in here.

And the most profound thing in this section of Vitvitskaia is Gurdjieff's installation that music is a way of working, and installs that in a very esoteric point of the whole, Vitvitskaia story. The fact that it's female means that it needs the development of the emotional center.

Participant 19: Yes, My super word for this chapter is Search. And the next thing I would say is that Search is a process and it has to follow a music, waltz. And this points again to the Enneagram which I think, it is not that close to what you have said, but this map, this map is Enneagram. It is Prince, from the beginning of the discussion, who ... very solid person, and his strength is that he has an aim and he has all the possibilities to diverge from this aim, he has a lot of money, he can go into the world and do all kinds of things, he has the means to remain in ordinary life. He doesn't do that. He uses his wealth, whatever that means, for the purpose of this ... aim.

And then he comes to almost the ... (hold) of this map. But with the means he had ... it was not enough. He couldn't get hold of it. So he continues, even though he met ... in that not having enough, he continued. And then he comes to the map anyway. That is something that even if you seem to fail you must just go on and on and on. That is very informative for me. Persistence.

And then at the end it seems like, he is just going so well to die. For me that was a very strong impression, it stood out, that, that is what you have to do. You have to go on and on and finally turn totally, absolutely, to your inward journey. And that is so different from just go in somewhere and die.

And then, why was he called a Prince? What does a Prince do? We inherit the kingdom.

Participant 20: That's a point I always wondered ... may be princess. I don't know, does anyone know? ... Have the right to name a Prince?

Participant 1: Prince is not emperor; it's much higher than this.

Seminar 2: Chapter 7 - Meetings with Remarkable Men

Participant 20: Yes, I know. But who names the prince? Bolkansky in war & peace.

Participant 1: Yeah, It is done by higher level of...

Participant 20: Yes, I just want to clear that out because it isn't as in English or Norwegian, an heir to the throne...

Participant 21: But in my world he'd inherit it... (laughing) We name dogs in US, "prince", and pets...

Participant 1: Well, just again a short remark about the three years account of Prince Lubovedsky's life. Everything was wonderful, especially the notion of the last part of the journey and turning inward, sometimes it is seen as death sometimes as rebirth, but there was a place, I don't remember details, where almost near the end of his journey, before he discovered the monastery, he was completely in, completely ... He lost interest in life he was thinking that his search was meaningless.

So he did not gradually grow in his Being. He was fluctuating, going up and down. So, it was not ascent, permanent ascent, but a sort of waves that he went through.

Participant: Can I just say that, this is also according to Law. And this is what you mention, according to Law. It can be said that this agony or the difficult ... They have to be there, they are there, they are what we experience as ... It does not mean that things stand still. It means that you have a new possibility, but you really have to work through it. If you don't do that, then your direction will diverge. But it has to be there. It is according to Law.

Participant: It was interesting that in finding the map ... with Prince Lubovedsky, it is not written what they did with the map, or how they continued with that. The lot is developed to how they got it. Prince Lubovedsky to purchase this and Gurdjieff made a copy...

But it seems that the whole point of the map was brought in, so they would together look at it by the Giza Pyramid, and then, and then it's never mentioned again.

And then, saying that the Prince by the end of his life was satisfied and happy ... But what happened to the map? Did they go and find something? Or did they drop it altogether?

Participant: It's an interesting situation, when standing in front of the Pyramid. And it's forgotten. And I remember reading something that Orage says, where he describes that whole plateau, that the temple is the place where we prepare, the temple before Sphinx. And Sphinx is how we should approach the efforts. And the Pyramids are what we become when we ... So that for me is a very important metaphor.

(Coffee Break)

Facilitator: Yes, going to the subject of Lubovedsky immediately I would like to sum up a few things - make some comments. To me the thought occurs that somehow Lubovedsky represents something of the second conscious shock. This was supported by comments that were made here by other people, that in their lives they had misfortunes and negativity, befallen by negative and unpleasant situations, and yet they found their way to positive emotions. I believe that's what the second shock is all about. There are a few questions I have, which could be used to further the discussion, but I will ask them in case there is nothing else to be said and I see that the conversation lags behind. So, please I think that whoever has comments that he believes might interest us to go ahead and place them.

Participant 1: To pick up on what Dimitri just said I propose the possibility that the chapter points at the way through the desert in terms of following his heart I see that the prince having followed his curiosity even almost, perhaps disharmonized … this phrase that resonates this seems to be the thought of the chapter and each of these relationships and stories seem to involve that following of the heart even without understanding what it is about, or where it's going, that passion, follow that, leading these characters to the higher place within themselves and closer to the place in the inner journey they were searching for.

Facilitator: I see.

Participant 2: I just wanted to comment on a question that was raised in the last session about a map, you know the map that wasn't followed up, I had a feeling, when there was a mention of an apparatus with the high priest in the monastery, that apparatus reminded me of a sort of a map, if you remember the apparatus had a column … on a tripod and in it there were seven segments attached to this apparatus, each one of these segments had itself seven segments, somehow reminiscent of the enneagrammatic emblem and there were inscription tablets in the cabinets that you could attach to these segments and by that the dancers could learn how to dance and communicate truths from ancient times and another key point for me there was that he says these dances correspond precisely to our books so almost there is a hint there that if you know how to use these apparatuses you could read the dances, learn the dances and you can read the books or know how to use the books, so it seems to me that these apparatuses are worthy of further attention, maybe because I am a good enough artist, I'm going to try to draw this to see how it looks like.

Participant 3: There is a couple of things I thought, one is the second conscious shock which I think that the second conscious shock is conscious and intentional suffering…at a certain point that second conscious shock can only take place on completion of the Kidman body and then I'm at the far bridge … which is I think, perhaps it's this very dangerous bridge which crossing this deep chasm and they have to be brought to this bridge with their heads covered, so if my head is covered it means one of two things that I am not at this moment conscious because my head is covered so my consciousness can't operate or it could mean something else, that my head is covered so at that time there is no more … and I am not sure which one I prefer, and I cross this far bridge over this deep chasm and I cannot cross the far bridge without help, and that help has to

Seminar 2: Chapter 7 - Meetings with Remarkable Men

come from a higher level. And an interesting passage is about this apparatus and I looked it up in the dictionary and I looked at apparatus, yes it means this physical thing but as Orage says we have to look for the essence of the word, and the essence of the word … means to prepare, which is a far more significant interpretation of apparatus and now it opens up something which is very important because I can't cross the far bridge unless I am prepared and once I enter into the Sarmoung brotherhood once I have prepared that I am also required to prepare, exactly ... as the two princes ... created the apparatus alla-attapan which to me means prepare because 'Allah – God', 'pan - is everywhere' so this is a very important symbol and it is connected with what I have to see for and be prepared before I can enter into this Sarmoung brotherhood state.

Facilitator: Just a second, I feel I have to say something about what you just said, because in a way it is your response to what I said and because we should both acknowledge of being accurate in the terms we use, in the terminology.

If one practices, if one practices intentional suffering this in itself cannot be the second conscious shock, it can be the preparation for it, the shock itself comes as a mystery because the level that is higher is a mystery to the ordinary mind, to the ordinary state of mind, so we can talk about it and possibly one could say that we can talk about it with examples, like the example of Prince so and so, or Mr. Soloviev, or…because we cannot implement the second conscious shock, it has to come from a higher source. We can prepare for it but we cannot implement it. So the shock itself could not be conscious suffering. Conscious suffering can only be the preparation. The decision, when it actually comes, belongs to a higher level, does not belong to me. This is the differentiation that has to come to what you say, in my mind, about the chapter leading to the second conscious shock, it deals with the preparation and giving oneself up, like exactly dying to the old reality.

Participant 3: But in this case, we are not dying to the old reality; we are dying to our Kidman body, if I have already completed my Kidman body, at the si, do, so it is complete, the next level or the next octave is the far bridge, sol, do, re, mi, fa. Si, do, on the Kidman body, so my preparation is complete, now in order to cross the far bridge, sol, Kidman has to die in order to complete the … but yes, I am all ready by conscious labor and intentional suffering; the emphasis is not on the suffering, the emphasis now is that I intentionally go out to suffer, the emphasis is not on the suffering it's on the awareness of something higher…

Facilitator: Yes, but there is a transcendental shock that completes the process, there is a transcendental occurrence that I cannot implement. It can only be implemented by the will of God, by grace, by something higher, so it cannot be the suffering itself because I can implement the suffering. I can choose when to suffer.

Participant 3: Yes, I agree.

Participant 4: Just something very quick, I think it's important, I have this image that crossing this chasm wherever it may be…at the end of this list of sections of this particular chapter, I measure myself crossing this chasm on one of those narrow bridges we have seen in the movie. So I am blindfolded, the hood is something like that so we can't see, so what comes alive what we have to be doing to cross this bridge, to me, there is a lot of sensation, we have to be sensing and we have to have balance.

Participant: It's also a leap of faith.

Participant 5 : I want to point out that this morning, that the friends here, the men tell you gobble, gobble, and this is something very sentiment, in all his life he did a lot of things and he couldn't see, this characteristic of him, he needed another person from outside to show him what is wisdom, that he can have the touch with the higher level, curiosity, so I think this is very important because everyone of us has something like that, that he can't see the reality, and I'd like to talk about it, how everyone sees it.

Participant: I think that this blindfoldedness was part of…but the crossing was too difficult and too dangerous …no ropes and with no handrails, nothing, so that was something important that I would like to point out.

Participant 6: But he described in detail how he would feel to look down and looking up in the mountains and he says it's hardly possible to bear.

Participant: Very strong.

Participant 22: I'd like to say something about the book, about my surprise when I read it, especially this chapter. Gurdjieff's teaching is usually associated with some sequence of methods like self-awareness, self-remembering, the main feature in a personality, analysis, sequence step to step…When I was reading this chapter of the book I was surprised to see a quite different type of people…Lubovedsky is taken as an ideal for all. I see them as people passionate, not the type of people willing to follow the type of regular exercises or methods. You remember that she was biting her finger and bit it through to the blood; this is a certain proof that she did not remember. At the same time Gurdjieff describes as an example of a person who gave all the life and efforts to the search of the truth. And I was surprised at this…

Facilitator: I would like to say something. You know, we are not exercising. Exercise is like a stick, you pick it up to help you walk for a distance, but what is real is your life that has all these problems and all these questions. For instance, do we really believe that we are mechanical automatons? Do we really believe in the Work? All these are questions that wait for an emotional involvement to work on ourselves, to work inside us. The system, the Work, is not a machine that we jump into and be processed into nice meatballs.

Participant 22: But usually people understand Gurdjieff's teaching as a … machine.

Facilitator: That the Work is a machine? That the Work is a machine, that we fall into the Work and the machine takes us and transforms us automatically into nice meatballs? That's not the real

Seminar 2: Chapter 7 - Meetings with Remarkable Men

image we have about Work. The image we have is that people go to a group meeting without knowing if they want to be there, that they have doubts about what they do. This is the reality of what is happening. And then we have this help, the exercise, like a stick that we can take a few steps with, for a new thing to develop within us, a new faith that it is possible to Work. This is what we need, we need to have faith that it is possible to Work, that it makes sense, that there is such a thing as Work, we are not sure about that. That's the reality of it.

Participant 7: We have to support in any sense what Elm said because, for example, of one side in Russia, in Moscow, we should devote to Fourth Way, it's his name is System, System could tell, System, so it's may be the second name of Fourth Way, as they name it, when they speak to each other, System. So it's like something very detailed and constructed and I think that a lot of people who I'm looking at, I'm knowing them. They think that this System, this organization, is advantaged Fourth Way and its strict System, something like that, I just want to say that this impression of Elm is correct, I met people like that.

Facilitator: This is a discussion that is moving our way from the topic that we are dealing with, but at the same time, for questions like that I think we have common sense. One has to be critical and unless one has a critical mind his place is not here. So one has to be real critical, one has to understand "Does he believe in a System?" If you believe in the System, the system will say in, I guarantee.

Participant 7: What if we know this is not right, Lubovedsky and the things with the system, is a system of our changing and it describes the system and it describes the materials from which the system is created and the cheap material of the system is amber surrounded by reels of platinum. What does that mean? It means the system is a spaceship; it is the vehicle I take to go from Earth to Karatas, my real goal. So if the system has the real material, this amber, then I need to follow it, to the end of the process. This describing, this magnificent space, which has to conquer the world, to lengthen the line. The neck and the head are segregated from the rest of the body, that amber, which amber signifies impartiality.

In the chapter of Ekim Bey, Ekim Bey loses his chaplet into the deep waters of the Bosphorus, he offers a great reward by anybody who will find his chaplet. So everybody else gives up except Gurdjieff, he's going to find the chaplet because he is attracted by the reward. So he dives and he dives and dives deeper and deeper and deeper until he finds his chaplet and he brings the chaplet up and what's this chaplet made of? It's made of amber surrounded by precious stone like in the arch, the system of archangel Hariton, it is surrounded by platinum, which is the most precious metal, he's not finding sensation, he's diving deeper and deeper to find impartiality, the lost chaplet to talk is the inevitable result of impartial mentation, not the inevitable result of sensation.

Facilitator: I object to what you just said because it is an opportunity to put opinions that, you know like would have to be, you know like discussed further to acquire meaning and it is art of, flux of the conversation. You know, we have to talk now about sensation and impartiality.

Participant 7: I didn't bring it up.

Facilitator: No, but you think that this is part of the system. So you really believe that. But anyway it's not really so, it's not really so. This is a point of view which I appreciate very much, correct, but I would like to go back, if we can to Lubovedsky itself.

Participant 8: I want to say too, there is something about the "Philos", it's a character, it's my character. If you have a dog you can see your character. It's very interesting, can I say this? My character? This is "Philos".

Participant: Mirror.

Participant 8: Yeah.

Participant 9: " Philos" is following ever round, watching him, paint his canaries, clip them and sell them and make a lot of money from them and suddenly "Philos" is going out and bringing in dead canaries.

Participant 10: Just something about Vitvitskaia. Although you just suggested she is the ideal of the perfect woman, there are also some things that are not quite good about her. She seems quite impatient she does these experiments and then she's sort of frustrated and moves on to something else and I wonder whether he really means what he says, whether he really thinks she is that great, she has some weaknesses , also her name might suggest something to do with speed, quickness, speed, impatience.

Participant 11: Vitvit, It's associated with the French.

Participant 10: Right.

Participant: But, if that was a French name, for example, it's sort of Russianised French name, would that have any suggestions of speed?

Participant: It's still a Polish name, like Lubovedsky. These are polish names.

Participant: Right. Right. Also is there something about her dying in Samara? She dies in Samara. Samara has lot of mention. Where people die is that important? Soloviev dies in a gloomy desert, she dies in Samara. Lubovedsky dies in Tibet?

Participant: Samara.

Participant: To me Vitvitskaia is also a symbol of character.

Participant: Is she the ideal woman to you, would you say?

Seminar 2: Chapter 7 - Meetings with Remarkable Men

Participant: Well, I think her function in this chat is.

Participant: Will you tell us, what is her function?

Participant: Well, it's so many things because this music, her impatience and so on, you know it's very complex. Look, I'd like to say there's different sights and different aspects of the emotional center and you mentioned speed, and this was something to be connected with the moving center and because the most of our emotions, which are disturbing character. It's a stronger image. It may be a strong body layer, the emotional center and the mechanical. All these seem different aspects of the emotional. And I just want to say, that she dies, that function, that automatic function has to part.

Participant: That of the thought on Soloviev's death, that Algerian expedition, which is really important to her, then the rest and Soloviev may be, has followed his character he takes a ride and he goes on hunting, well this is a distraction that basically holds up and following cancels the whole expedition and I thought this could be a mourning against such distractions because he just took it up profound and then he made fool of anything. He just became interested first and that interest was minor it was not important to … so he went out and he died and starved and he prevented the others from attaining their goals. He lost his way; almost he was half-eating.

Facilitator: There is a question I have, about this idea of dying to one's life until that point. Lubovedsky is told to die to his life, which is the condition by which he moves on and receives the help that is important for him to advance. We can make all sorts of different comments about what it means to die to one's life. I remember an orthodox monastery, on Mount Athos, there was a frame on the wall with this phrase in it "to live you must first die". But I have a question. What does it mean to each one of us in his real life, to die to his life until that point? And if we have any opportunity to receive the kind of help that will, without any doubt, move us on, what kind of things would we be willing to sacrifice and which things would be not willing to sacrifice.

Participant: I think dying to one's life may have the meaning of dying to meaningless life, to careless life. Also it could mean initiation to one's life, to real, one's real life. We can see our way to see Consciousness; there is the life of an ordinary man that it's nowhere and the life of a wakened man that is completely different life. So I suggest a lot that dying for one's life is initiation to one's life.

Participant: Because this the inner, not a necessary leave one's fairway or monastery, seems to me, may be more question of a shift in evaluation, a shift in what the sense machine will be in. So that it might open a possibility of it, in life that's not outer life. So that the responsibility is an extra situation all to distract an extra sense of ourselves, that is allowed to be carried out into life, in the higher and in the vibrations. It would open to a level, perhaps surrender to, and unscrew the eager personality.

All & Everything Conference 2011

Facilitator: Yes, this is what we would see from a distance, but there is a question, how will this affect me, I remember reading this thing for the first time. Let's forget about this that and the other thing. What would he say "No, what I meant was that I'm willing to live my life within life and die to the superficiality of what I am so far and who's to judge this superficiality, What I try to provoke in my question is the dramatic death to which this question touched me initially. Where do I stand to this total sacrifice?

Participant 3: I think it's a step of different levels like everything in this world. Finally we have to die to our Kidman body; we have to die from all the things which prevent us from moving higher but through the simple way. I walk across the room to my refrigerator and I'm going to get some butter and at that moment I see my mechanicality and I stop, I get in touch with my wish and I make a mental check to make sure that my ordinary life is not moving around at that moment and then make Work everything. When one's dying, all my ordinary thoughts and feelings must die at that moment and that be regenerated after my effort is proper, as long as I can't sustain my effort and my ordinary mind is rejumbled into constrain. So I think it has all on a practical level, a practical application which grows bigger and bigger.

Participant: We have one more minute.

Participant: I think that what Steve is saying is very important. For me this dying, is dying to the picture of myself and then much care now than before, I can say that the picture of myself, has so much been connected with the conservatory restoring paintings. That it's gradually slipping away. Sometimes I think that this movement is so slow, although it is moving it is unnoticed, in what goes on all the times, it goes very quick and lately I have been freer from this than I ever have and I think it has to do with accumulation of some insights about the emptiness of this self-picture. Practically it means that I've become in certain respect without going in detail, still there is a fan, at that this change in the way of looking at myself is moving away from certain personification, has made in me, the outer world a manifestation a flexibility that I couldn't foresee and I don't think I should say anything.

Participant: Could I say something? From my experience this dying, this painful, I mean the image I have of myself, it's very strong and every time comes from in to outside is destroyed I will pain. So I have to work with this pain and it's not to die, just to decide to die, this is to can accept what's happening and to work with the energy that arises and accept the shock. To be able to accept the energy that affects me so.

Participant: I thank you very much.

End of Session

The Ray of Creation Revisited

Seymour B. Ginsburg

The Ray of Creation Revisited: A Suggested Revision to the Presentation of the Ray of Creation from How It Was Initially Received by Ouspensky from Gurdjieff

The purpose of this suggested revision to the presentation of the Ray of Creation is two-fold:

1. To accommodate the idea that the descending Ray of Creation in the materialization descends in the first instance into multiple universes. Recent theories in astrophysics suggest that there are multiple universes just as there are multiple galaxies within our universe. William James in 1895, coined with word "multiverse" to describe multiple simultaneous universes.

2. To eliminate the idea that the planets taken as a whole represent a greater level of freedom from the operation of the Sacred Triamazikamno (law of 3 forces) than does Earth taken as a single planet. All our planets revolve around the Sun. Therefore, all of them are subject to the same level of limitation of freedom. The group is no more free than is an individual planet.

Like most students of Gurdjieff's teaching, I was introduced to the concept of the Ray of Creation through the book In Search of the Miraculous, by P.D. Ouspensky, who recorded it as part of the oral teaching given him by Gurdjieff in 1915 and which is recounted in this book. I was at once excited and dismayed by this presentation of the Ray of Creation. (See Figure 1)

I was excited because of the idea of scale and relativity that was presented. The Ray shows that at each level higher, there is a marked increase in the relativity of freedom, or operation under a significantly reduced number of orders of laws which restrict that freedom. While the Ray is presented astronomically in terms of the relativity of freedom of cosmic entities, of even more importance for us, is the idea that the Ray can be seen as presenting relative degrees of freedom in our inner world, the world of the psyche. The Gurdjieffian idea is that in our state of "ordinary consciousness" in which we identify with everything, we are under 48 orders of laws, equivalent to the number of laws under which is also the Earth. In the state that Gurdjieff calls "self-consciousness" or "self-remembering" we are under only 24 orders of laws, equivalent to the number of laws under which are the planets of the Sun when taken as a whole. In the state that Gurdjieff calls "objective-consciousness" we are under only 12 orders of laws, equivalent to the number of laws under which is our Sun as it relates to greater and lesser cosmic bodies. Our Milky Way Galaxy, for example, is said to be under only 6 orders of laws. The Sun is a captive of the Milky Way and is therefore less free than is the Milky Way Galaxy, just as our Earth is a captive of the Sun and is therefore less free than is the Sun.

THE RAY OF CREATION

As initially received by Ouspensky in 1915 from Gurdjieff's oral teaching. In Search of the Miraculous[1]. The Ray is shown in this form as a descending octave.

O	ABSOLUTE = ENDLESSNESS = THE GREAT BEING	1	DO
O	ALL WORLDS = OUR UNIVERSE	3	SI
O	ALL SUNS = OUR GALAXY (The Milky Way)	6	LA
O	SUN = OUR STAR	12	SOL
O	ALL PLANETS	24	FA

(The organic coating on planet earth, of which humanity is a part, fills the FA-MI Interval in the descending octave of energies from the ABSOLUTE.)

O	EARTH = OUR PLANET	48	MI
O	MOON = OUR EARTH'S SATELLITE	96	RE

Figure 1

But as valuable as is the insight into scale and relativity of freedom presented by the Ray, I was dismayed by a glaring inconsistency. In astronomical terms there is no reason to expect that the planets as a group are any more free of the Sun than is the planet Earth. The Earth is a captive of the Sun and all the other planets are likewise captives of the Sun. But because the insight into scale and relativity is so valuable to our understanding the different levels of human

---

[1] Ouspensky, P.D. *In Search of the Miraculous* (London: Routledge & Kegan Paul, 1950) pp. 80, 82, 94, 137.

consciousness, I set aside this inconsistency as relatively unimportant. There were several occasions during the many years I facilitated Gurdjieff Study Groups when the matter of this inconsistency was presented to me by a pupil. I had to fudge my replies in defence of the Ray as presented, because I could find no valid rebuttal to the charge of inconsistency. My primary reply was that we should value the immensity of the concept of relativity and scale as it applies to the inner world of the psyche, as illustrated by the Ray when applied to cosmic entities.

During the past year 2010, I along with several other of his pupils began to edit a heretofore unpublished manuscript of stories recollected and recorded by the spiritual teacher Sri Madhava Ashish. Many of these recollections were of his teacher Sri Krishna Prem (nee Ronald Nixon 1898-1965) and incidents that Prem confided to him. Among these was the following story related by Prem to Ashish, of an incident that occurred while Prem was a Reader in English at Cambridge University. The year was 1920:

"Something happened to Ronald that was of great significance to someone who would later dedicate his life to the inner quest. Call it fact. Call it dream. Call it vision. Ronald found himself at night rushing out into space in company with a guide or teacher. They seemed to rush outwards at great speed and for a long time. At last they stopped and turned round. Before them was a vast, roughly egg-shaped glowing mass, glowing with the light of myriads of stars. The light was irregularly distributed, following the distribution of the stars. Ronald asked which of the concentrations of stars was our solar system. Pointing to a smallish cluster towards one end of the total mass the guide said 'That is your universe.' The shock produced by the attack this statement made on Ronald's concept of scale sent him back to his room in Cambridge." [2]

The implication of this vision is that there are multiple universes within the Absolute existing simultaneously, just as there are multiple galaxies existing simultaneously within our universe. This is but one man's vision, and having such a vision does not make it true. While it might have been true for Ronald, it is hearsay for us. But the idea is not new. Others have also seen it and/or speculated about it. For example, the philosopher and psychologist, William James suggested it in 1895, and coined the word 'multiverse' to represent that, within which exist multiple simultaneous universes. The current state of thinking within the astrophysicist community is rife with speculation about multiple universes. And my own insight into this matter, although it admittedly would also be hearsay to others, reveals multiple simultaneous universes.

None of this changes the great value of the idea of scale and relativity of freedom brought to us by Gurdjieff as he explained it in terms of the Ray of Creation. And one does not lightly propose a revision to received wisdom from a Bodhisattva as I believe Gurdjieff to be. But the following suggested revision in the presentation of the Ray (See Figure 2) takes into account the idea of multiple universes and eliminates the inconsistency that had previously been necessary to explain the octave by artificially differentiating between degrees of freedom of the planets taken as a whole and any one planet such as Earth. Surely Gurdjieff would have known about multiple

---

[2] Ashish, Sri Madhava Ashish, *Unpublished Recollections* (2010).

All & Everything Conference 2011

simultaneous universes descending from the Absolute (Endlessness). But at the time of his revelation of the Ray of Creation in 1915, although there had been minor speculation about a multiverse such as in the thought of William James, this idea had almost no support within the scientific community at that time. Perhaps Gurdjieff interposed the idea of the planets taken as a whole to be at a different level of freedom from the Earth taken alone in order to fill out the octave. Now, that science is coming around to the idea of a multiverse, such an interposition is no longer necessary.

SUGGESTED REVISION TO THE PRESENTATION OF THE RAY OF CREATION

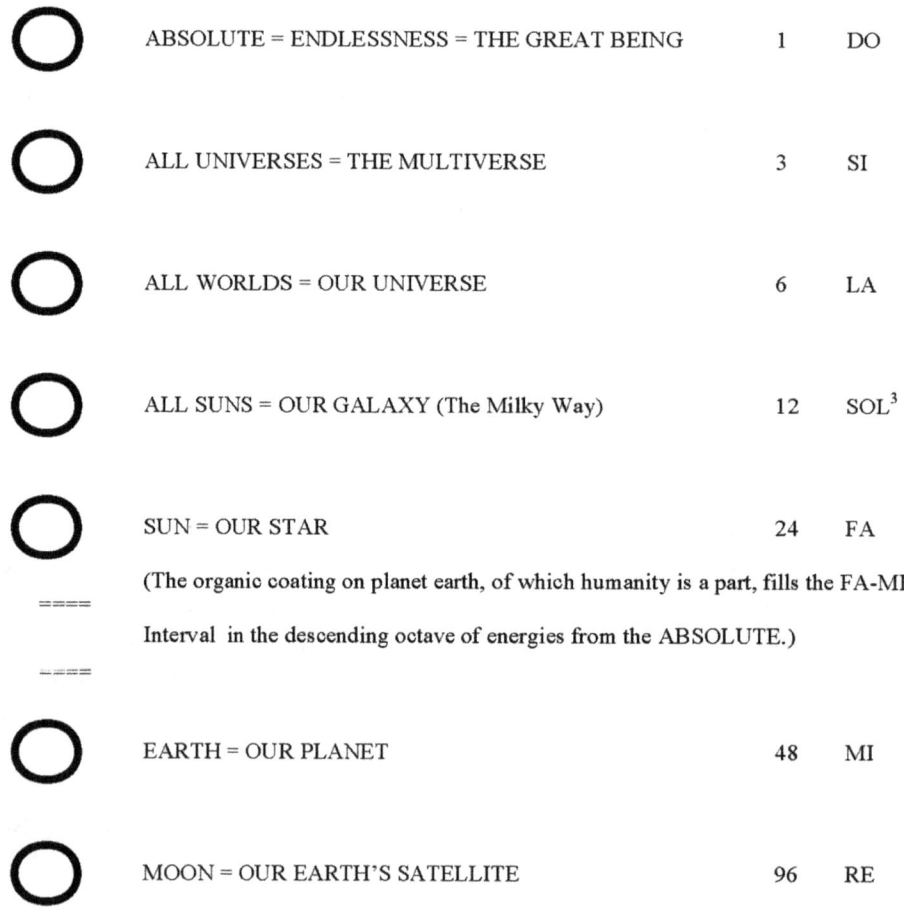

○	ABSOLUTE = ENDLESSNESS = THE GREAT BEING	1	DO
○	ALL UNIVERSES = THE MULTIVERSE	3	SI
○	ALL WORLDS = OUR UNIVERSE	6	LA
○	ALL SUNS = OUR GALAXY (The Milky Way)	12	SOL^3
○	SUN = OUR STAR	24	FA

(The organic coating on planet earth, of which humanity is a part, fills the FA-MI Interval in the descending octave of energies from the ABSOLUTE.)

○	EARTH = OUR PLANET	48	MI
○	MOON = OUR EARTH'S SATELLITE	96	RE

Figure 2

(Lest anyone think that the note 'sol' in the musical octave must be equated with the position of the sun in the great cosmic octave, it must be noted that the word 'sol' in musicology, comes not from the word for 'sun', but from the names of the musical notes derived by an Italian monk who used the first two letters of an ancient hymn to name the notes. See Endnote [3].)

© Copyright 2011 - Seymour B. Ginsburg - All Rights Reserved

---

[3] The note SOL in musical notation does not specifically refer to our star, the Sun. This notation from Wikipedia explains the source of the names of the notes: The founder of what is now considered the standard music stave was Guido d'Arezzo an Italian Benedictine monk who lived from 995–1050. Guido D'Arezzo's achievements paved the way for the modern form of written music, music books, and the modern concept of a composer. He named musical notes based on an ancient hymn dedicated to Saint John the Baptist, called Ut Queant Laxis, written by the lombard historian Paul the deacon. The first stanza is:

1. Ut queant laxis
2. resonare fibris,
3. Mira gestorum
4. famuli tuorum,
5. Solve polluti
6. labii reatum,
7. Sancte Iohannes.

Guido used the first letters of each verse to name the *Solfège* syllables: Ut, Re, Mi Fa, Sol, La, and Si (the exception being Si, which has the S of *Sancte* and the I of *Iohannes* - it also helps in that if two adjacent notes had the same vowel, verbal communication errors would become more likely). In the 17th century, Ut was changed in most countries except France to the easily singable, "open" syllable Do, said to have been taken from the name of the Italian theorist Giovanni Battista Doni.

The Ray of Creation Revisited - Questions & Answers

Note: Seymour B. Ginsburg, the presenter of this paper was not able to be physically present at the conference due to medical reasons. The paper, therefore, was read by Nick Bryce. Following the presentation, for the purpose of the Question and Answer session, a Skype hookup was arranged so that the presenter could address comments and questions from the participants and exchange thoughts about the subject.

Questioner 1: Two questions and a comment. The first question is: do you think that we are subject to energies from these other universes? The second question is: at what level in your scheme do you place the influence of the planets, our planets, on us? The third is a comment: do you think that Ouspensky's step-downs compensate or possibly compensate for these other universes?

Sy Ginsburg: The first question, what effects are influenced by these other universes? It would seem that in the scheme of things we are in a very bad place, in a muddle. Gurdjieff would say we are way, way down low in the Ray of Creation so that the influences directly affecting us would come from the sun. But in *Beelzebub's Tales* Gurdjieff refers at one point to our receiving influences from the stars, that is, other suns, and they influence us a bit. In terms of the planets as a whole, in astrology obviously the planets are important. And there are all kinds of astrological influences. But as opposed to the sun and the moon, even in astrology, the influences of the planets are very minor. So, the scheme I am proposing, can never justify that the planets as a whole are more free than planet Earth. It seems to me that in terms of levels of freedom these are equated with cosmic bodies in the Ray of Creation. Since all the planets go around the sun, they are all under the same controlling influence of the Sun. As to the other planets affecting each other, they have nowhere near the level of mass and weight and therefore nowhere near the kind of influence that the sun has on the earth. In psychological terms, it seems to me that the level of freedom as equated with these cosmic bodies would be the sun under 24 orders of law and this will accommodate the idea that there are multiple universes to fill out the octave. In current science there is speculation about all kinds of parallel universes, so we have to account for this additional level in the Ray of Creation. I don't know if that answers all of your questions but that's the view that struck me about this and it reinvigorated my thinking when I saw the quotation from Sri Krishna Prem.

Questioner 2: I like that you propose a revision. I think that revision is a necessary element in every teaching especially in a teaching like Gurdjieff's. I find inconsistency in what you are doing to the planets and not doing to the sun. You said that our planet has the same degree of freedom that has any other planet in our solar system. But our sun which is #24 (in your proposed revision) has the same degree of freedom as all suns #12. So why don't you reduce this #24 and don't say all suns or all stars or just leave our star? It is the same thing. There is no difference in the degrees of freedom of all stars in our galaxy and our star, the sun. There is no difference in the degree of freedom of our planet than any other planet of our system. That's the question.

Sy Ginsburg: I think you have answered the question. All stars in our Milky Way galaxy are under the control of the Milky Way galaxy so they would all have the same degree of freedom or be under the same number of orders of laws as our star, the sun.

Questioner 3: Yes, but you eliminated the level of all planets from Ouspensky's Ray of Creation. In your Ray of Creation there are no all planets, but you have all stars.

Questioner 4: I will try and repeat A's question, then I have an observation. A said that in the new schema you retain a level for all stars and then a level for our sun but you eliminated the level of all planets and compressed that to the level of the earth and one of the planets. Is that correct?

Sy Ginsburg: That's correct. The way I am proposing this suggested revision is to eliminate the idea of the planets as a group being under half as many laws as the earth. In the scheme that I am proposing our sun is under 24 orders of laws and the next step up is all stars or our galaxy, the Milky Way galaxy or any galaxy and that's under 12 orders of laws, and then there is our entire universe which is under 6 orders of laws. This would allow for the multiverse which would be the initial manifestation or materialization by Endlessness and would be under only 3 orders of laws. Then Endlessness or the Absolute or the great being, whatever we wish to call it, is still under only 1 law. That's the will of the Absolute as Ouspensky presumably got it from Gurdjieff.

Questioner 5: But there seems to be an inconsistency in that all suns would be under 6 orders of law, and our sun would be under 12 but our planet and all the other planets are under the same number, 48. So, I think the question is: why would we separate our sun out from all the other suns but not separate our planet out from all the other planets?

Sy Ginsburg: I don't believe I am being inconsistent. I am including our planet as the same as all other planets. But in this scheme of things it starts at the bottom with 96 which would be the satellite of the earth or the satellite of any other planet. Then the next level up, 48, would be any of the planets not singling out earth for some special consideration. Then the next level up is our star, and this would apply to every star in the Milky Way galaxy, and would be under the same number of orders of laws, 24 in this case. Going up a little further, not only the Milky Way galaxy but every galaxy would be under 12 orders of laws, and our universe, and this would apply to every universe, would be under 6 orders of laws. And all of these universes are contained in this concept called the multiverse which it seemed to me is this vision that Sri Krishna Prem had, looking at what was described as a glowing globe. He was looking at all of the universes and the guide pointed out one little distant speck within that globe and said, "That is your universe." So, I don't think there is any inconsistency at all. It is just that the way we received this from Gurdjieff, the planets as a group were singled out to be of under less domination by the sun than is the earth. That's the inconsistency we have heard for many years.

All & Everything Conference 2011

Questioner 6: Agreement on that, but I'll make one more attempt at this question. Given that the earth should not be singled out from the other planets in terms of orders of laws, why would our sun continue to be singled out as under more orders of laws than all of the other suns?

Sy Ginsburg: It's not being singled out. There are some diagrams in the paper that show this. The sun is in the same position in terms of levels of freedom as all the suns or all the stars in the Milky Way Galaxy. It's not being singled out at all. For example, the star Arcturus or the star Sirius, the brightest object in the summer sky, these are all stars within the Milky Way Galaxy and would all be under the same number of orders of laws which in the case of this proposed scheme is 24. I'd like to just add here that I wrote this paper with some reluctance because it does question what I have called, received wisdom. What I really was hoping to do was to simply give folks who are interested in this, to give them material to really think about. We don't know for sure that there are multiple universes. So, you might say that is a theory at this time. It does appear from what I have read in the scientific literature that more and more astrophysicists are coming to the position that there are multiple simultaneous universes.

Questioner 7: I am not an astrologer, although I think we have some here. I wonder if what you are proposing has not more to do with the single great Ray and the levels of influence on the entities, galaxies, stars, planets in the single Ray. Perhaps the other formulation has something more to do with the individual Ray. Because it does seem to me just from our current scientific knowledge that the other planets in our solar system influence life on the earth much more directly than possible planets much further away in other solar systems. So perhaps in the sense of the particular aspect of the Ray that influences us, the other planets of our solar system might be somewhat above the Earth in terms of their influence to the degree that we operate under laws of the collective planets of our system. So perhaps in some way both of these might have an application, although I agree with you that the possibility of other universes could be added to the schema. But other than stimulating our minds and hearts I don't see the practical value except for stimulating my head and my heart.

Sy Ginsburg: I agree with you that in terms of the practical value nothing has changed. You are a psychologist so you would be interested, I presume, more in the idea of the differences of levels of freedom between what Gurdjieff called negative identification which is under 96 orders of laws, ordinary identification under 48, and self-remembering under 24. Hopefully all of us in this Gurdjieff Work who understand about self-remembering are able to verify that when we are in the state of self-remembering, and presumably we should all be intentionally making an effort to be in that state all the time, we are clearly more free than in our ordinary states of identification. It is something that I have been able to verify and I suspect most everyone else has been able to verify too. So, that's the important thing and nothing has changed psychologically. Also, the Work requires us to make this intentional effort in accordance with Gurdjieff's aphorism to remember ourselves always and everywhere. So, none of that has changed. This proposal is a way to accommodate the idea of multiple universes when science finally says, yes we are able to verify that there are multiple universes. I don't know how many people beyond the ones that are in the room now would even be interested in this. But for those of us who have thought about this, I think it is worth considering. I am not saying that this is absolutely how it is because we do not yet have scientific confirmation that there are multiple universes.

Questioner 8: One reason I can see for sustaining the diagram of the Ray of Creation as Ouspensky presents it and not bring the earth to the level of the planets, would be that on Earth it seems to be from what is said in *Beelzebub's Tales,* that it is the only place where it possible to not remember ourselves whereas on the level of the planets that is from where we can receive substances, for example, those substances that build up our Kidman body. So to me it seems the most important differentiation is that it is possible to forget oneself only on earth.

Sy Ginsburg: Yes, Gurdjieff talks in many places in *Beelzebub's Tales* about normal three-brained beings existing on all other planets in our universe, and in terms of normal three-brained beings he saw the strange three-brained beings on earth who have taken Hassein's interest as mis-educated. But I don't think he is talking about three-brained beings on other planets in our solar system because we have pretty good evidence at this point that there are no other planets in our solar system that are populated by three-brained beings. So, these other planets where life is mostly normal would be planets perhaps like the earth going around other stars in the Milky Way galaxy. I believe that is what he was referring to.

Questioner 9: I'd like to ask a question about your change in your change in the Ray of Creation. Could it have any relationship to the step-down of the hydrogen table that Ouspensky reports about Gurdjieff in *In Search?*

Sy Ginsburg: About the step-down in the hydrogen table, in terms of if we go to higher numbers, is that what you mean, like if we go 192 and 384?

Questioner 10: Well, I hate to admit that I don't know really enough to ask this question clearly, but I'm trying to understand with the study of three-brained beings and the step-down in the hydrogen table, the third step-down which relates to us. Is it possible to consider these multiple universes in relation to the hydrogen table step-downs?

Sy Ginsburg: That's what I'm trying to do in this proposed revision, is to say that the multiple universes which are speculated about in science right now, that those multiple universes, you can call them the multiverse, that's the term that William James applied to it in 1895. The multiverse you could say is the first emanation of Endlessness's intention to have materialization so that Endlessness can know itself. But that's the beginning rather than simply saying "our universe" is that first division of the one into three. What this proposal says is that the multiverse, that is all of these multiple universes, is the first step down of the one into three. It's the first materialization. Does that answer your question or address it?

Questioner 11: It helps. I'm still unclear about all of this and just trying to become more clear. In relation to our own personal work and our three brains and the potential of creating a Kidman and higher being body, do you see a relationship between that striving of three-brained beings that would encompass more and more these multiple universes?

Sy Ginsburg: In terms of our own personal psychological work, trying to self-remember, nothing has changed. This doesn't suggest any change in that. The only thing it does do is change the numbering system that we've become accustomed to, based on the argument that the earth as well as all the other planets going around the sun are under the same equal domination by the sun. So it doesn't change our psychological work at all. It would just say that in our ordinary states of identification we are equivalent to the earth which is under 48 orders of laws and in our state of self-remembering, we are at the equivalent of the sun, now that's the big change that I am proposing here, which would then be under 24 orders of laws in this proposed scheme. The numbers would be different but the work is still the same. The whole purpose of this idea of thought is to accommodate the multiple universes that have been speculated about in science. It clears up what appeared to me to be an inconsistency, and I think Gurdjieff may have done it intentionally by giving the planets as a group a higher level of freedom than any one planet simply to fill out the octave in his scheme of the Ray of Creation because we are dealing with an octave here. But the same interval, the Mi-Fa interval, is where the work on ourselves applies.

Questioner 12: Yesterday in A's paper, he proposed a very interesting idea that I won't go into any detail here, but the idea was that what we know as Endlessness from *Beelzebub's Tales* is not the ultimate Endlessness, but is itself subject to other forces that suggest that maybe, I believe A said, the demiurge rather than the ultimate. For instance, even Endlessness himself is subject to the effects of the merciless Heropass and had to create this universe in order to accommodate the flow of time which even Endlessness himself could not eliminate. So here we now have this idea of other universes and we also have had two questions about the step-down in the table of hydrogens which does seem to provide for levels above any universe that we can conceive of. So perhaps this idea of the multiverse could be considered above Endlessness, above world one; oh, you don't like that. (laughter) Suppose the God of our universe is one of all Gods. Suppose the Endlessness of our universe is not the ultimate I but part of a multiverse of I's that collectively make up something much larger. If we are going to scientifically consider the possibility of infinite numbers of universes than we must also consider the possibility of infinite aspects of a larger whole, something that each of these universes are an aspect of. Multiple Absolutes, A says, or multiple universes which collectively themselves would make up the realm of all possible universes with their collective wisdom into one larger something. Is it too early in the morning there for this? (laughter)

Sy Ginsburg: If this paper, and of course I am not familiar with A's paper, but in a sense they are kind of coincidental because they seem to be dealing with the same issue. One thing that comes to mind that I should mention is that in Chapter 47 of *Beelzebub's Tales* there is something called a Hymn to our Endlessness. Maybe some of you have the book there. I think, in that Hymn, part of it suggests thanking Endlessness for vanquishing the Merciless Heropass. However, that is just an aside. I guess A's paper has to do with ultimately is there something that we could call One or is there not something that we would call One? Now, I know that even in spiritual literature, which may not help a whole lot because it has become so distorted, the most famous Old Testament prayer in Judaism is based on a statement in Deuteronomy that the Lord is One. Now, I don't know if you can go by that, but that does suggest the idea that ultimately there is a One something, whatever we want to call it, the Great Being, the Endlessness, the Absolute. Apparently A's paper brings that into question and I think that is worth considering just like what is in this paper might be worth considering in terms of our common thinking. Is that what you are getting at?

Questioner 13: I think that as with the idea that our universe which we believed was all there was, now may be seen to be a small part of a larger whole, perhaps the God that we think controls our universe is much larger. So, I don't think this in any way eliminates the sense of an ultimate One. It just keeps becoming pushed back further and further and further and becomes larger and larger. And that each level that we thought was the whole subsequently turns out to be part of something else, as our universe may now turn out to be part of something else, our galaxy has turned out to be part of something else. I think psychologically each one of us experiences ourselves inside of the universe and perhaps in some small way try to relate to other psychic entities inside our bodies. They are like other galaxies although there is a sense that somehow collectively we are all one and as our minds and hearts meet sometimes we can feel something of that quality. So, as below, so above.

Sy Ginsburg: Certainly, my proposed idea fits in with that, the idea that our universe is part of something larger; in this case we'll call it a multiverse. I didn't hear A's paper but maybe it is in the same direction, certainly causing us to think more broadly about the subject in cosmic terms or astronomical terms. But again from a psychological perspective the Work would be exactly the same. It wouldn't make any difference at all as far as I can tell.

Questioner 14: Yes, it just adds the problem of more distracting speculation when we try to pay attention.

Sy Ginsburg: Are there no more questions, in which case let me just wish you all a wonderful conference, apparently it's been wonderful already and I certainly hope that it will just continue that way. I'll look forward to seeing all of you in Salt Lake City next year. I've been told that that is where we are thinking of having the conference and it is something that I should be able to do, I hope to do anyway. (Applause).

(The discussion continued after the presenter signed off of the Skype transmission.)

Questioner 15: I found very interesting this idea of revising something in the Work, both interesting, difficult and perilous. For example, the concept that Sy put forth of incorporating the idea of multiple universes into the Ray of Creation scheme, I think is a very positive way of thinking. There will be things that will be discovered, images that would be created by scientists of how the universe works that would be different from what prevailed when Gurdjieff came and gave his teaching. If the teaching is anything above forms than it has to recognize what is there objectively and make the forms conform, use the forms to incorporate and make the data conform to the general overall scheme of things. And, of course, it is more than possible to have this thing done with the Ray of Creation which incorporates the octave, which goes back so many thousands of years, and has survived so many civilizations as a model of structuring levels because that's what it is. It's a model of structuring levels combined with Fourier's theorem about what is able to be expressed mathematically. It is an interesting way of structuring this. Fourier's theory which was developed in the 18th century has not died out as a tool regardless of the fact that numerous new theories have been put forth. So the idea of revision would be an attempt to preserve the method of using the central core to adapt to our vision that the problem is changing according to scientific data all the time. And we need to change. We are not even in the final form of scientific interpretation. I think it is a very positive thing, and the perilous part lies in the fact of trying to alter the core like some wiseacre coming up with the idea that the octave should have five intervals or that Re should be after Mi or something. So revision, I believe, is absolutely necessary to keep the thing informative with data coming in and this is really the idea I was trying to put forth when I spoke about religion and science meeting together in the sense of religious beliefs and physical speculation or the physical practice incorporating the data that we have, not being in conformity with the data that we have from science. But the other change one has to be wary about, I believe.

Questioner 16: Yes, I agree to a certain extent, but I don't think we have to revise anything. I think we have to be able to incorporate in whatever system we have. If you read someone like Hawking, we don't only have multi-universes, we have negative universes and we have negative numbers as well. So, we are going to have to worry about that. In a sense, what we have to be able to do is to understand or incorporate in whatever system Gurdjieff gave us, we can incorporate what we know, into the new data that comes out and ultimately affects.

Questioner 17: Yes, as you were speaking, I was just thinking about the strong perspective to revise Gurdjieff from the early 20th century. Are you thinking that we revise the Old Testament, Shakespeare, Beethoven's Late Quartets? I think we have to accept things as they are and use them as we can.

Questioner 18: It is an interesting problem and dilemma, whether we should revise the existing teaching or we should incorporate new data into the existing system. I think we should do both. We should incorporate new data and new considerations, new elements, and today Sy gave us a new element, incorporating it into an existing system. But we may come to the point when our new understanding and new data will not fit the old system. And in this case we have a dilemma. Either we change the basic elements of the old system or think of possible replacement of the old system. This happens constantly in the world of ideas, of metaphysics. This happened with Kant who could not go along with the old system, with the old way of looking at time and space. He suggested that time and space are our own properties, not properties of the world. And this happened to Christianity that eventually replaced Judaism and Islam that came to criticize Judaism for one thing and Christianity for another thing. This happens with Gurdjieff who actually gave a new system and put it in the place of Blavatsky's theosophy. So let us not absolutize any system including Gurdjieff's system. It works beautifully today but it should be constantly renovated, revised, changed and developed, so that it will stay on target, balanced and continue to work. It is not that we should keep it forever as it is, and it is not that we should revolutionize everything every day.

One more theme I hope to attract your attention to. I look again at the Ray of Creation and I notice that we are playing with two types of energies. Some are individual and some are gross. Moon is individual. Earth belongs to all planets. Sun belongs to all stars. Our galaxy belongs to all worlds. All worlds belong to multiverse or all universes, and all universes are topped with one Absolute. Sometimes we think in terms of one and sometimes we think in terms of a group. It is our mentality; it is how we perceive reality. There are many people and there is one person whom we revere most of all, one Gurdjieff, one Christ. Sometimes we prefer to see singular objects, sometimes we prefer to see things as a group. And we have to figure out why and how we work with this reality.

Questioner 19: I think we have to be careful. For me the discussion of this kind of subject is probably going to turn us all into a madhouse. (laughter) Because Gurdjieff never ever meant anything like that as far as I am concerned. Because he says what is a Megalocosmos and I am a Microcosmos of the Megalocosmos. So I have to find out within myself what the Sun-Absolute is, what do the planets correspond to in myself, what is the earth in myself, what is the moon in myself, what is Anulios in myself? Now, if I added a multi-universe, I am going to go crazy because it is absolute nonsense because I can't use it. I can't experience the universe. I can only experience my own little tiny solar system. So, if we intellectually decide to add and revise anything we are certainly headed for some cataclysm absolutely not known. (laughter)

Questioner 20: I believe that in order to be able to think, we have to realize what thinking has to be done in a state of some mental relativity. When it comes to the question of whether there are more than one Absolute, I cannot follow it simply because even if there is one more and not ten more Absolutes, both of them will exclude themselves in the Absolute.

Questioner 21: It is really very straight forward to me that it is not conflicting that the Absolute is One. As Sy was saying, it's One. It's very clear.

Questioner 22: I just want to add something to what R said before and which I agree with very much and I think it is the same point that N was saying, that we have something to work with. Now a plan to work a system is a blueprint maybe. It is something given to work with and then there is a bridge or something to be constructed. So, what are we going to do, construct or revise the plans? I think the plans are there for us to make an effort to connect them to our reality and build them. The central fact is on the building.

Questioner 23: I think there is a point of view that might not have been expressed. There is also a matter of perspective. One is the perspective of looking at the Ray from our perspective and our octave and then there is the perspective of the great Ray of itself and the Absolute of itself. Let me make this more simple. Can we eliminate or put on the same level, planets? Do the planets influence us? That's a perspective. Or should all the planets be taken together? That's a perspective outside that system. So, with our minds, we can have thought experiments that ask where are we standing when we look at these perspectives.

Questioner 24: I feel that Gurdjieff has given us so much material for thought, and this proposition of the Enneagram is an immense task, and is truly for understanding. So, I'm not sure that we have to revise. I think we have to try to understand more.

Questioner 25: We are always revising, we cannot stop.

Questioner 26: Gurdjieff was called the second most dangerous thinker of the age because he developed a cosmology that did not answer the scientific fact. If we are going to judge all this by scientific fact, we are lost.

Questioner 27: He revised everything through all his life.

Beelzebub Alien

Paul Beekman Taylor

Abstract

It is not unusual for a reader of Beelzebub's Tales to His Grandson to be so taken up with the story that he forgets the spatial point of view of the narrator, who is an alien, an extra-terrestrial, if you will, with non-human physical and mental characteristics, including narrative orders of action, place and time. Every word he relates to his grandson Hassein is spoken in outer space aboard an intergalactic vehicle, though most of what he relates concerns his experiences on Earth, where he is both listener and teller of tales. Although the Tales are stories related in space about space, as far as I have been able to discover, Gurdjieff's work seems not merit more than cursory notice of in of the countless studies of the plurality of worlds and travels to and between them. Gurdjieff's reader is also likely not to care that Beelzebub, as an extra-terrestrial voyager observing the activities of humans on Earth, is just one of a legion of otherworldly beings who have been visited and engaged humans in recorded story. The striking difference, however, is that Beelzebub is a visitor to Earth rather than a receiver of visits from Earth.

The stages in the development of stories of aliens in the western world develop from Aristotle's, Plato's and Heraclitus's scientific inquisitions into the shape and content of space. Following them, scientists and story-tellers consider possibilities of travel by inhabitants of the Earth into space in order where they find a fresh view of present, past, and future mortal activities of mankind from an extraterrestrial point of view. In more recent times, writers have portrayed aliens from superior cultures who, like Orson Welles' Martians, invade Earth, or like Swedenborg's angels, Gurdjieff's Beelzebub and Ashiata Shiemash, visit Earth for the good of mankind.

Gurdjieff had many models in the long history of extra-terrestrial travel to draw upon for the form and function of his protagonist Beelzebub. The science fiction and fantastic story of more recent times do not concern him. He is, rather, interested in delineating a historical trace of human civilizations and an "objective" criticism of man's behaviour. He accomplishes this by widening and deepening the genre of spatial travel by conjoining with it fresh ideas about human culture from a perspective that is reminiscent of the writings of Emmanuel Swedenborg.

Beelzebub the Alien

The purpose of this brief review is to look at G. I. Gurdjieff's *Beelzebub's Tales*, the first series of Gurdjieff's *All and Everything,* in the context of the ageless tradition of stories of other worlds, especially those that have philosophical, theological, sociological and psychological purport.[1] Besides primal creation myths in which sky deities shape the world, there is a rich body of story that features alien observers and visitors to the Earth. Curiously, *Beelzebub's Tales* has not been noted or little noticed, as far as I know, in the record of the countless stories and studies concerning other worlds that have filled scientific journals and shelves of fiction since Gurdjieff died in 1949. This is all the more puzzling considering the number studies that have followed space voyages and the sightings of satellite telescopes. I would not add Gurdjieff's work to the expansive corpus of science fiction, for it is not exactly that,[2] but I would suggest that *Tales* constitutes an encyclopaedic cultural scope on extraterritoriality that goes far beyond its predecessors.[3]

One can trace the evolution of studies and stories of extraterritorial forms through three broad and overlapping stages. First and earliest were investigations into the size and substance of outer space and the existence of plural worlds in the universe. Second were speculations of travel possibilities between worlds, some of which may hold life forms either like or unlike those on Earth. A third and more recent stage comprises possibilities of present and future exchange between Earthlings and extraterritorial beings. In our time, scientists, or natural philosophers, have increased observation and calculation of plural worlds, while moral philosophers, story-tellers, and mythographers consider cosmic flight and engagements with alien beings. The scope of Gurdjieff's *Beelzebub's Tales* sweeps over both fiction as science and science as fiction.

In brief, the ancients contrasted finite with infinite space. Aristotle and after him Ptolemy described a finite symmetrical universe with Earth at its center and the seven visible planetary bodies - Moon, Mercury, Venus, Sun, Mars, Jupiter, and Saturn - moving around it in circular orbits. Ptolemy posited an eighth sphere, the *Stellatum*, or fixed stars, a ninth Empyrean, or crystalline sphere, and a tenth sphere, the *Primum Mobile* marking God, First Mover, or Creator. These universe designs were mathematically ordered, as is Beelzebub's.

The universe described by Beelzebub in his exposition of the creation and maintenance of the Universe has a center (524) but no definite boundaries. This universe corresponds to the cosmos

---

[1] This paper has profited substantially from Michael Benham's information about Russian science fiction and Walter Driscoll's bibliographical material. Both have lent their critical eye to the text and suggested revision.
[2] Martin Seymour Smith, *The 100 Most Influential Books Ever Written,* Secaucus, NJ: Carol Publishing Group), 1998, Chapter 94 calls *Tales* "Gurdjieff's own 'science fiction' style exposition."
[3] Boris Mouravieff claims that ideas in *Tales* can be found in the novels of a Mme. Krzanowska, "much in vogue among Russian youth before the first world war. These also dealt with interplanetary trips and with excursions in the darkest unreachable past, as well as into the future beyond the XXIst century": *Gurdjieff, Ouspensky and Fragments* (1997), 24–25. Michael Benham has given me this reference (see Bibliography). Neither any evidence for the assertion nor the cited novels have been found.

proposed in *de rerum natura* by Titus Lucretius (d. ca. BCE 50). Gurdjieff, in the epilogue to *Beelzebub's Tales*, "From the Author," lists theories about the nature and bounds of the universe, while Beelzebub assures his grandson that according to Objective Science "everything without exception in the universe is material" (138). If the Universe is infinite, so is the amount of material and the number of planetary bodies in it; i.e., it contains a plurality of worlds. One recalls that according to Plutarch's *Moralia* the Greek astronomer Anaxarchus (380–320 BCE) told Alexander the Great, to the conqueror's dismay, that there were an infinite number of worlds. Putting aside Einstein's calculation of the size of our universe, a boundless Universe containing an infinite number of worlds is a fundamental concept.[4] The idea that there were earths before ours has been advanced in poetry and fiction since the Renaissance, notably in the *Democritus Platonissans* of Thomas More (1474–1535).

Galileo Gallilei (1584–1642) mapped the moon and the satellites of Jupiter in *Sidereus nuncius* (*Sidereal Messenger*, 1610), the first scientific treatise based upon telescopic observations. The astronomer and mathematician Johannes Kepler (1571–1630), who worked with Tycho Brahe, defended the Copernican design of a solar system in *Mysterium cosmographicum* (1596), in which he illustrated the tight geometric order of the solar system in a drawing that shows the planets as polyhedrons, each fitting within another. Observations through telescopes in the seventeenth century suggested a limitless Universe and, inevitably, countless stars and worlds.

It was inevitable that in taking account of new and radical views of space and time, many of which were distinct from orthodox religious teachings, scientists and philosophers speculated widely on observation of the Earth from above, the possibility of life elsewhere in the Universe, and travel between worlds. In general, the astronomer focused attention on evidence of the plurality of worlds, and the writer of fiction on travel between worlds. In fact, from the moment mankind charted the skies he considered possibilities of investigating cosmic elements directly or in visions. The Greco-Roman historian Plutarch (CE 46–120), best known for his biographies, wrote *de facie in orbe lunae* (*The Face of the Moon*), in which he suggested that the moon serves a universal purpose in the cosmos that affects the life-cycle of human souls.[5] This echoes the Stoic conception of the moon as a repository for souls, an idea that foreshadowed Gurdjieff's view that the energy of those who die without improving their consciousness serves to stabilize the moon's position. It is not unlikely that Gurdjieff knew of both the work of Plutarch and his Stoic antecedents.

---

[4] As early as 1584, Giordano Bruno (1548–1600) posited an infinite universe and number of worlds. His concept of infinity entered the charge of heresy which resulted in his burning in 1600. More recently, the plurality of worlds was popularized by the astronomer Thomas Wright (1711–1786) and the philosopher Emmanuel Kant (1724–1804). In the light of current space exploration, the concept has been brought up to date by the astro-biologist Steven J. Dick and the philosopher David K. Lewis (1941–2001) who argues logically, following Gurdjieff and a host of others, that an infinite universe must contain an infinite number of worlds.

[5] *Moralia* 920a–945d. Plutarch, whose Roman name was Lucius Mestrius Plutarchus, assumed the moon populated.

The conception of a multitude of earths, or worlds in the universe stirred interest in interplanetary and intergalactic travel. Lucianus of Samasota (ca. 120–190), wrote in Greek of interplanetary flight in *Alethe diegamata* ("A True Story") that records visits to the moon and Venus, and a war between planets. His *Icaromenippus*, in which the god Zeus looks down at the earth with disfavor, describes an aerial expedition made possible by carefully calculated distances between celestial bodies. His *Macrobii* discusses the remarkable longevity of ancients and credits the trans-sexual Tiresias with six hundred years of life. All in all, there is little in Lucianus that could not have served as a distant model of concepts for *Beelzebub's Tales*.

A popular description of the world seen from a point far above in space appears in an episode in *De re publica* by Marcus Tullius Cicero (BCE 106–43), a dream vision in which Scipio Africanus is carried high above the earth by his dead grandfather who, in the course of their observation, comments from a Stoic point of view on the world's history, time, the music of the spheres and the cosmos.[6] About 1380, Geoffrey Chaucer, who knew Macrobius's commentary, wrote *The House of Fame*, a dream vision in which the poet is carried through the planetary orbits and the houses of the Zodiac by an Eagle who lectures him on relations between celestial signs and man's life. Over a century later, in 1535, Pier Angelo Manzolli (1500–1543), under the pseudonym Marcellus Palingenius ("born again") Stellatus, printed *Zodiacus Vitae* ("Zodiac of Life"), a Latin hexameter poem which describes travel through the twelve houses of the sky, and identifies the meaning of signs and their significant reflections on the life of mankind below.[7]

Incited by what he observed through his telescope, Kepler wrote *Somnium* (published after his death in1634), a story of an Icelander Duracotus whose mother is in contact with the moon Daemon of Lavania. Able to resisting the pull of gravity, he reaches the moon where he observes the monstrous Privolvans. In another of his works of "science fiction," *Dissetatio cum nuncio sidereo* (1610), Kepler portrays Galileo in conversation with a celestial messenger who speaks only with breath. Independent of Kepler's tale, an English bishop, Francis Godwin (1562-1633), composed *The Man in the Moon* (1638) which describes a chariot, drawn by forty wild geese to the moon where the lunanaut finds a serene and peaceful society of superior beings.

The pioneer of probability theory Christiaan Huygens (1629–1695) expanded the idea of other civilizations in a work that appeared in English in 1698 entitled *Celestial Worlds Discover'd: or, Conjectures Concerning the Inhabitants, Plants and Productions of the Worlds in the Planets*. Even before Huygens' work appeared, the French dramatist, Cyrano de Bergerac (1619–1655) had produced *L'Autre monde: l'histoire comique, les etats et empires de la lune* (*The Other*

---

[6] The work is lost, but a Platonic commentary on it by Ambrosius Theodosius Macrobius (A.D. 395–423), well-known in the Middle Ages, is extant. Coincidental in relation to Gurdjieff's concept of long life for those who achieve a higher conscious is the etymology of the name of Macrobius: *macro* "great" + *bio* "life."

[7] Sophia Wellbeloved's *Gurdjieff, Astrology & Beelzebub's Tales* (New Palz, NY: Solar Bound Press, 2001), is a study of Gurdjieff's astrological sources and use of the Zodiac as a structural principle in *Tales*.

World: A Comic History of the States and Empires of the Moon), first staged in 1657. In it, Cyrano speculated on alien technology and space flight by means of magnetism. One recalls that magnetic currents are used aboard Beelzebub's spaceship Karnak (168) which functions by means of laws of Physics. Gurdjieff also adds wireless communication to Karnak's machinery.

Later, a contemporary of Huygens, the French writer, Bernard le Bovier de Fontellelle (1657–1757), nephew of the dramatist Pierre Corneille, published *Conversations on the Plurality of Worlds* (1686) which popularized the notion of life elsewhere in the solar system. More recently, *Auf Zwei Planeten* (1897) by Kurd Lasswitz (1848–1910), describes a trip from Earth to Mars in anti-gravity space ships.[8] His Martian civilization, clearly superior to that of our world, is protected by angelic guardian angels. The Russian playwright, scientist, and philosopher, Alexander Vasilyevich Sukhovo-Kobylin (1817–1903) proposed an "All-the-World" cosmic philosophy that supposed three types of civilizations: one based on Earth energy, another on the energy of the entire solar system, and the third upon galactic energy.[9] Closer to our era, C. S. Lewis published *Out of the Silent Planet* (1938) in which a Dr. Ransom, kidnapped to Mars, observes a superior civilization before returning reluctantly to Earth.

I have cited only a handful of the works produced in Europe, both scientific and fantastical, that concern life elsewhere in the universe.[10] From a psychological point of view, the search for life elsewhere in the universe can be seen as a quest for superior life forms, material and immaterial. Psychological engagement with aliens is prominent in the work of the mystic Emmanuel Swedenborg (1688–1772) who reported that he had had visions of Angels bearing him messages from above with whom he conversed. In *De Telluriberus in Mondo Nostro Solari, quae Vocantur Planetae* (*Concerning the Earths in our Solar System which are Called Planets*), published in 1758, Swedenborg scanned the various worlds of the solar system. His Martians, who possess a clear sense of reality, converse with inhabitants of our world.

---

[8] Published in English in 1971 under the title *Two Planets*. A recent example of comparable studies is the scientific study of the astronomer and astro-physicist Carl Sagan (1934–1996), *Intelligent Life in the Universe* (1966). Several contemporary religious sects, including the Seventh-Day Adventists, Latter Day Saints, and Scientology entertain beliefs in superior extraterrestrial beings.

[9] Michael Benham has given me this reference.

[10] For a detailed scan of the various speculations on other worlds, see Karl S. Guthke (1933–), *Mythos der Neuzeit* (Bern, 1983), translated into English as *Imagining Other Worlds From the Copernican Revolution to Modern Science Fiction*. It is clear that, since the beginning of the 20th century, American writers have taken the lead in tales of alien life, though Russian writers are not far behind. The syllabus of a 2007 UCLA seminar "Russian Science Fiction,", given by Vyacheslav Ivanov in the Department of Slavic Languages and Literature, mentions Ouspensky's work on multiple dimensions and draws attention to his association with "Gurdzhiev" without mentioning the latter's work.

In describing visitors to Earth from utopian civilizations that may exist elsewhere, Swedenborg differs from his predecessors and contemporaries who speculate on possibilities of visits *from* Earth to other worlds. Recently there have been a large number of stories of planetary colonization.[11] Following World War II reactions to the development of the Atom Bomb included sightings of unidentified flying object sightings that evoked descriptions of visits and invasions from other planets.[12] In this respect, *Beelzebub's Tales,* composed between 1924 and 1928, and published in 1950, is far ahead of times in providing an encyclopaedic coverage of a geographical and cultural history of the earth recorded by an extraterrestrial being in the course of six descents to Earth from different cosmic locations after leaving the "perfected world" of His Endlessness on the Most Holy Sun Absolute.

Distant superior worlds have been have always been a typical feature of myth. In the Christian monotheistic scenario, God abides in a Heaven with a population of nine orders of angels, intelligent extraterrestrial beings who are sent on missions to Earth. The Christian scholastic view recognizes Jesus as an Agent sent by the Principle to create the world and its kind. Gurdjieff's Beelzebub is also an agent whose travels and whose tales are attributed to "a legend I had heard in childhood about the appearance of the first human beings on Earth and of which I had made Beelzebub, as a likely witness of this appearance, the principal hero" (*The Herald of Coming Good*, 45). Beelzebub witness to the beginning of man's inhabitation of the world, and his recitation to his grandson of its history comprises an alien's analysis of the course of human development from its inception. The characterization of narrator-observer Beelzebub as an extraterrestrial being with supra-human physical and mental attributes (horns, tail, extreme age, memory of all time, broad knowledge of human science and morals) is more philo-anthropological than science fictional. In having an alien agent narrate his story, Gurdjieff draws upon what he might have known of the literary history of alien observers and visitors to the earth. His likely sources are beyond my ability to trace, but there is a rich heritage of such myths and legends in the lore and language of areas Gurdjieff knew well. His father must have chanted many of those current in Transcaucasia.[13]

From the beginning of recorded time, that is, since human beings first expressed beliefs and hopes in visual, oral and written story that assumed universal truths, or "myth," the source of all life has

---

[11] Philip Dick has written extensively about planetary colonies.

[12] Writers of fantastical tales of otherworld visitations are divided in considering extraterrestrials as either invaders or helpers. *War of the Worlds* (1898) by a Gurdjieff contemporary, H. G. Wells (1866–1946), is the first notable example of an invasion version. H. P. Lovecraft (1890–1937) has written horror tales of aliens occupying Earth. An alien threat to Earth is displayed in the film *The Day the Earth Stood Still* (1952). *Close Encounters of the Third Kind* (1977) and *Cocoon* are notable examples of helpful aliens. A Psychological view of extraterrestrials is *Flying Saucers: A Modern Myth of Things Seen in the Sky* (1958) by C. G. Jung (1875–1961), who understands the sightings as mankind's myth-making needs.

[13] Walter Driscoll tells me that he suspects that the tales Gurdjieff heard came from Yezidi legends. In Plato's *Timaeus,* "a likely account" of creation is given.

been attributed to extra-terrestrial forces. An appropriate starting point for an exploration of myths of alien powers is Christian Scripture, which opens: "In the beginning, God created the Heavens and the Earth. . . God said 'Let us make man in our own image.'" The order of creation in this and other sacred story - first universe, then world, then living inhabitants on it - is archetypal. Gurdjieff's cosmogony, expounded by Beelzebub in his exposition of the Holy Planet Purgatory to his grandson, is comparable, though there are significant differences. First of all, the God of the three Semitic monotheistic religions, Yahweh, Deus, and Allah, creates the universe by fiat; that is, by an act of conscious will, while Beelzebub's Endlessness sets in operation a group of primal laws which effect an evolutionary formation of the three-brained beings we call humans. Secondly, the single God-force of religions engages himself in the lives of the peoples he creates.[14] The Jewish, Christian and Muslim Creator judges the transgression of Adam and Eve, weighs the ritual offerings of Cain and Abel, orders Abraham to sacrifice his son, and tests Job's spiritual faith.

The Christian God can view the earth and impregnate a mortal woman, and the gods in the myths of the Greeks, Romans, Hindu and Norse traverse all worlds in humanoid form. Like Greek gods, the Norse deities couple with mortals and giants. What sets the God of Judaism, Christianity and Islam apart from the gods of pantheistic myth is their exercise of spiritual judgment and punishment. The ultimate arbiter of human life is its primal source.

So, it is not surprising that Gurdjieff, in his invention of a cosmogony, should attribute creation and maintenance of the Earth to an absolute force, and observation and criticism of the human race to his agents. This collaboration is comparable to the relation between a monotheistic God and his various agents, such as the archangels Michael and Uriel, and the hypostatic Jesus. Both the gods of mid-eastern scripture and Gurdjieff's creator figure are, from the point of view of Earth's inhabitants, "aliens" who scrutinize their creations. As such, Beelzebub appears to be one of scores of aliens, or extra-terrestrial beings, who in myth and story serve as a Creator's deputy to visit and participate in human activities. The Christian God would have his emissary, Jesus, redeem mankind and restore his maker's intention to have mankind replenish Heaven.

Beelzebub's Tales is radically different from mainstream science fiction in that the narrator is not a human who observes aliens, but an alien who observes humans.[15] As an alien, Beelzebub is free of the stereotypical mentality inherent in humans due to influences of family, school and religion. It attributes to him a memory of the beginnings of things that are hidden from the reader, and whose "facts" are beyond their comprehension, though we are led to believe that his grandson, Hassein, does understand them. Not being limited by the point of view of a human in his descents

---

[14] Christian doctrine, in general, accords with Aristotle's argument that the hand of the Maker no longer touches that which it thrusts into being. The *Torah* and the *Koran* recognize God's presence on Earth, though Spinoza asserted that any participation of God in human affairs abrogates the Free Will with which he endows mankind.

[15] Beelzebub's narration is introduced by Gurdjieff's setting of the scene in chapters I and II, and interrupted by Gurdjieff's account of the honoring of Beelzebub in chapter forty-seven.

to our world, Beelzebub has the knowledge of all Earth languages and, as far as his interlocutors realize, earthly forms: race, height, weight, etc. He has lost his horns temporarily and while on Earth his tail is well hidden under various apparels (*BT* 608).[16] When he achieves the highest grade of reason, his horns are restored to signal his deserved supernatural authority (*Tales* 1176 ff.).[17]

It is rare in religious story to find those fallen from God's grace restored to eminence. In Greek myth, Prometheus is freed from his punishment by Zeus, and in the Yezidi-Kurdish mythological tradition to which that Walter Driscoll has directed me, fallen angels are redeemed.[18] The Apostle Paul was transformed from scourge of Christians to the principle transmitter of the teaching of Christ. As the avatar Vishnu mediates between Brahma the Creator and Siva the Destroyer in Hindu mythology, Beelzebub mediates between Endlessness the Creator and mankind the destroyer of creation. In effect, Beelzebub is an allegorical figure of perfected human consciousness, knowledge and memory.

In *Beelzebub's Tales,* though Beelzebub is not identified as one of them, His Endlessness has sent a number of "messengers from above" (*BT* 53–54). Beelzebub remarks that only Ashiata Shiemash, among others, succeeded in fulfilling the Creator's purpose on Earth (*BT* 347–48); yet curiously Ashiata is not an alien by birth, but has been infused with alien force.[19] Beelzebub does not identify himself as agent or spy, so to speak, in the service of His Endlessness on Earth. He is simply one of the Cherubim and Seraphim who attend His Endlessness on the Sun Absolute (*BT* 749). We discover that, in the course of his six visits to Earth, Beelzebub works, as Ashiata Shiemash does, to instruct human beings way toward a higher consciousness.

This said, at the least, *Beelzebub's Tales* in part of the corpus of writings on alien spatial travel. Whether the story is science, science fiction, fantasy or vision, is inconsequential, for it is all these within an encyclopaedic "Objective Criticism of the Life of Man." Gurdjieff's fiction of "likeliness," however, conceals a deep and broad truth, for his habit was "always to keep deep thoughts under ordinary . . . outer expressions" (*Life Is Real*, 123).[20] The "ordinary" story has Beelzebub on earth, as well as on other planets, reporting on and abetting the operations in the universe which maintain Sun Absolute. This function is a "minor feature" of the tale, while its major feature is the instruction of his grandson Hassein, who is "everyman" on a path toward

---

[16] Though Beelzebub masters English, he makes good fun of exposing popular means of teaching it.

[17] See Exodus 34: 29–35 and Deuteronomy 24: 29, for the horns (*cornuta*) of Moses.

[18] See Giuseppi Furlani, *Religious Texts of the Yezidis* (Bombay, 1940).

[19] An alien force taking on human form, a common feature of science fiction would refer to the Buddha.

[20] When a listener to a reading of *Tales* in New York City asked Gurdjieff if the "system" in "Planet Purgatory" is to be believed, Gurdjieff laughed and said something brief in Russian. Madame de Salzmann translated this into: "The foundation of belief is doubt." Does a novelist offer fiction as fact?

higher consciousness of the purpose of human existence, individually as well as generally. If Beelzebub represents perfected actuality of being, Hassein represents humankind's potentiality of being. He is all of us.

The universe of space and time through which Hassein is carried with his grandfather is boundless if not infinite. Its measured expanse is a function of the laws of three and seven that the endless Creator has projected outward from his presence on the Sun Absolute by force of will. One can find philosophical content in both scientific treatises and fanciful stories of cosmic travel, but none cover the range of "all time" and infinite space. Aquinas coined the word *Æviternity* for such a conjuncture of eternity and time. The "now" of eternity is not the "now" of time; that is, the flow of "now" is what we conceive of as time. As Aristotle argued, time is *potential* infinity, while measurable time is *actual* infinity. The "now" of a still source is eternity.

Beelzebub's Tales has the scope of Holy Scripture in its characterization of time. Ashiata's and Beelzebub's adventures on Earth are typological reflections of the story of Jesus. The good work of Ashiata, like the good work of Jesus, was subsequently undone. In Scripture a second and terminal coming of Christ is foretold. In *Beelzebub's Tales,* the titular protagonist's sixth descent is his terminal message from above. One can see Scriptural analogies and echoes throughout Gurdjieff's tale, but his work does more than shadow Holy Writ. Gurdjieff shapes a cosmogony to fit his cosmology into his hero's exposition of witnessed events from the sinking Atlantis to the rising of America, as well in his recollection of the beginnings of planetary formation and life elsewhere in the universe. Beelzebub's observations are critiques of human society and its cultures, religion, philosophy, astronomy, and social behavior. He traces the development of music, mathematics, medicine, and technical developments throughout Europe, Asia and Northern Africa with a goodly dose of humor. He recognizes "holy" teachers of mankind, Saints Moses, Jesus, Mohammed, and Lama. He distinguishes between "objective" and "subjective" art. We need not agree with all the facets of Beelzebub's critique of human behavior through the ages, but what he reveals for Hassein is worth our reflection. We need not question the "truth" of his science, for holy words, Beelzebub tells Hassein, tend to be understood by contemporary man "only 'literally,' without any awareness of the inner meaning put into them." The burden of extracting "fact" from fiction is our task.

Considering into which line of thought concerning plural worlds *Beelzebub's Tales* falls, I would cite the ideas of Emmanuel Swedenborg, who not only describes visitations of instructing and advising alien spirits (angels) to Earth, but elaborates a general correspondence of thought about creation, the Creator's plan for mankind's place in the Universe and how to ameliorate it, though it is hardly< necessary to argue a direct influence on Gurdjieff.[21] According to his visionary perception, Swedenborg was designated by God as His spiritual emissary to explore and observe worlds, just as Gurdjieff's Beelzebub, though initially banished into exile (52), serves his god in his visitation to planets of the universe.

---

[21] Swedenborg's visionary writings had an extensive influence on English poets William Blake and W. B. Yeats, as well as on the theosophist Elena Blavatsky whose works Gurdjieff knew well.

For Swedenborg, Creation is a manifestation of the effort of an infinite and pure motion, similar to Endlessness's emission of formative laws into space. Swedenborg assumed a new revelation of God would be a "Second Coming." Accordingly, Gurdjieff's Beelzebub, following Ashiata Shiemash, is a second messenger from above (*Tales* 348, 1126). Gurdjieff's materiality of all things echoes Swedenborg's material plane of the trinity love, wisdom and physical motion. Gurdjieff's instance on breath as life reflects Swedenborg's findings that activities of the brain synchronize with breath rather than with pulsations of the heart.

Beelzebub's Tales, like Swedenborg's texts, conjoins the genre of tales of extraterrestrials with an objective critique of terrestrial life and thoughts. As an encyclopaedia, or compendious text of the life of mankind, as well as a space science, it is too vast a work, too full in its historical and scientific scope to be considered fantastical. It is a monumental work of philosophic and social criticism, and deserves notice as social history, philosophy, and literary history of plural worlds.

Select Bibliography

Crew, Michael J. *The Extra-Terrestrial Debate 1750–1900.* Cambridge: Cambridge University Press, 1988.
Cyrano de Bergerac. *The Other World: A Comic History of the States and Empires of the Moon.* London: New English Library, 1976
Dick, Steven J. *Plurality of Worlds: The Origins of the Extraterrestrial Life Debate from Democritus to Kant.* Cambridge: Cambridge University Press, 1982.
Fontenelle, Bernard Le Bovier de. *Entretiens sur la Pluralité des Mondes.*
Griffiths, John Charles. *Three Tomorrows: American, British and Soviet Science Fiction.* Totowa, NJ: Barnes and Noble, 1980.
Gurdjieff, G. I. *All and Everything.* New York: Harcourt Brace, 1950.
——— *Life Is Real Only Then, When "I Am."* New York: Viking Arkana, 1991.
Guthke, Karl (1933-). *Mythos der Neuzeit* (English: *Imagining other Worlds From the Copernican Revolution to Modern Science Fiction.* Trans. Helen Atkins. Ithaca: Cornell University Press, 1990.
Lewis C. S. *Out of the Silent Planet.* New York: Scribner's, 1936.
Lewis, David K. *On the Plurality of Worlds.* Oxford: Blackwell, 1986.
Mouravieff, Boris. *Ouspensky, Gurdjieff, and Fragments of a Forgotten Teaching.* Praxis Research Institute, 1997. Trans. Boris Volkoff, from "Ouspensky, Gurdjieff et les Fragments d'un Enseignement Inconnu." *Synthéses* 138, 1957.

Appendix: Extraterrestrials Populations on Earth

Beelzebub is an exceptional visitor to Earth from a distant planet, exceptional in the sense that he is invited there to help others of his tribe - natives of Karatas - there are an untold number of extraterrestrials from other planets, most notably Mars. Beelzebub makes his first descent to help one of his "tribe" who had "migrated . . . to Earth" (*Tales* 109). There was, apparently, a colony of migrants from Karatas already established on earth in the city of Samlios. Many if not all of those had moved from a temporary residence on Mars and, from among them and others that arrive from Mars (*Tales* 118), Beelzebub fills the administrative offices of King Appolios. The important point to note here is that the "aliens" offer themselves as the target of the anger of earthmen.

Ashiata Shiemash is one of many "messengers from above" dispatched to earth. Later, Providence decides to send another messenger from to rescue mankind from the "maleficent idea of good and evil" attributed to Markary Kronbernkzion. Markary is a rare example of an earthly impending saint, one who has earned qualification to migrate from Earth to a higher place in the universe.

In brief, the close relationships developed between the populations of the Earth and aliens were established eons before Hassein expressed an interest in the three-brained beings.

© Copyright 2011 - Paul Beekman Taylor - All Rights Reserved

Beelzebub Alien - Questions & Answers

Questioner 1: Did Cyrano de Bergerac speak of aliens?

Paul Beekman Taylor: He spoke of extraterrestrial engines and he spoke of planetary civilizations in a book entitled The Other World.

Questioner 2: Who is Beelzebub? Is he Lord of the Flies or Lucifer?

Paul Beekman Taylor: Lord of the flies is an epithet meaning ruler of the latrine. Lucifer means "bringer of Light." As such he is the morning star Venus, reflecting the goddess of love, and Christ, the God of Love. It was the bringing into existence of Jesus Christ that incited Beelzebub's rebellion.

Questioner 3: Yes, but who is the highest among the devils? Beelzebub was not alone.

Paul Beekman Taylor: He one of three principal devils that followed Lucifer, or Satan, as he was later called. The others were Moloch and Mammon, but Beelzebub was the highest of those but inferior to Satan.

Questioner 4: What are the meanings of the names of the spaceships?

Paul Beekman Taylor: Karnak has been explained as an Armenian word for "body," but the name echoes places Gurdjieff had been, like the Egyptian Karnac and Carnac in Brittany. Gurdjieff often uses names that have multiple meanings. His own family name has been explained in many ways: a Georgian, son of Gurdji (a Christian name for local Moslems), a son of Georgiades (a Greek name), and others, I am sure. [A very long digression on Gurdjieff's family records which have nothing to do with the paper, followed and took perhaps have of the question period].

Questioner 5: What is the point in having an extraterrestrial narrate the story?

Paul Beekman Taylor: A simple answer is that Beelzebub's voice represents an objective view of the history of the Earth. This is a tricky point that is not so simple since we have a double source of language. The first is Gurdjieff's and the second is Beelzebub's. We could assume that they are identical, but when Gurdjieff begins and ends the book in his own voice, and even interrupts Beelzebub's account once or twice, we are not realize a difference in perspectives between a fictional character and his creator. One is, so to speak, more objective than the other, to begin with. Then, the reader is challenged to understand two linguistic registers. I am reminded of the literary problems Milton and Dante had in representing God's speech in the same work as their own. Beelzebub, like Dante's and Milton's God, is objective, to be sure, but objective speech is humorless, lacking metaphor and figures of speech. Then again, man cannot very well reproduce the speech of God's since the language of a God is impossible to replicate by human beings. This said, the question arises whether or not we can understand Gurdjieff's language, for his language is a product of a perspective of human life that we do not have or share.

Questioner 6: Has anyone reported having contact with Gurdjieff since 1950?

Paul Beekman Taylor: Of course there are some who pretend to have had visitations with Gurdjieff. Anyone who has dreamed of Gurdjieff - and I imagine hundreds have seen and talked with Gurdjieff in dreams - can claim contact. I would be wary of claiming any sort of contact with Gurdjieff, and if I had heard him in dreams, would his voice communicate anything different from what he said to me and others before he died?

Seminar 3: Chapter 33 - Beelzebub's Tales

Beelzebub as a Professional Hypnotist

Facilitator: Terje Tonne

Introduction

Facilitator: Waking state - the usual, but not our normal state is, according to Gurdjieff, hypnotic. In this chapter Beelzebub uses hypnotism as a mean to reconnect man to parts/sides in himself that he is far from in his ordinary waking state. Hypnotism is in other words a manifestation with two entirely different consequences. In perspective of triads our hypnotic sleep will be that of corruption. Our real life has been put on hold in the passive position. In the active position (form) our thinking, feeling and acting has broken loose from higher purposes. The neutralizing factor then becomes the dead matter of mechanicality.

In order for him to proceed in his experiments without the harmful expenditure of his own hanbledzoin, he invented the new method. A method indirectly connected with the gradual arising of his objective love and directly connected with the need of others. What does this tell us about the nature of "love of kind"? Definitely that it is not a behavioral pattern stemming from an "I" in quotation marks.

His invented method was a consequence of the impulse "love of kind" - he said himself that it led him to seek for new means.

Central in this chapter and in "Beelzebub's therapeutic activities" seems to be the filling of the blood vessels. Through his new method a change became possible by making a contact with the unconscious and the pacifying part of our ordinary consciousness that usually has the upper hand. It is with this filling of the blood vessels that the free circulation of blood takes place and the sacred data that we originally possess are revealed to us.

After establishing himself as a hypnotist, Beelzebub was exposed to hate from his rivals. How can we view this psychologically? Can we find a leading thread in the fact that they were impatient - as we are?

We are also told that hundreds of patients attended his daily consultations and that further hundreds tried. Can we view this in perspective of our own psychological potential?

Beelzebub's therapeutic activities gradually interested certain most Very Saintly Individuals of a higher degree of reason. For me this is an underlining that his activities were that of a healing triad restoring a fragment on one level of the Unity. By hypnosis, matter rediscovers through new form, represented by the filling of the blood vessels, its normal vitality.

The people that Beelzebub helped through his method did not have gratitude -they almost had it. What does this tell us about what is required of us, if we ourselves are to be delivered from "pernicious habits", not alone by hypnotism, but by will. Towards the end of this chapter, Beelzebub informs us that the Akhaldans, through their persistent labors, obtain from their own atmosphere, and from certain surplanetary formations, substances that helped them to perform their experiments. Why is this brought into this chapter? Is he here referring to a next step - after hypnotism? Now, the neutralizing factor in the triad of healing is not only a restoration back to normality, but also a preparation for what I would call the next step, regeneration. When Beelzebub further speaks of the descendants of the learned members of the Akhaldans receiving their information, he speaks of "the knowledge of the ableness..." (p587). To me this ableness represents an initiative, intention, purpose, will and persistence - all cornerstones in the triad of regeneration where man recreates himself. So, if Gurdjieff is speaking of hypnotism as a part of a healing process, it seems to me, in other words, that he in this chapter is also pointing much further ahead.

And to Ulrike's question about hanbledzoin, Steven suggested that we maybe speak a little more about this today. And - I think it is appropriate, because at the first page, he speaks of that he is acting upon people with his hanbledzoin. Now, the hanbledzoin is the blood of the inner body. And I think that in order to understand something about how this blood can act upon others, I think one has to see from where these substances come. And it is said that they are derived from the level of the planets - world 24 - and the Sun. And that when these substances -active substances -act upon us, or when we receive them, and together with active substances from the body, they create an atmosphere. As I understand, this is how he acted upon others, it was through this atmosphere.

And the questions that I have posed - we can return to them, but they are my questions, and I thought they could serve as an example of other questions - or other views. And maybe Nick could add something to this with the blood.

Seminar Discussion

Participant 1: Do you want me to just say what I feel about hanbledzoin?

Facilitator: Yes.

Participant 1: Exactly from the chapter. I thought he'd just say in the chapter, the previous chapter <inaudible> on the separate localized part in us which was subconscious. So, for me that would mean that the subconscious or this something I <inaudible> or this "I", this objective "I" which I create, separates itself from me during a work effort, it acts as a catalyzer to convert the energy from the impression, which goes in from another localized part, which changes it into a substance

- and he talks about this in the chapter 33 - which goes down my spine, or down my neck, and into my heart. And that's, as far as I understand it, how it's done. But it must be this objective faculty that acts to convert the material (?). So, in other words, it comes from consciousness.

Participant 2: Just now in Terje's summary, I saw something - maybe - that is useful I've not seen before. Always been a puzzle to me about this <inaudible> filling up the blood vessels. I've talked to physician friends of mine about this <inaudible> physiological basis for this, <inaudible> in terms of the circulation of the extremities, of the circulation in the interior, that this can switch back and forth. So, I wonder when I <inaudible> centered, whether that change is taking place. <inaudible> another shift, that Gurdjieff talks about to approach us to hypnosis, first one <inaudible> and then gives it to the other. That as a professional hypnotist, he found a way to evoke such sincerity and trust in the others, that they were filled with gratitude and love for him.

And perhaps, that is an interesting, perhaps, analogy to a <inaudible> filling an empty <inaudible>. What is the difference for someone, if they are <inaudible> with an openness <inaudible> versus having it imposed upon by something much stronger from the outside, even if it's to defend it.

Sometimes <inaudible> God appeared in the middle of the, we would have no choice, but we have to seek God and say "yes" at our end. That then is a choice; something in us then changes, something in us shifts, it's nothing imposing. I wonder if this change in his work, in evoking the gratitude of others might be something useful to explore.

Participant 1: I don't hold the microphone, but I think it's in the second chapter, he changes his system <inaudible> began to worship and evolve <inaudible>. So he changes it, and he does this by a certain <inaudible> for the movement of blood, and by doing so he obtains the result, that although the mechanized <inaudible> blood circulation of their waking state remain in these <inaudible> same time that real consciousness, that is the one they call the self consciousness, began to function. And as far as I'm concerned, he's talking about how to work on yourself.

Because if I'm hindering something, I'm preventing or stopping the involutionary octave. So, in other words, if I walk across the room towards my refrigerator, to get something out of the refrigerator, and I see my mechanicalness, I stop. And by breaking up <inaudible> I can now get in touch with my real consciousness. How this stop hindering <inaudible> is a very important part of making a work effort. So he's changed and he's put the responsibility on us, and not on him.

<the rest of part 1 is inaudible.>

(Coffee Break)

Facilitator: So if we're all here and can continue, it was proposed that we change the format, and read the chapter. And I would say I hesitate, because the intention was that we all come here and be as prepared as we can, and share how we see the chapter. Then again, why not do both things.

Seminar 3: Chapter 33 - Beelzebub's Tales

And we don't have time for doing both things, that is, a mere exchange of views and reading, if we were to read the whole chapter, so we start reading a part of the chapter and go to the end. Another suggestion in this experiment is that when we come to the part where we are to share our views, that we try to make an effort to speak about what we just read, how we view this, not necessarily big pictures. Maybe there is a word that has puzzled you, that you have pondered and find very interesting for a particular reason. What is that reason? And so on - yes? So if we could do that two-sided experiment, it would be interesting - maybe.

Participant 1: Could I make a small comment?

Facilitator: A small one.

<general laughter>

Participant 1: I have recognized something - we all, or most of us, come from different lineages. And all these lineages, they come from the, what do you call the big thing of the tree?

Facilitator: Trunk.

Participant 1: And we sit here with parts of the trunk and try to understand some of it, and I have recognized that often there is used a lot of time and energy that the ideas are presented in the language of the different lineages, and there seem to be contradictions which are actually not there, and that there is used a lot of time to clarify the so-called contradictions. And I think that if especially some of the male members would try to make an effort to listen a little bit more carefully to one another, that could be - how to say...

Participant 2: Very useful.

Participant 1: Yeah - thank you.

Participant 3: That's only a suggestion.

Participant 1: Yes.

Participant 4: And could female members say more things? Too many males speak, not enough females.

Facilitator: We start with a man. So, if Nick can start.

Participant 5: So I'm going to start where Beelzebub is in Turkestan.

Facilitator: Maybe you can say what page this is. Because <inaudible> is going to write it.

All & Everything Conference 2011

Participant 2: Page 584.

Facilitator: Yes.

Participant 5: <inaudible> - if you've got a single volume, it's probably page 175. <inaudible>

Participant 5: So I'll begin. "But to remain in this Turkestan and to organize my existence there ..." <reads aloud from BT, page 584, to the end of the chapter.>

Facilitator: Thank you.

So where do we start? Turkestan? Black coffee? I mean, there are many.

Participant 6: Does anyone have an idea of what this last part of this chapter has to do with Beelzebub as hypnotist, or hypnosis, at all?

Facilitator: Yeah, it's fine if you can use the microphones, because we want to write this out.
Participant 6: So does anyone have an idea of what this last part, starting with what Nick read, has to do with hypnosis, or Beelzebub as hypnotist?

Participant 7: I can offer a suggestion. I'm checking is plausible (?). I think that this last part talks about imbalance, and the perils of imbalance. And I think that it is a warning, so to speak, of what happens if there is imbalance, vis-à-vis the first part, which is the possibility of building the higher being-body <inaudible> in that imbalance can end up in disastrous results. This is the way I see this part of the chapter. The imbalance, I think, is quite obvious - three parts in <inaudible> everything, and if they're not in the right proportions, then the result could be disastrous. And I think it's quite obvious that what he is alluding to <inaudible> historical facts, is opening up the tomb of Tutankhamen, and people dying from it because they were exposed to substances that were used in <inaudible> proportions <inaudible> evil.

Participant 8: So, this imbalance you're speaking of, Dimitri, then this substance force of the holy reconciling existing in these rooms did not properly blend, and so do we understand that the reconciling force was the substance that caused the death?

Participant 7: The imbalance of the three, I can not remember what it was, neither was I able to read the text before we - word by word. But <inaudible> I remember him say, it is the imbalance exactly causing the problem. Of any one of the three elements, this one in particular - that case.

Participant 8: Yeah, okay. Nick?

Participant 9: I also paid attention to the imbalance. And I would like to ask which three forces - I mean, Triamazikamno - where they lose their balance, lead to the death of three-brained creature. Because it was told, and that this question is - I am not sure that I can get the answer, because it's not so simple. I have never good understanding of this law Triamazikamno properly. It's difficult for me to find these real examples in my life, and here in this chapter, it was that. There is this specific case, and then it's told that when this balance disappears, a rascooarno takes place. So, which - maybe somebody can explain - in this specific case, which are these three forces? Which - can <inaudible> them, maybe to help me to understand that this law, and maybe somebody else - in general, not in only this specific case.

Participant 5: I looked at this for a long time, this particular section, and it almost came "why do I want to preserve my dead body?" Why - what would be the point of that. So clearly, it's got nothing to do with that. It's a story that I have to turn upside down, and say - what does it mean to me in my experience? So the third force, the reconciling force, is impartiality. Impartiality eventually becomes a substance. When that substance enters into the physical body, my physical body dies to its manifestations. So when my physical body is dead to my manifestations, it means the other two centers, the kesdjan body emotional center, or my soul body, are now in a position that all the attention and work goes into these two higher centers. But my physical body at that time is flooded with impartiality. And it's like everything else connected but Work the abnormal conditions of being-existence and make it extremely difficult to make any effort permanent. So this castor oil, which he talks about, is a purgative. So I purge my body of all its manifestations. It has to be something that I can experience in Work, not something that the Egyptians <inaudible> - that may have happened, I don't know. So, if I think castor oil is a purgative, that my body is now in the special state to receive the substance of impartiality, then there's no need for all the energy which I waste in my body and the manifestations, now goes to the creation of my kesdjan soul body. <inaudible> I would think, at that moment, when my body is full of impartiality, I'm in the state of freedom.

Participant 10: <inaudible> of something that is very interesting for me. That we don't respect to this energy. This is very, very heavy for me. I respect this that I know I need to trust someone else. To hood (?) and trust another person - to guide me. It's very difficult - very, very difficult for me. During this way, I put out the hood, and after a little I remember I wear this. I have a picture to my mind now, if I go through <inaudible>, so there is a palace there. I have my hand to push me, I have my body to walk and I have my mind to connect with this. So, maybe this energy comes. And I respect this.

Facilitator: He moves from Turkey, he started reading about Turkey - he moves from country to country and comes to Egypt. And to me, that is a sign that there is a process - he says about Turkey that one of the reasons he didn't, as I understand him, didn't want to stay there. Because - they become fixed pleasant memories and so he didn't stay there. And I wonder how you see this process, moving from country to country, and maybe in particular, why didn't he want to stay with these pleasant memories?

Participant 11: Is it because he was hounded, overwhelmed, by too many customers. He had all these customers who wanted his service as a physician hypnotist. Too many of them, so he couldn't rest. And again, when he goes to Egypt - again he seems to accumulate <inaudible>, more or less for the same reason.

Facilitator: So if Turkey is somewhere in ourselves, and Egypt is somewhere in ourselves, how do you see that?

Participant 12: So you go from Turkey to Egypt, and then - but you have to go somewhere else, called Europe. So you go from consciousness to subconsciousness, and then go somewhere else.

Participant 1: I have this idea which is in the beginning of what we read. If we go back to what Terje just said about - what did he say - pleasant memories?

Participant 12: Pleasant memories, yes

Participant 1: ... that may be related to living in a world of imagination. Living in the world of dreaming. And in relation to that, I wonder if when he moves, or when he explains why he is going to Egypt, and he relates to the many three-brained beings there which are possessing what is called material wealth. I wonder if that could be related to valuation, higher valuation, higher sort of values in oneself. Because, a little bit later he says that he has been there earlier and that he has been there to pick up freaks called "apes", and it came to me that that could be a picture of wrong attitudes. And somehow it struck me that that would be a way of maybe understanding, looking

Facilitator: If you turn the "material wealth" - twist it around - it will be "a wealth of material". And it was people with a wealth of material who went to Egypt. And the whole book is like that, you have to look at it upside down, in a way. And why not also - this word? So they had some things, those who went to Egypt - they had something. That's what's mentioned a little earlier - to make gold you have to have some gold.

Participant 13: I'm having lots of questions, one of them is: Do we understand what the mistake was he made? He says he was distracted by his pardon, and he made a mistake.

Participant 5: And he said that the mistake was that, he said that...

Facilitator: I'm going to write this down, so you better speak into the microphone. <laughing>

Participant 5: He said the mistake was that nothing had been left on our planet that had any value or any spiritual purpose.

Participant 13: No, he says he made a mistake.

Participant 5: He said in previous chapters, you see. So he comes now to realize he made a mistake, because he discovered that they had one - this one experience did exist. But he had said in previous chapters, not in this chapter.

Seminar 3: Chapter 33 - Beelzebub's Tales

Participant 13: Well. Yeah, sure.

Participant 13: One more thing - if I am to take this discussion of Triamazikamno and the sacred Okidanokh and the three elements as having something to do with Work - and this story about preservation, it seems to me that there's another - and this is his last sojourn, right, it's the sixth descent - that he could be alluding to something else, which has to do with the sustaining of the third body. The sustaining of whatever is being built, so that it doesn't decay. And it also seems to me that there could be something in the business about being drained by so many people coming to him, that he needed to go to a place where he could separate himself from those demands. I don't see this clearly, but I think that that could be another way of looking at this question of the preservation and hermetically sealed and so on and so forth.

Participant 14: So that we could ask - what are the demands that I accede to agree to? That I must begin to separate myself from, so when - try to translate the outer to the inner, so this responsiveness to the outside. Now even though it's helpful out here, it's helpful in the moment, it's not helpful perhaps in eternity. And - so I'd have to ask myself - how would I have to rethink my amount of energy, or attention, or something I'm putting into my relationship or service to the outside world. And begin to preserve that - something. For an inner usage. And I think that might relate allegorically to Terje's question about - what is the attitude or behavioral <inaudible> pattern of Turkey - in me? Where I'm known, beloved, and it's comfortable, and I can just relax here forever in a kind of comfortable paradise. And what is the Egypt in me that I would then go to? Egypt is used in so many metaphors and myths, now, with its great deserts and its struggles, as well as its buried treasures.

Participant 13: And two kinds of sand there, too.

Facilitator: The Akhaldans they were able to stop the decay and make it permanent, and crystallize qualities. So, maybe it refers back to what they were doing. How did they get in the position of being Akhaldans? Has it something to do with me moving from Turkey and into Egypt?

Participant 24: I think it's Turkestan? <inaudible>

Participant 5: Turkestan.

Facilitator: Turkestan, all right.

Participant 15: So - perhaps interesting to look at this image of the sealed tube. And there is the - to hermetically seal something. And who breaks into the hermetically sealed place where there is this superfluidity of reconciliation force?

Participant 16: A couple of academics. <general laughter>

Participant 17: I have been thinking about this question about hypnotism, and the situation is that we are hypnotized all the time. So we are not able to accumulate the higher bodies. So that is a connection. So to get out of hypnotism, we have to engage this process of Triamazikamno, the threefoldness. Out of which the neutralizing force is the very specific force that will oppose this decay that otherwise would happen.

Participant 18: I have a question concerning the coffee

Facilitator: Can you please speak into the microphone?

Participant 18: Yes. First time the coffee is mentioned, first is a black coffee, and after he returns, the coffee is mentioned again, so I start "what this could mean?" So coffee is pushing up the energy, so after that he's leaving Turkestan with the black coffee, and I also thought about the sealed space - what this could mean. I think for certain aspects of myself need some time to develop in silence or in isolation. And part of my - don't like this so much - or to give time for this - and so this is <inaudible>, yes? Who would like to have results much faster, to see something? So part of me would like to get conscious much faster. But, on the other hand, I know I have to be - with myself, part of myself, passive. Much more passive as my usual life, my coffee life is. And this <inaudible> is my interpretation for myself, there's a process, needs it's time, does not <inaudible> destruct to early. And after that, one can return also to the life of the coffee, so this is this post (?) part.

<several different conversations going on>

Participant 19: This question that in this chapter <inaudible>, I put the question to myself: What means to keep the balance, for example now? For about ten minutes. And suddenly I saw all this association that comes, because I hear something or someone, and from someone. And all this, it's something that comes without my will, it just comes from outside impressions, I accept. So for me to keep the balance, was just watch at this, and have attention in my body, when all this proceed - happens. I can't believe anything from these associations, because they're not mine. If they just come, I don't know from where, but they don't come up with my <inaudible>. I think this is mechanicality.

Facilitator: We are getting close.

Participant 20: Okay - I would like to speak about something quite different <inaudible> talked so far. And - it touches upon the question when we dig into this text - what exactly are we digging it for? One could say that we dig in it to find paradigms for Work, metaphors related to Work et cetera. Sure, we do that. And I think this is its major objective <inaudible>. At the same time, one has to see possibly one wishes to talk about. I wouldn't mind talking about how this <inaudible> up with organized picture of Gurdjieff's own reality. This text in this particular chapter, for example. One example for this is that Beelzebub here acts like a professional hypnotist. Now we know Gurdjieff himself worked with freeing people from habits of drinking and smoking opium, and things like that. In Paris, people would get their sons and their relatives to him - with their request to free them from such habits.

So in a way, there's also a circle, a review of this book that defines a circle of what happened with his professional hypnotist career. I think this something of an autobiographical dimension - in <inaudible> his life in France. At the same, there's another aspect to it, I believe. The aspect of - talking about, I think there is no question of the fact that he alludes to the Tutankhamen experience of the archaeologist who dug up Tutankhamen's tomb. I suppose most of us are familiar with that story - he dug up the tomb, and then they started dying - the ones who were present there, the ones who got into the chamber. All died within a year or so. And there was also speculation in the newspapers, how was this possible? And in a way, Gurdjieff takes this story and gives an explanation to what happened; of course using the story to pass to the reader his image of what I think is the dark consequences of imbalance. And it is interesting that he has then several occasions, I believe, Gurdjieff, this thing in his text, he's taken things that were, at the time that he was a young man, a boy, possibly - things that were in the news, so to speak, of his time. The Gobi desert and secret cities of the Gobi desert were a subject of very wide publicity some time in the late nineteenth century, when he was <inaudible> reading avidly all the newspapers and everything, and there were east people travelling to the East in search of cities which they found, some German guy, as a matter of fact, <inaudible> excavation to the Gobi desert, and established the idea of cities being buried there. And - same thing was true with zilnotrago, which is like the track of the Haley comet. And there was lots of speculation that it carried cyanide, which could be killing all life on earth. That was speculation around the turn of the century - right before the twentieth century. Again it was hysteria, like <inaudible> the centennial bug. It was hysteria <inaudible> with the 2000 bug. This is, you know, something very much beside the point of esoteric approach to this text, that Gurdjieff uses these historical facts to spice up, I believe, the story.

Facilitator: I think we are getting very, very close to the end of this. I am grateful for this opportunity that came about through your suggestion.

Participant 20: Thank you, thank you, thank you.

Facilitator: Yes. I just wanted to mention what <inaudible> we don't have the time, but this black coffee puzzled me for a long time, and still does. The closest I've come to it, is that it has something to do with modern society.

Participant 21: Excuse me - it doesn't say black coffee.

Facilitator: No - I'm sorry - I say black coffee. This liquid - who knows what. Well, it doesn't matter, does it? In modern society, all the influences from modern society - the last thing I want to say it was mentioned here that we are hypnotized all the time. I would say no - we are hypnotized most of the time, but I am not hypnotized all the time, and that must not become a habitual attitude. Most of the time, not all the time. If I were hypnotized all the time, and I'm speaking of the triad of corruption, there would be no possibility. There is a possibility, and the possibility is in those moments where I'm not hypnotized.

Participant 22: I was not speaking <inaudible> truth, then.

Facilitator: That would be the last word.

Participant 13: So here's one last puzzling thing to consider. That is that this has to do with Beelzebub - the title is "Beelzebub as Hypnotist". And the previous chapter, "Hypnosis" - and a discussion of hypnosis, and the one kind of hypnosis, at least, having to do with the blood flow. Beelzebub is described as having one nature - a three-brained being with one nature. This is in juxtaposition with him talking about his planetary body in this chapter. So, one thing to consider, is there another level of talking about Beelzebub here - a three-brained being - and what would be the hanbledzoin and the blood of Beelzebub's second body, if he has one nature. That is, <inaudible>.

Facilitator: Thank you.

End of Session

Seminar 4: Where Do We Go From Here?

Facilitator: Bonnie Phillips

A&E Prague 2011 - A Report

1. Introduction

The WDWGFH was held at 09:30 on the 10th of April in Prague and was chaired by Bonnie. As part of the introduction to this session she invited the participants to reflect on their experience at the conference and suggest what they may wish to change and improve upon. She informed the audience that the next conference will be held at Salt Lake City and invited suggestion for suitable venues for 2013 and beyond.

2. Scope and Mission of Conference

One theme that emerged in the discussion was the view that while the conference was unique with exceptionally attractive features such as its openness to all lineages and backgrounds; it has serious shortcomings in the limitations of its scope and ambition - leading to its stagnation. The view was expressed that it should he part of the mission of the Conference to reach out to a wider audience and it should actively seek to spread these teachings.

This view was countered by those of others that stated their firm preference for keeping the focus of the Conference on the study of Gurdjieff's book(s). The personal expectation of many for their engagement with the conference was an increase in personal understanding. Other goals and lines of work may be addressed through individuals' group memberships and through other channels. The Conference was compared to an annual gathering at a watering hole where different tribes meet and exchange and then separate enriched by their common experience to pursue their independent quests.

It was also suggested that the wider mission, suggested by some of the participants, does not need to he carried out by the A&E conference but can he handled by a setting up a new (international) organization that may he created by those who share the ethos of the A&E conference but wish to see its mission expanded.

However, the need for ensuring that the conference is put on an ascending octave was felt by many and suggestions were made to consider how this could he achieved. These included making more time available for the study and reading of *The Tales* and exploring alternative techniques for such a study including exploring music, movements, drama, and alternative forms of presentation as they relate to and inform such a study.

In particular the issue of including a study of movements within the scope the conference was discussed. It was suggested that this might not be contradictory to the focus of the conference on the texts but may also support and enhance it.

3. Decision Making

Another theme that emerged during discussions was the questioning of the process of decision-making that governs the Conference and the authority of the WDWGFH session to make decisions and recommendations. There was a call to vote to determine if the Session believe it has the right to set policy at the session.

This view was strongly contested as it was pointed out that, not withstanding the requirements of the Conference Charter, many of the participants in the session do not have the necessary background and experience to he able to weigh the proposals adequately and in any case the present participants are not representatives of the whole constituency of the Conference.

It was suggested that the Conference should formally review its Charter and Bylaws to ensure they are still fit for purpose and address its mission. This view had wide support and although no vote was taken.

4. Communication and Community

In order to support collective deliberations and the evolution of consensus it was suggested an online forum should he set up for all the alumni of A&E conferences. Such a forum, working as an easy to use electronic mailing list, could help with keeping up the connections (creating a Virtual Watering Hole) between participants in between the yearly meetings and help promote discussions such as those that have begun during this session. Any proposals emerging from such an exchange could be considered by the Conference Committees for formal adoption.

This proposal had strong support and it was recommended that the PC should consider its adoption to set up a Friends Forum formally associated with the Conference. An alternative approach may be for an informal forum he set up by some of the participants without formal connection to the Conference but nevertheless for the purpose of discussions related to the conference by those who have participated and may wish to participate again.

5. Future Venues & Timing

The planning horizon has now been extended to two years ahead and therefore consideration should now he given to the conference venues for 2013 and 2014. Moscow and Istanbul were mentioned as two possible future venues for the Conference and members willing to prepare proposals for each venue were identified.

Seminar 4: Where Do We Go From Here?

It was also suggested that extending the length of the conference should he considered -possibly to four or five days instead of 3 1/2.

Appendix

The diagram on the next page was handed out at the beginning of the WDWGFH seminar.

All & Everything Conference 2011

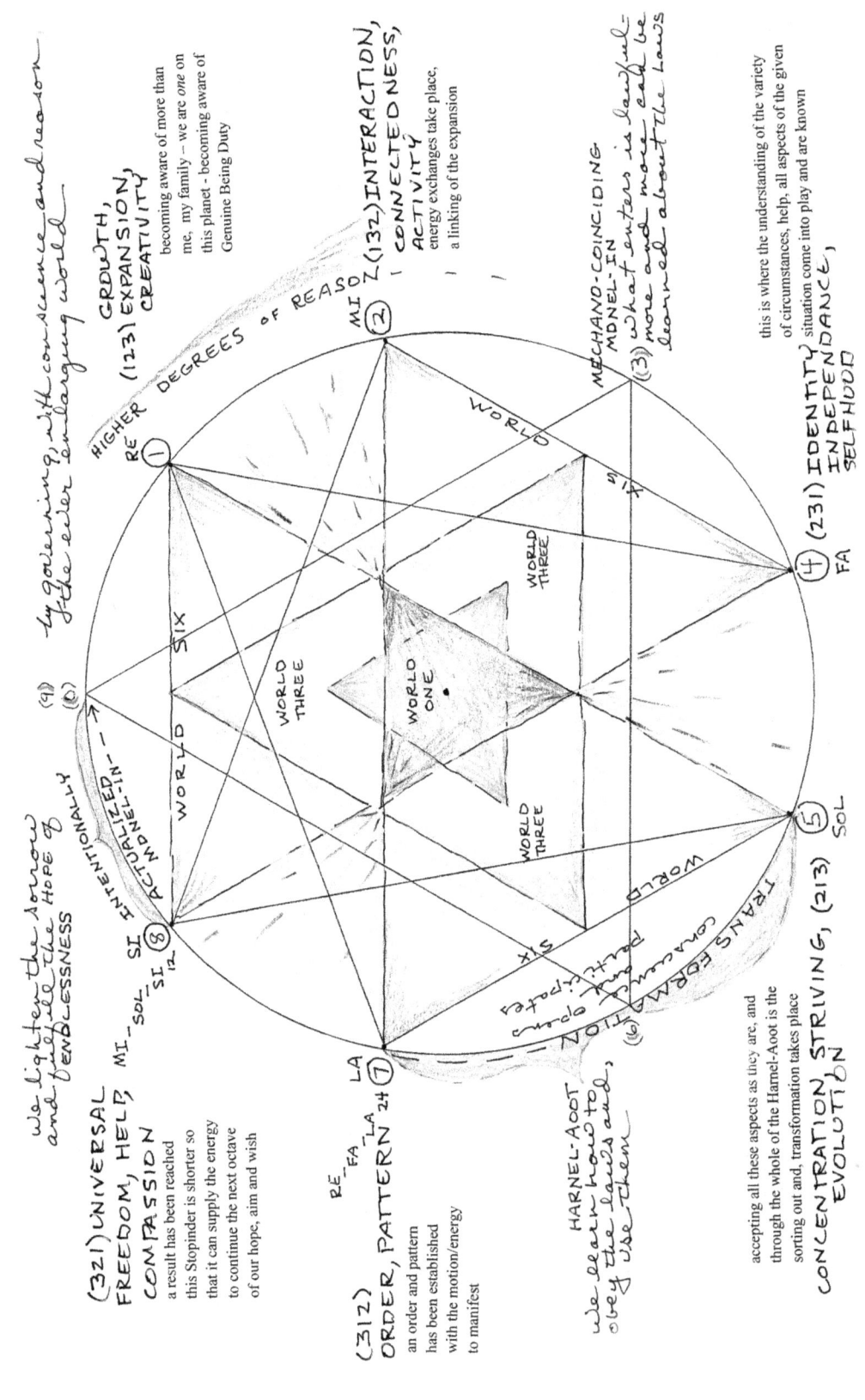

Appendix 1: List of Attendees

John Amaral - USA
Steve Aronson - USA
Popi Asteri - Greece
Hilde Brottveit - Norway
Nick Bryce - Canada
Farzin Deravi - UK
Dmitry Dobrovolski - Russia
Eduazd Ermilov - Russia
Sezgey Ezmilov - Russia
Irina Fomintseva - Russia
Mani Gerlach - Germany
Feliks Komarov - Russia
Alex Lisitsa - Russia
Tao McQuade - Norway
Eugeniy Milyavskiy - Russia
Clare Mingins - UK
Cyrie Mouravieff - Russia
Anu Paseka - Russia
Dimitri Peretzi - Greece
Maria Peretzi - Greece
Bonnie Phillips - USA
Vadim Potiy - Russia
Michael Readshaw - UK
Arkady Rovner - Russia
Tatiana Rovner - Russia
Oyvind Ruud - Norway
Robert Schuck - USA
Paul Taylor - Switzerland
Terje Tonne - Norway
Ulrike Tonne - Norway
Vlad Voroniv - Russia
Orjan Waldenstrom - Russia

Index

A

Absolute, 86, 115, 116, 119, 123, 125
active, 52, 54, 57, 140, 141
Adrenaline, 76
Advaita, 87, 90
affirm, 25, 62
Africa, 135
Aieioiuoa, 68, 71, 75
Aiëssirittoorassnian, 45
Aim, 37, 38, 48, 77, 101, 104
Alchemy, 39, 41, 84
Salzmann, de, Jean; Michel, 14, 15, 93, 94, 100, 134
Alla-attapan, 107
allegorical, 85, 134
allegory, 65, 69
Amber, 109
America, 15, 79, 92, 94, 131, 135, 136
Ananda, 95
Angel, 73, 77, 127, 131, 132, 134, 135
Antkooano, 45
Anulios, 52, 125
Archangel, 77, 81, 88, 109, 133
Aristotle, 127, 128, 133, 135
Armenia, 81
Armenian, 81, 84, 89, 93, 97, 138
ascending, 151
Ashiata Shiemash, 20, 22, 63, 69, 70, 71, 127, 134, 136, 137
Ashish, Sri Madhava, 14, 115
Assyrian, 85
astral, 19
Astrology, 118, 130
Atlantis, 46, 47, 52, 53, 135
Atom, 37, 132

Attention, 30, 31, 34, 35, 36, 37, 39, 41, 43, 44, 53, 67, 71, 74, 75, 80, 81, 106, 123, 125, 129, 131, 144, 145, 147, 148
awareness, 14, 33, 42, 46, 57, 61, 66, 107, 108, 135

B

Beekman Taylor, Paul, 13, 15, 127, 137, 138, 139
Beelzebub, 3, 4, 14, 16, 17, 20, 21, 22, 27, 28, 35, 45, 49, 50, 56, 62, 77, 78, 79, 80, 81, 82, 83, 84, 85, 86, 87, 90, 92, 93, 95, 101, 118, 121, 122, 127, 128, 130, 131, 132, 133, 134, 135, 136, 137, 138, 140, 141, 143, 144, 148, 150
Beelzebub's Tales
The Tales, 3, 34, 53, 58, 62, 63, 68, 69, 73, 127, 151
Being, 3, 16, 17, 19, 20, 21, 22, 23, 24, 27, 29, 30, 31, 32, 41, 43, 45, 46, 47, 48, 49, 50, 51, 52, 53, 54, 57, 59, 61, 64, 65, 66, 67, 68, 69, 70, 71, 72, 73, 74, 78, 81, 82, 86, 87, 88, 89, 90, 91, 97, 99, 100, 102, 105, 107, 117, 119, 120, 122, 123, 124, 132, 133, 135, 145, 147, 149, 150
Bennett, John G., 31, 35, 57, 78, 84, 85, 86, 89, 90, 91, 95, 98
Blake, William, 135
Blavatsky, Helena P., 57, 77, 79, 88, 89, 124, 135
Bodhisattva, 115
Boehme, Jacob, 89
Bogachevsky, 103
bone, 77, 78, 82
Brahe, Tycho, 129
Brahma, 134
Brain, 33, 41, 60, 62, 121, 136
breath, 30, 91, 130, 136

Index

breathing, 86
Brother Sez, 155
Buddha, 20, 48, 50, 59, 73, 84, 95, 134
Buddhism, 44
Buddhist, 57, 85
Buzzell, Keith, 13, 35

C

Canada, 4, 13, 80, 83, 93, 155
Celestial, 94, 95, 130
center, 50, 55, 57, 63, 81, 98, 104, 111, 128, 145
Cerebellum, 61
Chakra, 74
cherubim, 134
child, 53, 76, 101
children, 14, 59, 95, 101
Chinese, 86
Christ, 44, 73, 75, 88, 90, 95, 125, 134, 135, 138
Christian, 57, 65, 77, 85, 86, 89, 90, 91, 132, 133, 138
Christianity, 35, 50, 73, 87, 88, 89, 90, 124, 133
coat
coating, 83
comet, 53, 149
Commission, 88
compassion, 39
concentrate, 36
concentration, 36
Conscience, 3, 20, 22, 42, 52, 61, 62, 65, 66, 68, 69, 70, 71, 73, 75, 86, 88, 100
conscious, 25, 28, 36, 42, 52, 53, 54, 61, 62, 64, 67, 69, 71, 72, 84, 94, 106, 107, 130, 133, 148
Conscious Labor, 42, 107
consciousness, 3, 14, 17, 18, 19, 22, 23, 24, 25, 27, 28, 33, 45, 46, 47, 51, 52, 53, 54, 62, 63, 64, 65, 66, 67, 69, 70, 71, 72, 73, 74, 75, 91, 106, 111, 113, 115, 129, 134, 135, 140, 142, 146
constate

constated, 46, 48, 56
contemplate
contemplation, 45
contemplative, 68
cosmic, 60, 61, 88, 89, 95, 113, 115, 117, 118, 123, 128, 129, 131, 132, 135
cosmology, 85, 89, 90, 95, 126, 135
Creation, 31, 42, 43, 61, 77, 81, 85, 86, 87, 88, 90, 113, 116, 118, 119, 124, 128, 132, 133, 134, 135, 136, 145
creative, 4, 87, 88, 91
Creator, 81, 85, 86, 87, 128, 133, 134, 135, 138
crystallize, 147
crystallized, 16, 19, 20, 46, 47

D

Dante Alighieri, 77, 79, 80, 138
death, 54, 85, 91, 97, 98, 103, 104, 105, 111, 112, 130, 144
Demiurge, 87, 88, 122
Demiurgic, 88
Dervish, 85, 97, 98
descending, 113, 114, 116
descent, 49, 50, 135, 137, 147
Descent, 63
die, 98, 100, 102, 104, 107, 110, 111, 112, 129
digest, 20
dimension, 32, 71, 149
disharmonized, 106
dissonance, 40
Djartklom, 40
dog, 77, 78, 82, 97, 99, 103, 104, 110
dream, 48, 59, 67, 115, 130, 139, 146
dying, 98, 107, 110, 111, 112, 144, 149

E

Earth, 16, 20, 45, 46, 47, 77, 81, 88, 109, 113, 114, 115, 118, 119, 120, 121, 122, 125, 127, 128, 129, 130, 131, 132, 133, 134, 135, 137, 138, 149

Ego, 42
egoism, 19, 52
Egoaitoorassian, 45
Egypt, 97, 101, 145, 146, 147
Egyptian, 85, 138
Einstein, 129
Ekim Bey, 109
electromagnetic, 35
element, 22, 70, 80, 85, 86, 89, 118, 124, 129, 144, 147
emanation, 121
emotion, 74, 111
emotional, 28, 50, 51, 55, 74, 104, 108, 111, 145
Endlessness, 31, 35, 58, 87, 88, 116, 119, 121, 122, 132, 133, 134, 136
England, 14
Enneagram, 104, 126
esoteric, 14, 57, 64, 98, 104, 149
Essence, 14, 17, 18, 19, 23, 25, 46, 47, 49, 53, 62, 64, 72, 76, 101, 103, 107
Eternity, 135, 147
Etherokrilno, 87
Evil, 86, 137, 144
Evolution, 62, 128, 152
evolutionary, 133
Evolve, 142
Exercise, 29, 30, 31, 32, 33, 34, 35, 36, 37, 39, 40, 41, 42, 43, 44, 59, 74, 108, 109, 133

F

Faith, 33, 45, 70, 71, 75, 108, 109, 133
father, 34, 35, 44, 87, 100, 132
feeding, 85, 86
Feeling, 29, 36, 66, 79, 99, 106, 140
Fire, 64
First Conscious Shock, 52
Food, 36, 57
force, 28, 51, 52, 57, 85, 88, 133, 134, 135, 144, 145, 147, 148
Formatory, 67, 68
Foundation, 14, 15, 91

Fourier, 124
Fourth Way, 64, 89, 109
France, 14, 93, 117, 149
friction, 19

G

Galileo, 129, 130
Galumnian, Elsaveta, 93
genital, 40
Germany, 4, 155
Gilgamesh, 79
Ginsburg, Seymour, 1, 2, 13, 14, 113, 117, 118, 119, 120, 121, 122, 123
Giza, 105
Gnostic, 87, 88
Gob, 56
Gobi, 97, 103, 149
God, 31, 35, 73, 77, 80, 81, 85, 86, 87, 88, 90, 107, 122, 123, 128, 130, 132, 133, 134, 135, 136, 138, 142
Goepfert, Louise, 93
Goethe, Johann Wolfgang von, 86
Good, 102, 132
gravity, 130, 131
Great Nature, 21, 23, 45, 58, 86
Greece, 4, 13, 14, 155
Greek, 53, 54, 84, 85, 90, 129, 130, 133, 134, 138
Gurdjieff, G. I., 3, 4, 14, 15, 16, 17, 18, 19, 20, 21, 22, 23, 24, 25, 26, 27, 28, 29, 30, 31, 32, 33, 34, 35, 36, 39, 40, 41, 42, 48, 49, 51, 53, 55, 57, 58, 60, 61, 62, 63, 64, 65, 66, 67, 68, 69, 70, 71, 73, 76, 77, 78, 79, 80, 81, 82, 83, 84, 85, 86, 87, 88, 89, 90, 91, 92, 93, 94, 95, 97, 98, 100, 101, 102, 103, 104, 105, 108, 109, 113, 114, 115, 118, 119, 120, 121, 122, 123, 124, 125, 126, 127, 128, 129, 130, 131, 132, 133, 134, 135, 136, 138, 139, 140, 141, 142, 148, 149, 151

Index

H

Hanbledzoin, 49, 60, 61, 140, 141, 150
Hands, Rina, 14
Hariton, 109
harmonic, 29, 33, 35
Hawking, Stephen, 124
heart, 22, 40, 44, 51, 61, 74, 88, 99, 100, 106, 120, 136, 142
heaven, 132, 133
Hebrew, 77, 80
Heptaparaparshinokh, 55, 87
Heropass, 85, 86, 87, 122
higher being-body, 122, 144
Hindu, 14, 133, 134
Hope, 21, 40, 45, 64, 70, 71, 75, 91, 102, 123, 125
hydrogen, 30, 35, 121
Hypnosis, 45, 48, 49, 50, 51, 52, 53, 54, 57, 58, 59, 61, 141, 142, 144, 150
hypnotise, 50, 51, 55, 57, 58, 59
hypnotised, 51, 54, 55, 59, 148, 149
hypnotism, 4, 18, 45, 48, 49, 55, 60, 63, 101, 103, 140, 141, 148
hypnotist, 51, 61, 140, 142, 144, 145, 148, 149
Hypnotist, 4, 140, 150

I

I Am, 3, 29, 31, 32, 35, 39, 41, 44, 136
Identification, 55, 58, 59, 60, 120, 122
Idiot, 78
imagination, 146
impartial, 24, 27, 109
impressions, 20, 25, 29, 30, 33, 41, 56, 57, 61, 72, 99, 148
In Search of the Miraculous, 24, 26, 58, 63, 113, 114, 121
Fragments, 128, 136
India, 50
Individual, 19, 31, 40, 72, 113, 120, 125
inexactitude, 69
initiation, 111
insight, 33, 49, 114, 115
Institute, 14, 29, 35, 63, 101, 136
Intellectual, 50, 51, 74, 89, 91, 104
intention, 14, 121, 133, 141, 142
intuition, 28, 68
Involution, 88
involutionary, 142
Involve, 106
Islam, 88, 89, 124, 133
Itoklanoz, 53, 56, 59

J

Jesus, 50, 75, 84, 90, 132, 133, 135, 138
Jew, 65, 133
Jewish, 65, 133
Jung, Carl G., 132

K

Kant, Immanuel, 124, 129, 136
Karatas, 109, 137
Karnak, 131, 138
Kars, 34
Kepler, Johannes, 129, 130
Kesdjan, 42, 51, 60
Krishnamurti, 58, 89, 90
Kundabuffer, 16, 19, 20, 45, 61, 70

L

labyrinth, 103
laughter, 122, 125, 143, 147
Law, 29, 30, 54, 62, 87, 90, 113, 119, 120, 122, 131, 133, 135, 136
Law of Three, 30, 57
lawful, 69
Legominism, 17, 18, 19, 21, 22, 70
Libet, B., 63
Life is Real, 29, 32
light, 39, 68, 69, 71, 73, 76, 87, 115, 129, 138
Logos, 87
Love, 45, 70, 71, 75, 86, 97, 99, 100, 101, 103, 136, 138, 140, 142

Lubovedsky, 4, 97, 98, 99, 100, 101, 102, 104, 105, 106, 108, 109, 110, 111
Lucifer, 35, 138

M

machine, 79, 92, 108, 111
Macrobius, 130
Magician, 61
magnet
magnetic, 131
Mahayana, 77, 85
maintenance, 86, 89, 128, 133
mammon, 138
Maralpleicie, 56
Mars, 128, 131, 137
material, 25, 51, 55, 56, 68, 85, 101, 109, 120, 126, 128, 129, 131, 136, 142, 146
matter, 26, 39, 43, 51, 64, 66, 102, 104, 115, 125, 140, 141, 149
Maya, 65
mechanical, 25, 67, 90, 95, 108, 111
mechanicality, 52, 60, 100, 112, 140, 148
meditate, 74
meditation, 28, 74
Meetings with Remarkable Men, 3, 4, 34, 35, 97, 100, 101, 102
Megalocosmos, 83, 125
mentate, 67
mentation, 18, 19, 25, 36, 62, 109
Mesmer, 48, 49, 50, 51, 59
Mexico, 102
Microcosmos, 125
mind, 14, 19, 50, 52, 60, 62, 64, 65, 66, 67, 71, 86, 90, 99, 100, 102, 107, 109, 112, 122, 145, 148
Mohammed, 48, 135
monastery, 97, 98, 102, 105, 106, 111
monk, 14, 26, 117
Moon, 52, 88, 118, 125, 128, 129, 130, 131, 136
Moral, 68, 71, 128, 132
Morality, 68
Moscow, 15, 80, 98, 109, 152

Moses, 134, 135
mother, 93, 103, 130
Mount Athos, 111
Mouravieff, Boris, 128, 136, 155
Moving, 18, 51, 109, 111, 112, 128, 145, 147
Mozart, 40
music, 4, 13, 14, 28, 33, 34, 40, 41, 55, 99, 104, 111, 117, 130, 135, 151
mysticism, 15, 73, 98
myth, 57, 58, 59, 85, 86, 87, 88, 89, 90, 91, 92, 132, 133, 134
mythology, 89, 134

N

Naqshbandi, 98
Nature, 2, 24, 34, 55, 58, 64, 65, 66, 76, 79, 84, 90, 103, 129, 140, 150
Negative emotion, 27, 28, 52, 75
Neologism, 83
nervous system, 64, 65, 76
Neutral
Neutralizing, 140, 141, 148
New Age, 63
nine, 98, 100, 101, 102, 103, 104, 132
ninth, 128
nothing, 18, 23, 25, 40, 46, 47, 50, 51, 58, 63, 67, 72, 75, 82, 86, 94, 100, 106, 108, 120, 122, 138, 142, 145, 146
Nothingness, 44
Nott, Stanley and Rosemary, 82, 84, 85, 92
Nyland, W, 14, 33, 40

O

Objective, 17, 20, 22, 23, 37, 45, 60, 70, 74, 77, 81, 84, 86, 113, 127, 129, 134, 135, 136, 138, 140, 141, 148
octave, 107, 114, 115, 117, 118, 122, 124, 125, 142, 151
Okidanokh, 88, 147
Opium, 41, 55, 148
Orage, Alfred, 84, 105, 107
oral teaching, 113, 114

Index

organic, 71
Ors, 88
Orthodox, 85
Ouspensky, P. D., 15, 24, 26, 27, 52, 58, 63, 89, 90, 91, 95, 113, 114, 118, 119, 121, 128, 131, 136

P

pagan, 51
Parable, 50
paradise, 65, 79, 147
Paris, 15, 78, 149
Partkdolg-duty, 17, 21, 22, 23, 48, 66, 67
passive, 140, 148
Patanjali, 73
patience, 22
Pentland, John, 14, 15
Peretzi, Dimitri, 1, 13, 14, 62, 72, 74, 76, 92, 97, 155
personality, 14, 19, 45, 48, 49, 50, 54, 56, 57, 59, 61, 68, 71, 72, 76, 108, 111
physical, 20, 29, 40, 50, 104, 107, 124, 127, 132, 136, 145
physics, 131
Pistis Sophia, 79, 80
planet, 16, 20, 36, 46, 47, 49, 56, 70, 81, 87, 88, 113, 114, 115, 118, 119, 120, 121, 122, 125, 129, 130, 132, 134, 135, 137, 141, 146
planetary, 128, 129, 130, 132, 135, 138, 150
Plato, 65, 127, 132
politics, 49
Popoff, Irmis, 14
Positive emotion, 106
Prana, 51
Prayer, 123
Prem, Sri Krishna, 115, 118, 119
presence, 18, 22, 23, 24, 25, 36, 37, 46, 47, 53, 67, 83, 133, 135
Priest, 87, 97, 106
psyche, 46, 47, 52, 56, 70, 72, 86, 113, 115
psychological, 68, 118, 122, 123, 128, 131, 140

psychologist, 49, 115, 120
psychology, 51, 84
Ptolemy, 128
Purgatory, 61, 133, 134
Pyramid, 97, 105

R

Rabelais, 77, 84
Ramakrishna, 73
Rascooarno, 19, 145
Ray of Creation, 3, 31, 43, 113, 115, 118, 119, 121, 122, 123, 125
Real, 29, 36, 41
Reason, 16, 19, 26, 31, 43, 45, 49, 56, 60, 64, 66, 67, 68, 83, 89, 90, 91, 93, 99, 100, 114, 121, 134, 140, 143, 146
Reciprocal, 85, 86
Reconcile
Reconciliation, 147
Reconciling, 144, 145
Relativity, 43, 113, 114, 115, 125
religion, 68, 80, 90, 124, 133, 135
Remember, 20, 27, 52, 57, 67, 84, 101, 102, 105, 106, 108, 111, 112, 120, 121, 122, 144, 145
Remembering, 24, 27, 57, 120
Remorse, 68, 75, 88
Repentance, 86
repetition, 30, 36
resonance, 40, 79
resonate, 29
Russia, 4, 13, 15, 40, 73, 80, 81, 82, 83, 84, 89, 91, 92, 93, 94, 97, 98, 102, 103, 109, 128, 131, 134, 155

S

Sacred, 16, 19, 20, 30, 32, 37, 45, 46, 48, 49, 58, 61, 69, 70, 71, 80, 84, 86, 88, 90, 97, 113, 133, 140, 147
Sacred Individual, 16, 19, 20, 88, 90
sacrifice, 111, 112, 133
Sakaki, 88

Sarmoung (also Surmang), 97, 98, 107
Satan, 138
Saturn, 128
Science, 45, 56, 62, 63, 64, 65, 66, 67, 73, 74, 75, 78, 116, 118, 120, 121, 122, 124, 127, 128, 129, 130, 131, 132, 133, 134, 135, 136
Scientific, 64, 65, 66, 67, 73, 74, 116, 120, 121, 124, 126, 127, 128, 129, 131, 135, 136
Second Conscious Shock, 30, 35, 41, 42, 52, 106, 107
seeing, 60, 123
Self, 27, 71, 88
Self Observation, 27, 30, 40, 71
Self Remembering, 24, 27, 30, 60, 108, 113, 120, 122
Self-consciousness, 113, 142
sensation, 30, 34, 36, 37, 46, 48, 54, 56, 61, 71, 74, 108, 109
senses, 57, 61, 65, 90
Sensing, 29, 30, 71, 72, 108
seraphim, 134
seven, 21, 106, 128, 133, 135
seventh, 100
Sex, 127
sexual, 130
Shiva
Siva, 134
shock, 42, 52, 57, 106, 107, 112, 115
sin, 65, 90
sing, 34, 40
Sitting, 100
Skridlov, 97
Sleep, 45, 48, 49, 51, 52, 55, 58, 60, 61, 67, 140
solar plexus, 29, 36, 37
Soloviev, 89, 97, 98, 102, 103, 104, 107, 110, 111
son, 87, 100, 133, 138, 149
Sophia, 130
Soul, 42, 88, 101, 145
sound, 30, 40, 41, 63, 83

sounding, 33
spine, 61, 142
Spirit, 42, 74, 80, 88
spiritual, 3, 50, 58, 61, 63, 64, 65, 66, 68, 77, 78, 79, 80, 87, 89, 90, 91, 92, 93, 102, 115, 122, 133, 135, 146
spirituality, 98
St. Petersburg (also Petersburg), 102
Staveley, A.L., 14, 78
Steiner, Rudolf, 89
subconscious, 17, 18, 19, 20, 23, 24, 25, 26, 27, 28, 58, 62, 65, 66, 67, 69, 71, 141
subconsciousness, 46, 47, 53, 67, 69, 70, 72, 146
subjective, 32, 66, 74, 135
substance, 41, 43, 51, 54, 55, 59, 60, 61, 87, 128, 141, 144, 145
Suffer, 42, 107
Intentional Suffering, 42, 106, 107
suffering, 42, 101, 107
Sufis, 98
suggestibility, 19, 27, 46, 47, 48, 49
Sun, 87, 113, 114, 117, 118, 119, 120, 122, 125, 128, 132, 134, 135, 141
Sun Absolute, 132, 134, 135
Swedenborg, 127, 131, 132, 135, 136
Symbol, 107, 110
symbolism, 100

T

Table of Hydrogens, 122
Tail, 132, 134
Tao, 4, 155
telepathy, 101
Theomertmalogos, 87
Theosophical, 14, 89
Theosophist, 135
Theosophy, 90, 124
third being-food, 20
Third Force, 145
three-brained, 20, 21, 29, 45, 46, 47, 48, 56, 69, 70, 71, 72, 83, 121, 122, 133, 137, 144, 146, 150

Index

Tibet, 97, 102, 110
Timaeus, 132
time, 16, 19, 20, 21, 22, 25, 26, 27, 28, 30, 32, 33, 34, 40, 46, 47, 48, 50, 51, 52, 53, 55, 63, 71, 73, 75, 78, 82, 83, 84, 85, 86, 87, 89, 90, 91, 95, 101, 102, 106, 108, 109, 112, 115, 116, 120, 122, 124, 127, 128, 129, 130, 132, 135, 142, 143, 145, 148, 149, 151
Toomer, Jean, 15
Transapalnian, 101
transform, 16, 17, 18, 19, 21, 22, 23, 24, 28, 83
transformation, 3, 16, 17, 18, 21, 22, 23, 24, 26, 27, 62, 86
Transubstantiate, 46, 47
Transubstantiation, 52
Travers, Pamela, 15
Triad, 32, 33, 141, 150
Triamazikamno, 57, 87, 113, 144, 147, 148
Triangle Editions, 83
Trinity, 87, 136
Trogoautoegocrat
Trogoautoegocratic, 85, 86
Turkey, 145, 146, 147

U

unconscious, 48, 49, 53, 60, 75, 86, 140
unconsciousness, 50
understanding, 14, 16, 19, 21, 26, 27, 29, 30, 36, 39, 51, 54, 60, 64, 65, 66, 71, 73, 74, 76, 78, 81, 85, 95, 106, 114, 124, 126, 145, 146, 151
universe, 18, 37, 46, 47, 68, 81, 85, 86, 87, 92, 113, 115, 119, 121, 122, 123, 125, 128, 129, 130, 131, 133, 134, 135, 137
Upanishads, 77, 87
USA, 13, 155

V

Vacuum, 14, 28
Vedanta, 44, 87, 90
Venus, 128, 130, 138
vibration, 29, 36, 40, 43, 57, 58, 111
Vishnu, 134
Vitvitskaia, 97, 98, 99, 102, 103, 104, 110
vivifyingness, 34

W

Water, 101
Welch, William and Louise, 14
Wellbeloved, Sophia, 130
Will, 29, 35, 80, 87, 111, 133
Wisdom, 80, 85, 90, 108, 115, 120, 122, 136
wiseacre, 81, 124
wiseacring, 91
Word, 87
Work, 4, 14, 15, 30, 33, 42, 57, 62, 65, 67, 69, 70, 71, 74, 78, 98, 108, 112, 120, 123, 145, 147, 148
world, 4, 15, 18, 20, 21, 23, 30, 33, 34, 40, 45, 48, 49, 50, 52, 55, 61, 64, 65, 71, 72, 74, 80, 85, 86, 87, 101, 103, 104, 105, 109, 112, 113, 115, 122, 124, 125, 127, 128, 129, 130, 131, 132, 133, 134, 135, 136, 138, 141, 146, 147

Y

Yelov, 97
Yezidi, 132, 134
Yoga
Karma, 103

Z

Zen, 50, 85
Zodiac, 130
Zoostat, 45, 46, 47, 51, 53, 54, 60, 61
Zoroastrian, 87

163

www.ingramcontent.com/pod-product-compliance
Lightning Source LLC
Chambersburg PA
CBHW081920170426
43200CB00014B/2783